Settler Colonialism

Also by Lorenzo Veracini

ISRAEL AND SETTLER SOCIETY

Settler Colonialism

A Theoretical Overview

Lorenzo Veracini

Queen Elizabeth II Fellow, Institute for Social Research,
Swinburne University of Technology, Melbourne

First published 2010 by
PALGRAVE MACMILLAN

Palgrave Macmillan in the UK is an imprint of Macmillan Publishers Limited,
registered in England, company number 785998, of Houndmills, Basingstoke,
Hampshire RG21 6XS.

Palgrave Macmillan in the US is a division of St Martin's Press LLC,
175 Fifth Avenue, New York, NY 10010.

Palgrave Macmillan is the global academic imprint of the above companies
and has companies and representatives throughout the world.

Palgrave® and Macmillan® are registered trademarks in the United States,
the United Kingdom, Europe and other countries.

ISBN 978–0–230–22097–3 hardback
ISBN 978–0–230–28490–6 paperback

This book is printed on paper suitable for recycling and made from fully
managed and sustained forest sources. Logging, pulping and manufacturing
processes are expected to conform to the environmental regulations of the
country of origin.

A catalogue record for this book is available from the British Library.

Library of Congress Cataloging-in-Publication Data
Veracini, Lorenzo.
   Settler colonialism : a theoretical overview / Lorenzo Veracini.
      p.   cm.
   ISBN 978–0–230–22097–3 (hardback)
   1. Colonies—History.   2. Land settlement—History.   I. Title.
   JV105.V35 2011
   325'.3—dc22   2010034610

10   9   8   7   6   5   4   3   2   1
19   18   17   16   15   14   13   12   11   10

Transferred to Digital Printing in 2014

Contents

List of Figures

Acknowledgements

This research was supported under Australian Research Council's *Discovery Projects* funding scheme (project number DP0986984). This support was seriously enabling; without the fellowships the Council provided, researching and writing this book would have been impossible. Many in my generation had to leave Italy to find opportunities and dignity elsewhere. I was lucky and ended up in Australia. At the same time, Australia is also a great place to get to know about settler colonialism.

Part of Chapter 1 has appeared in *Native Studies Review*, an earlier version of Chapter 3 was published in the *Journal of Intercultural Studies*, and an abridged version of Chapter 4 will appear in *Thinking Settler Colonialism: Essays on Settler Colonialism and its Consequences* (Palgrave Macmillan). The jacket reproduces a painting by William Ludlow Sheppard entitled "Wives for the Settlers at Jamestown" (1876). I believe this painting identifies the moment when colonialism turns into settler colonialism. The cover image is reproduced with permission from the New York Public Library.

And I want to thank the shower for a number of decent ideas that came up while I was having one. Had we not had water restrictions all along, this book would have probably been a better one. Blame climate change.

Introduction: The Settler Colonial Situation

The expectation that every corner of the globe would eventually become embedded in an expanding network of colonial ties enjoyed widespread currency during the long nineteenth century. A theoretical analysis of what is here defined as the settler colonial situation could perhaps start with Karl Marx and Friederich Engels' remark that the "need of a constantly expanding market for its product chases the bourgeoisie over the whole surface of the globe", and that it "must nestle everywhere, settle everywhere, establish connections everywhere".[1] "Nestle", "settle", "establish connections": Marx and Engels were effectively articulating in 1848 what had become a transnational system of diversified colonial intervention. It was a typology of colonial action that depended on local circumstances and opportunities: there were different colonial empires, and there were different *modes* of empire. Settler colonialism, "the colonies proper", as Engels would put in 1892 underscoring analytical distinction between separate forms, was one such mode of colonial action.[2] Sometimes capable of displacing established colonial traditions, more rarely giving way to other colonial forms, settler colonialism operated autonomously in the context of developing colonial discourse and practice.

Another point of departure for this analysis could be Charles Darwin's voyage, which, as well as an exploration into the evolution of the species, was also a journey into what had become a geographically diversified system of intertwined colonial forms. On the issue of settler colonialism, he had specifically noted in 1832 that the

Argentinean war of extermination against the Indians, an episode he had personally witnessed during his voyage, was too much.

> The Indians are now so terrified that they offer no resistance in a body, but each flies, neglecting even his wife and children; but when overtaken, like wild animals they fight, against any number to the last moment. [...] This is a dark picture, but how much more shocking is the undeniable fact that all the women who appear above twenty years old are massacred in cold blood! When I exclaimed that this appeared rather inhuman, he [general and temporarily out of office national leader Juan Manuel de Rosas] answered "Why, what can be done? They breed so".[3]

dialectical
ingenuity

Personal dispositions are often surprising. Whereas one could argue that (especially the later) Marx was not a "Marxist" in suggesting that traditional, indigenous, and colonised societies could follow historical trajectories that did not necessarily reproduce the evolution of the metropolitan cores, at the same time, one could maintain that Darwin was not a (social) "Darwinist" when he regretted the deliberate targeting of the reproductive capabilities of the indigenous community and the horror intrinsic to what was otherwise understood as a globally recurring approach to indigenous policy. In both cases, a colonial imagination had failed to ultimately convince them. This book is a theoretical reflection on settler colonialism as distinct from colonialism. It suggests that it is a global and genuinely transnational phenomenon, a phenomenon that national and imperial historiographies fail to address as such, and that colonial studies and postcolonial literatures have developed interpretative categories that are not specifically suited for an appraisal of *settler* colonial circumstances.[4] The dynamics of imperial and colonial expansion, a focus on the formation of national structures and on national independence (together with a scholarship identifying the transoceanic movement of people and biota that does not distinguish between settler and other types of migration), have often obscured the presence and operation of a specific pan-European understanding of a settler colonial sovereign capacity. *Settler Colonialism* addresses a scholarly gap.

"Colony" as a term can have two main different connotations. A colony is both a political body that is dominated by an exogenous agency, and an exogenous entity that reproduces itself in a given environment (in both cases, even if they refer to very different situations, "colony" implies the localised ascendancy of an external element – this is what brings the two meanings together). Settler colonialism as a concept encompasses this fundamental ambiguity. As its compounded designation suggests, it is inherently characterised by both traits. Since both the permanent movement and reproduction of communities and the dominance of an exogenous agency over an indigenous one are necessarily involved, settler colonial phenomena are intimately related to both colonialism and their migration. And yet, not all migrations are settler migrations and not all colonialisms are settler colonial: this book argues that settler colonialism should be seen as structurally distinct from both.

Both migrants and settlers move across space and often end up permanently residing in a new locale. Settlers, however, are unique migrants, and, as Mahmood Mamdani has perceptively summarised, settlers "are made by conquest, not just by immigration".[5] Settlers are *founders* of political orders and carry their sovereignty with them (on the contrary, migrants can be seen as *appellants* facing a political order that is already constituted). Migrants can be individually co-opted within settler colonial political regimes, and indeed they often are. They do not, however, enjoy inherent rights and are characterised by a defining lack of sovereign entitlement. It is important that these categories are differentiated analytically: a very different sovereign charge is involved in their respective displacements; not only do settlers and migrants move in inherently different ways, they also move towards very different places. As New Zealand historian James Belich has noted, an "emigrant joined someone else's society, a settler or colonist remade his own".[6] Migrants, by definition, move to *another country* and lead diasporic lives, settlers, on the contrary, move (indeed, as I suggest below, "return") to *their* country. A diaspora is not an ingathering.

Indeed, an analytical distinction could also be made between settler colonial and other resettlements. Imperial, national, and colonising (including internally colonising) states frequently promote "settlement" with the aim of permanently securing their hold on specific locales. On the contrary, the political traditions *Settler Colonialism* focuses on concentrate on autonomous collectives that claim both a special sovereign charge and a regenerative capacity.

Settlers, unlike other migrants, "remove" to establish a better polity, either by setting up an ideal social body or by constituting an exemplary model of social organisation. Of course, even if I propose to see them as analytically distinct, colonialism with settlers and settler colonialism intertwine, interact, and overlap.

Ultimately, whereas migration operates in accordance with a register of difference, settler migration operates in accordance with a register of sameness, and one result of this dissimilarity is that policy in a settler colonial setting is crucially dedicated to enable settlers while neutralising migrants (real life, however, defies these attempts, with settlers recurrently failing to establish the regenerated communities they are supposed to create, and migrants radically transforming the body politic despite sustained efforts to contain and manage their difference).[7] In this context, refugees – the most unwilling of migrants – can thus be seen as occupying the opposite end of a spectrum of possibilities ranging between a move that can be construed as entirely volitional – the settlers' – and a displacement that is premised on an absolute lack of choice (on a settler need to produce refugees as a way to assert their self-identity, see below, "Ethnic Transfer", p. 35).

At the same time, settler colonialism is not colonialism. This is a distinction that is often stated but rarely investigated. And yet, we should differentiate between these categories as well: while it acknowledges that colonial and settler colonial forms routinely coexist and reciprocally define each other, *Settler Colonialism* explores a number of structuring contrasts. In a seminal 1951 article – a piece that in many ways initiated colonial studies as a distinct field of scholarly endeavour – Georges Balandier had defined the colonial "situation" as primarily characterised by exogenous domination and a specific demographic balance:

> the domination imposed by a foreign minority, racially (or ethnically) and culturally different, acting in the name of a racial (or ethnic) and cultural superiority dogmatically affirmed, and imposing itself on an indigenous population constituting a numerical majority but inferior to the dominant group from a material point of view.[8]

Balandier's definition remains influential.[9] Jürgen Osterhammel's more recent and frequently quoted definition of colonialism, for

Demography Key to understanding colonialism / Settler colonialism [handwritten annotation]

example, also insists on foreign rule over a colonised demographic majority. In his outline, colonialism is

> a relationship of domination between an indigenous (or forcibly imported) majority and a minority of foreign invaders. The fundamental decisions affecting the lives of the colonized people are made and implemented by the colonial rulers in pursuit of interests that are often defined in a distant metropolis. Rejecting cultural compromises with the colonized population, the colonizers are convinced of their own superiority and of their ordained mandate to rule.[10]

Historian of British imperialism A. G. Hopkins's definition of settler colonialism as distinct from colonialism is also premised on demography: "Where white settlers became numerically pre-dominant, colonial rule made peoples out of new states; where indigenous societies remained the basis of government, the state was fashioned from existing peoples", he concludes.[11] Similarly, D. K. Fieldhouse's seminal classification had also privileged demography. He had placed "mixed", "plantation", and "pure settlements" colonies on an interpretative continuum: in the "mixed" colonies, settlers had encountered a resilient and sizeable indigenous population and asserted their ascendancy while relying on an indigenous workforce; in the "plantation" colonies, settlers relied on imported and unfree workers; and in the "pure settlement" colonies, the white settlers had eradicated and/or marginalised the indigenous population.[12]

Settler colonial phenomena, however, radically defy these classificatory approaches. As it is premised on the domination of a majority that has become indigenous (settlers are made by conquest *and* by immigration), external domination exercised by a metropolitan core and a skewed demographic balance are less relevant definitory traits. According to these characterisations, colonisers cease being colonisers if and when they become the majority of the population. Conversely, and even more perplexingly, indigenous people only need to become a minority in order to cease being colonised.

At the same time, while Osterhammel's interpretative framework emphasises the antagonisms pitting colonising metropole and colonised periphery, "settler colonial phenomena," as I argue in

settler colonial phenomena [handwritten annotation]

Chapter 1, complicate this dyad by establishing a fundamentally triangular system of relationships, a system comprising metropolitan, settler, and Indigenous agencies. But there are other structuring distinctions. For example, whereas settler colonialism constitutes a circumstance where the colonising effort is exercised from *within* the bounds of a settler colonising political entity, colonialism is driven by an expanding metropole that remains permanently distinct from it. And again: as settlers, by definition, stay, in specific contradistinction, colonial sojourners – administrators, missionaries, military personnel, entrepreneurs, and adventurers – return.[13]

And yet, while the "colonial situation" is not the settler colonial one, and as *Settler Colonialism* programmatically explores a systemic divide between the two, the political traditions outlined in this book are contained *within* the space defined by the extension of Europe's colonial domain. Even if they defy it by espousing a type of sovereignty that is autonomous of the colonising metropole, this book focuses mainly on *European* settlers.[14] I do not want to suggest, *situation* though, that non-Europeans have not been, or cannot be, settlers. If settler colonialism is defined as a "situation", it is not necessarily restricted to a specific group, location or period (or, as I emphasise throughout the book, to the past).

Even though they placed colonialism and settler colonialism within the same analytical frame, reflections on colonial orders and their historiographies have traditionally acknowledged the distinction between colonies of settlement and colonies of exploitation and between "internal" and "external" colonialisms.[15] Classificatory attempts have repeatedly emphasised this separation. For example, Ronald Horvath's analytical definition of colonialism distinguished between "colonialism" and "imperialism" on the basis of a settler presence, Moses I. Finley's argued against the use of "colony" and associated terms when referring to the act of settling new lands; George M. Fredrickson's distinguished between "occupation colonies", "plantation colonies", "mixed colonies", and "settler colonies"; and Jürgen Osterhammel's identified a unique "New England type" of colonial endeavour.[16] Despite this acknowledgement, however – indeed, one result of this acknowledgement – settler colonial phenomena have been generally seen as a subset, albeit a distinct one, of colonial ones.[17] Alternatively, an approach dedicated to highlighting the transcolonial circulation of ideas and practices

Dialectics are described as the tensing [defined] an individual feels when experiencing paradoxical desires that our need / want.

Introduction 7

has placed the colonies of exploitation and settlement – as well as the metropole itself – in the same analytical frame.[18] The notion that colonial and settler colonial forms actually operate in dialectical tension and in specific contradistinction has not yet been fully articulated.

In the 1960s, Louis Hartz's *The Founding of New Societies* proposed a theory of "fragment extrication" (that is, the founding of a new society out of a fragment of the old one) that was entirely unconcerned with colonial and imperial phenomena. Hartz insisted on the separate development of the "fragments", a development that detached them from, rather than subordinated them to, the colonising core: when it came to the founding of new societies, settler colonialism, like the indigenous peoples it had been assaulting, disappeared entirely.[19] Later, in a 1972 article for the *New Left Review*, Arghiri Emmanuel convincingly criticised available theories of imperialism by identifying settler colonialism as an irreducible "third force" that could not be subsumed into neatly construed oppositions. He defined settlers as an "uncomfortable 'third element' in the noble formulas of the 'people's struggle against financial imperialism'", and called for the elaboration of dedicated categories of analysis.[20] Conflicts involving settlers demanded that traditional approaches to understanding colonial and imperial phenomena be revised and integrated. Even in a call to account for an intractable specificity, however, the settlers and their particular agency were detected only as they operated *within* a colonial system of relationships: when it came to the actions of settlers, it was the settler societies that disappeared entirely. The settlers were entering the analytical frame but not settler colonialism; the two terms could not yet be compounded.

Nonetheless (also as a result of the renewed global visibility of indigenous struggles), calls for the study of settler colonialism were repeatedly issued during the following decades. In the late 1970s and early 1980s, Donald Denoon called for a systematic exploration of the specificities characterising settler economic development as structurally opposed to the dynamics of colonial de-development. There is "something distinctive about settler societies, marking them off from metropolitan societies on the one hand, and the rest of the 'third world' on the other", he concluded.[21] Denoon was placing Anglophone and non-Anglophone and developed and developing countries in the same analytical frame: as his analysis encompassed

contradistinction — distinction made by contrasting two things.

colonial and settler colonial settings, this was a crucial passage in the development of a truly global focus. Without concentrating specifically on the development of a settler economy, but still insisting on an intractable systemic specificity, David Prochaska similarly concluded in 1990 that "settler colonialism is a discrete form of colonialism in its own right", and that it should be recognised "as an important and legitimate subtype of imperialism and colonialism".[22] Presenting settler colonialism as a discrete category (even if a subtype), Denoon and Prochaska emphasised again the need to develop dedicated interpretative categories.

In 1990 Alan Lawson proposed the notion of the "Second World", a category equally distinct from the colonising European metropoles and the colonised and formerly colonised Third World (indeed, during these years, a particular branch of postcolonial studies focused on the specific circumstances of settler colonial subjectivities).[23] In line with this interpretative trajectory, Daiva Stasiulis and Nira Yuval Davis have also emphasised in their 1995 comparative overview that settler societies complicate the dichotomy typical of colonial and postcolonial studies between Europe and the rest of the world.[24]

However, these insights have more recently been the subject of sustained analysis. Patrick Wolfe's 1998 definition of settler colonialism distinguished structurally between colonial and settler colonial formations. Wolfe drew a crucial interpretative distinction: settler colonialism *is not* a master–servant relationship "marked by ethnic difference" (as Osterhammel, for example, has argued restating a crucial discursive trait of a long interpretative tradition); settler colonialism *is not* a relationship primarily characterised by the *indispensability* of colonised people.[25] On the contrary, Wolfe emphasised the *dispensability* of the indigenous person in a settler colonial context.

> The primary object of settler-colonization is the land itself rather than the surplus value to be derived from mixing native labour with it. Though, in practice, Indigenous labour was indispensable to Europeans, settler-colonization is at base a winner-take-all project whose dominant feature is not exploitation but replacement. The logic of this project, a sustained institutional tendency to eliminate the Indigenous population, informs a range of

historical practices that might otherwise appear distinct – invasion is a structure not an event.[26]

Wolfe's *Settler Colonialism and the Transformation of Anthropology* could thus be seen as a crucial moment in the "extrication" of settler colonial studies from colonial (and postcolonial) scholarly endeavours: no longer a subset category within colonialism, settler colonialism was now understood as an antitype category. As such, settler colonial phenomena required the development of a dedicated interpretative field, a move that would account for a structuring dissimilarity.

Similarly, in 2000, Anna Johnston and Alan Lawson conceptualised a specifically *settler* form of postcolonial theory. "There are always two kinds of authority and always two kinds of authenticity that the settler subject is (con)signed to desire and disavow", they noted (i.e., the authentic imperial culture from which he is separated and an indigenous authenticity that he desires as a marker of his legitimacy). "The crucial theoretical move to be made is", they argued,

> to see the 'settler' as uneasily occupying a place caught between two First Worlds, two origins of authority and authenticity. One of these is the originating world of Europe, the Imperium – the source of its principal cultural authority. Its 'other' First World is that of the First Nations whose authority they not only replaced and effaced but also desired.[27]

Following a similar trend, during the subsequent decade, a growing number of scholars have approached settler colonialism as a distinct category of analytical inquiry. "Settler" and "colonialism" were now routinely compounded. One tendency was to comparatively appraise legal history, international law, land tenure, judicial institutions, and environmental histories.[28] Edited collections of essays and monographs exploring comparatively specific issues characterising the history of the settler colonial polities (with particular attention dedicated to indigenous–settler interactions) have also appeared.[29] International academic conferences dedicated to settler colonialism in 2007 and 2008 and a special issue of an academic journal published in 2008 confirm that "settler colonial studies" may be consolidating into a distinct field of enquiry.[30]

Transnational character

Besides comparative approaches, in recent years, scholarly activity has continued to focus on the need to distinguish between colonial and settler colonial phenomena. One line of inquiry has placed an emphasis on settler colonialism's inherently transnational character.[31] As settlers and ideas about settlement bypassed the imperial centres and travelled and communicated directly, settler colonialism requires, as suggested by Alan Lester, a "networked" frame of analysis: an approach that inevitably displaces the metropole–periphery hierarchical paradigm that had previously underpinned the evolution of colonial studies.[32] Marilyn Lake drew attention in 2003 to the imaginative coherence of settler colonial formations and emphasised the inadequacy of definitory approaches based on demography. The "defensive project of the 'white man's country' ", she argued,

> was shared by places as demographically diverse as the United States, Canada, New Zealand, Kenya, South Africa, Rhodesia (Zimbabwe) and Australia. Clearly their strategies of government were different – ranging from indirect rule to democratic self-government – but a spatial politics of exclusion and segregation was common to them all and the 'white man' always ruled the 'natives'. In this framework, immigration restriction was merely 'segregation on a large scale' as Stoddard observed in *The Rising Tide of Colour*. 'Nothing is more striking', he added, 'than the instinctive solidarity which binds together Australian and Afrikanders, Californians and Canadians into a "sacred union" '.[33]

Lake also focused on the conflict between settler national projects and their insistence on racial exclusion and imperial demands regarding the freedom of movement of British subjects within the Empire, a conflict crucially pitting colonial and settler colonial sensitivities against each other (a topic that she would later develop further with Henry Reynolds in *Drawing the Global Colour Line*).[34]

Two years later, Caroline Elkins and Susan Pedersen's theoretical definition of settler colonialism emphasised institutionalised settler privilege (especially as it relates to land allocation practices) and a binary settler–native distinction in legal and social structures (especially as it relates to a settler capacity to dominate government).[35] In the introduction to their edited collection they distinguished between twentieth-century "state-oriented expansionism", which was undertaken by "imperial latecomers", and nineteenth-century "settler-oriented semiautonomy", which was typical of colonies where settlement had happened earlier. Deploying a genuinely global perspective, Elkins and Pedersen produced an analysis that was ultimately inclusive of all the settings where settler projects had been operative at one stage or another. Settler colonial forms, they argued, had a global history, a history that could not be limited to the white settler societies or to the settler minorities that had inhabited colonial environments.[36] A further passage in this globalising trend was a new way of implicating the metropolitan core in the history of settler colonialism. In *The Idea of English Ethnicity* (2008), Robert Young suggested that the very notion of an English ethnicity is actually premised on settler colonial endeavours in an expanding British world.[37]

Finally, Belich's 2009 *Replenishing the Earth* outlined a "settler revolution" that had comprehensively transformed colonial practice. Enabling technological changes and a crucial shift in attitudes to migration had created the conditions for "explosive settlement". Without a crucial shift that allowed for the possibility of thinking about life in the settler locale as actually preferable to (and more important than) life in the metropole, this would have been impossible.[38] An awareness of the settler "transition" could in turn sustain an understanding of the relationships between settler peripheries and metropolitan cores that emphasised the immediate sovereign independence of the multiplying settler entities (Belich calls this phenomenon "cloning"). This was a transformation that had crucially *upturned* – not merely complicated in the context of a networked pattern of relationships – the hierarchical relationship between centre and periphery that is intrinsic to colonialism. Settler colonialism had turned colonialism upside down.

Settler Colonialism engages with this literature and aims to integrate it (indeed, as well as an attempt to define settler colonial phenomena and a call to establish settler colonial studies as an independent scholarly field, this book is intended as an entry point to a number of literatures, and in the endnotes I engage extensively with the work of others). Its aim is not so much to confirm a conceptual distinction, but, rather, to emphasise dialectical opposition: colonial and settler colonial forms should not only be seen as separate but also construed as antithetical. The aim is not to construct a coherent narrative, even less so to focus on specific locations. *Settler Colonialism* focuses on settler colonial imaginaries and *forms*; extraordinarily different circumstances are here juxtaposed on the basis of morphological contiguity. In an attempt to analytically disentangle what should be seen as discrete fields, and relying on very diverse sources and literatures, each of the chapters in this book thus deals with a specific aspect of the divide separating colonial and settler colonial phenomena.

Chapter 1 proposes a framework for the interpretation of the structural differences between the population economies of colonial and settler colonial formations. Chapter 2 outlines the specific nature of a settler colonial understanding of sovereignty, a political tradition that is crucially and immediately autonomous of colonial and imperial ones. Chapter 3 approaches the settler colonial mindset, a set of psychic states that are structurally distinct from those operating under colonial circumstances. Finally, Chapter 4 focuses on the different narrative forms underpinning colonial and settler colonial phenomena.

Identifying two separate forms, of course, does not mean that they should not be seen as regularly coexisting on the ground: reality is inevitably complex, and, as I repeatedly note throughout the book, colonial and settler colonial forms constantly interpenetrate each other and overlap in a variety of ways. On the contrary, as the foremost aim of the book is to develop an interpretative framework and language as a starting point for further, more thickly contextualised, research, *Settler Colonialism* is inevitably more programmatic and suggestive than conclusive. With these two crucial disclaimers in mind, the general argument that is developed throughout the book is as follows: on the one hand, the settler colonial situation is characterised by a settler capacity to control the population economy as a marker of a substantive type of sovereignty (Chapters 1 and 2); on the other hand, this situation is associated with a particular state of mind and a specific narrative form (Chapters 3 and 4). Under these circumstances, the possibility of ultimately discontinuing/decolonising settler colonial forms remains problematic.

Of course, even if it has not been the subject of sustained theorisation, the analysis of phenomena that characterise the settler colonial situation in one way or another has been approached from

If settler colonial studies becomes its own field, then what might this suggest about its capacity?

very different perspectives. Traditionally, there was an emphasis on geographical determination; climatic determinism had a significant and long-lasting impact. It was generally assumed that Europeans, and especially Anglo-Saxons, could only truly flourish in temperate zones. Other literatures have emphasised the gradual development of separate identities, focused on pioneering "frontier" activities and their effects, on racial exclusion, and concentrated on white conquering men and their body politics (in specific contradistinction against other colonisers and their habit of reproducing with colonised Others). Language has also been a traditionally emphasised feature, together with the gradual establishment of specifically European institutional and constitutional patterns and associated political institutions.[39] Alternatively, settler colonialism has been approached on the basis of its ultimate success: the eventual foundation of stable settler national polities.[40]

Settler colonialism has also been approached via a focus on a specific positioning in world trade patterns (settler economies operate in "areas of recent settlement" and concentrate on a limited number of "staple" commodities), the comparative analysis of the development of "settler capitalism", the transformation of local biota and landscapes, and a specific demography, where indigenous peoples are swamped by invading Europeans, and other migrations.[41] Specific patterns of land tenure, appropriation and distribution, a predominance of individual initiative over state-centred activities, and, conversely, state promotion and organisation of the settler enterprise have also been emphasised. Yet, other approaches have placed an emphasis on the coloniser's permanence (as opposed to expatriate colonisers and their ultimate departure), on particular spatial politics of exclusion, on specific reproductive regimes (the possibility of reproducing familial patterns is one fundamental defining feature of settler colonial regimes), and on a structural "logic of elimination" (of course, as mentioned, there was always the option of placing an accent on colonialism and conflating settler colonial phenomena within the context of Europe's expansion).[42]

Settler Colonialism argues that the study of settler colonialism should be framed *beside* the study of migrations, colonialisms, comparative economics, environmental transformation, "transplanted" European institutional patterns, "frontier" circumstances, and national formation. Obviously, scholarly debate surrounding

disavow – deny any responsibility or support for

one implication might be that we would, effectively, normalize it as deserving of study

these themes has been sustained and intense for generations – these literatures are massive. And yet, *settler colonialism as a specific forma-tion has not yet been the subject of dedicated systematic analysis.* How can this neglect be explained?

mimetic

disavow

Settler Colonialism suggests that settler colonial phenomena possess a mimetic character, and that a recurrent need to disavow produces a circumstance where the actual operation of settler colonial practices is concealed behind other occurrences (see Chapter 3). The settler hides behind the metropolitan coloniser (the settler is not sovereign, it is argued; "he is not responsible for colonialism" and its excesses), behind the activity of settlers elsewhere, behind the persecuted, the migrant, even the refugee (the settler has suffered elsewhere and "is seeking refuge in a new land"). The settler hides behind his labour and hardship (the settler does not dispossess anyone; he "wres-tles with the land to sustain his family").[43] Most importantly, the peaceful settler hides behind the ethnic cleanser (colonisation is an inherently non-violent activity; the settler enters a "new, empty land to start a new life"; indigenous people naturally and inevitably "vanish"; it is not settlers that displace them – in Australia, for exam-ple, it is the "ruthless convicts" that were traditionally blamed for

impt!

settler colonialism's dirty work).[44] Settler colonialism obscures the conditions of its own production.

A traditional distinction between "colonialism", as exercised over colonised peoples, and "colonisation", as exercised over a colonised land, for example, is a long-lasting and recurring feature of settler colonial representations, and a trait that contributes significantly to remove settler colonialism from view. While this differentiation is premised on the systematic disavowal of any indigenous presence, recurrently representing "colonialism" as something done by some-one else and "colonisation" as an act that is exercised exclusively over the land sustains fantasies of "pristine wilderness" and inno-cent "pioneering endeavour". Moreover, the very shape of the various national historiographies contributes to making settler colonialism difficult to detect. If, in metropolitan historiographies, the "settlers" are undistinguishable from the "emigrants", and these terms are used interchangeably, in the various national settler historiographies,

proto-x

the settlers are the inhabitants of a polity *to come*: proto-Americans, proto-Australians, and so on. In both instances, the settler can hide behind the emigrant and the future citizen and the transfer of a

Mimesis – representation or imitation of the real world in art and literature.

resilient mimetic quality

specific type of political sovereignty is blocked out by a failure to adopt a transnational perspective.

invisibility

Awareness of a resilient mimetic quality, on the other hand, can help explaining why settler colonialism remains currently most invisible where a settler colonial order is most unreconstructed (e.g., Israel and the United States).[45] In these instances, early settler independence ensured that the establishment of a settler colonial order would not need to contend with competing and distorting forms of imperial and colonial interference. And yet, it is in these two polities where (relative to public debate in other settler societies) the very invisibility of settler colonialism is most entrenched. The more it goes without saying, the better it covers its tracks.[46]

It is important that we focus on the settlers, on what they do, and how they think about what they do. True, they have been the traditional subject of historical inquiry, and only recently the experience of indigenous people in settler contexts has been the subject of extensive scholarly activity. And yet, there are also risks intrinsic in focusing primarily on indigenous peoples and their experience. In a seminal essay, and in another context, but underlying a similar dynamic, Ava Baron noted that if we only investigate women, "man" "remains the universal subject against which women are defined in their particularity".[47] We should heed this advice, and similarly focus on settlers as well in order to avoid the possibility that, despite attempts to decolonise our gaze, we continue understanding the settler as normative.[48]

A focus on the global history of settler colonial forms can sustain genuinely transnational approaches (and provide an antidote against parochialising national and state-centred histories).[49] A number of transnational paradigms have been proposed: Atlantic, North Atlantic, mid-Atlantic, continental, hemispheric, oceanic, colonial, comparative, neo-Imperial, and so on.[50] As settler colonialism is constitutively transnational, being essentially about the establishment and consolidation of an exogenous political community following a foundative displacement, establishing settler colonial studies as a distinct scholarly field would provide an inclusive direction for new research.

➔ decolonize our gaze

settler colonial studies a distinct field.

1
Population

A comprehensive body of historical and postcolonial literature highlights how the colonial situation is fundamentally premised on the
sustained reproduction of a series of exclusive dichotomies (i.e., good
and evil, civilised and primitive, culture and nature), the most essential being the one separating coloniser and colonised. In contrast,
in this chapter, I argue that the settler colonial situation establishes
a system of relationships comprising three different agencies: the
settler coloniser, the indigenous colonised, and a variety of differently categorised exogenous alterities. In this context, indigenous
and subaltern exogenous Others appeal to the European sovereign
to articulate grievances emanating from settler abuse, the metropolitan agency interposes its sovereignty between settler and indigenous
or subaltern exogenous communities (establishing "protectorates" of
Aborigines, for example), and settlers insist on their autonomous
capacity to control indigenous policy.[1] In its etymological sense,
"economy" refers to the act of governing a household. Settler
colonialism is about domesticating; "population economy" is used
here to refer to recurring settler anxieties pertaining to the need
to biopolitically manage their respective *domestic* domains.[2] Settlers
resent imperial interference; their capacity to manage the population
economy of a settler locale can be identified as one crucial marker of
settler substantive sovereignty.

Significantly, however, the settler colonial situation is generally
understood as an inherently dynamic circumstance where indigenous and exogenous Others progressively disappear in a variety of ways: extermination, expulsion, incarceration containment,

and assimilation for indigenous peoples (or a combination of all these elements), restriction and selective assimilation for subaltern exogenous Others, and an ultimate affirmation of settler control against exogenous metropolitan interference (or a coordinated devolution of responsibility that pre-empts the need for revolutionary disruptions on the other). Only the settler body politic in its ultimate sovereign assertion against metropolitan interference and against indigenous residues or other insurgencies is expected to survive an inherently temporary triangulation.

In this chapter, I interpret the settler colonial situation as primarily premised on the irruption into a specific locale of a sovereign collective of settlers. This chapter sketches the ways in which settler colonial projects interpret and set out to manage the population economy of their respective domains: the first section outlines the ways in which relations can be conceptualised within this situation; the second section focuses on "transfer" as a foundational trait of settler colonial formations.

Population economy and settler collective

As a self-constituted settler body politic is established through a foundational sovereign movement across space (see Chapter 2), two negatively defined alterities are brought into existence: they comprise those who *have not* moved out to establish a political order (migrants are not settlers), unlike those who belong to the settler collective, and those who *have not* autonomously moved in, unlike those who belong to the settler collective.[3] They are the exogenous and indigenous Others. Indeed, colonialism and settler colonialism should be seen as distinct especially because two is not three. Architect of Latin American independences Simón Bolívar poignantly commented in 1819 on an inherently triangular system of relationships:

> We are neither Europeans nor Indians, but a mixed species [sic] midway between aborigines and Spaniards. Americans by birth and Europeans by law, we find ourselves engaged in a dual conflict, disputing with the natives for titles of ownership, and at the same time struggling to maintain ourselves in the country of our birth against the opposition of the [Spanish] invaders. Thus our position is most extraordinary and complicated.[4]

And yet, considering the truly global spread of settler colonial forms, that position, while certainly complicated, especially in a Latin American context, is not particularly extraordinary: all settler projects need to manage in specific ways the triangular relationships involving settlers on the one hand, and indigenous and exogenous Others on the other.[5]

A relational system comprising three elements complicates the bilateral opposition between coloniser and colonised that is paradigmatic in the interpretative categories developed by colonial studies – what Jürgen Osterhammel defines in his typological classification of colonial phenomena as the inherent "construction of inferior 'otherness' ", and Partha Chatterjee calls the "rule of colonial difference" (of course, "inferior 'otherness'" is also present in a settler colonial circumstance; crucially, however, in this case, it is understood as a temporary rather than a permanent presence).[6] True, immigrant exogenous Others often benefit from the dispossession of indigenous people, even as their incorporation within the structures of the settler body politics remains pending (they are implicated; however, their positioning *is* distinctive). On the other hand, this triangular understanding of the settler colonial situation underlines the constitutive hegemony of the settler component: even if indigenous and exogenous subalternities are dialectically related to it, indeed, exactly because of these relationships, it is the settler that establishes himself as normative.[7]

How these agencies relate to each other, of course, varies dramatically. And yet, two fundamental variables can be identified. On the one hand, as the settler colonial situation is established via the movement across space of an exogenous collective of people, an indigenous/exogenous dialectic is established. (Sometimes, the indigenous/exogenous dialectic is complicated by settler claims to an "historical" right to the land, as in Zionism as a settler colonial project, or in the case of French constructions of Algeria and Italian imaginings of Libya as a locale destined to be transformed into settler colonial space. In these cases, settlers think of themselves as indigenous *ex abrupto*.)[8] On the other hand, settlers are righteous, and since their movement is performed in the context of a sovereign entitlement that travels with the settler collective, a righteous/degraded dialectic is also instituted. A series of explanatory diagrams describing heuristically the relational geometry characterising the settler

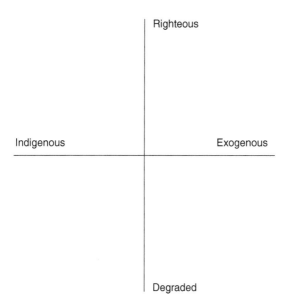

Figure 1.1 Population economy

colonial situation can thus be devised, where various groups can be plotted differently depending on their indigenous or exogenous character, and their supposed morality and potential for rectitude (Figure 1.1).

These categories and the people they endeavour to identify, of course, are open to ongoing and protracted contestation, are never neatly separate, mutually shape each other, and are continually tested and reproduced. And yet, even radically dissimilar representational regimes, as recurring contestations confirm, with debate focusing on the possibility of establishing regenerated communities through settlement and resettlement, ultimately share a perception of the fundamental structures informing the population economy of a settler colonial locale. The upper section of this system is thus characterised by the possibility of regeneration and improvability, the lower section is characterised by its impossibility.[9]

The idioms of settler colonialism confirm the high/low dialectic in accordance with a cluster of orientational metaphors (these metaphors, however, are not always systematic: settlers, for example, move *forward* towards the *back*woods, the *back*country, the *back*blocks, the out*back*, and so on; their claim becomes "higher" the closer it is to the soil, and the "depth" or "shallowness" of a settler claim is a recurring issue of great concern).[10] When settlers claim land, it is recurrently in the context of a language that refers to "higher use", and assimilation policies are recurrently designed to "uplift", "elevate", and "raise" indigenous communities. In modern Hebrew, *aliyah* means "ascent", and to settle on the land is, literally, "to ascend to the soil" (conversely but consistently, *yerida* – emigration – means "descent").[11] At the same time, the settler irruption is from the right of field, a movement that flattens the indigenous sector of the population system on "the past" and confirms what anthropologist Johannes Fabian has called in a different context "denial of coevalness" (this denial is relevant, as I will point out, to the conceptual strategies that settler colonialism develops *vis à vis* indigenous peoples).[12]

In a context where the settler collective is fundamentally defined by permanent residency *and* sovereign entitlement, there are, as mentioned, a number of differently categorised exogenous Others: those who are in place but have not yet been given access to political rights as settlers, those who are in place but cannot belong to the settler body politic (e.g., variously defined racialised Others in each settler context), those who could belong but have not committed to the settler political community (potential settlers who retain a permanent right to migrate to the settler locale), and those who are permanently restricted from entering the settler locale.[13] In other words: those who lack either one of the defining settler traits, and those who lack both – those who have *not yet* been admitted within the structures of the settler body politic, those who have *not yet* become permanently excluded, those who have *not yet* crossed the line separating inside from outside, and those who are *never* to cross that limit. The settler colonial situation is thus characteristically perceived as a dynamic environment where different groups are routinely imagined as transiting from one section of the population system to another.

The settler collective

Crucially, as it is coming from elsewhere *and* as it sees itself as permanently situated, the settler collective is indigenous *and* exogenous at the same time (this ambiguity is not reproduced, of course, in the context of the righteous/degraded dialectic: the settler collective invariably represents itself as virtuous). Ambivalent emotional strategies relating to location and origin are thus one consequence of settler colonialism's inherent ambiguity. Settler colonial nationalisms, for example, focus on at least two spaces of origin. On the one hand, the "Outback", the *"brousse"*, the "frontier", the "backblocks", the "True North" and so on provide a mythical reference for "indigenisation" processes, allowing for crucial settler investment in place and landscape.[14] On the other, settlers also routinely articulate diasporic identities via a focus on ancestral "roots" that are located elsewhere.[15] The settler has a filiative and an affiliative connection with "home", but "home" is alternatively (or simultaneously) both the "old" and the "new" place. The settler collective can thus be seen as occupying an indigenous/exogenous sector in the top section of the population system (see Figure 1.2).

In the context of a situation that is perceived as inherently dynamic, however, there are conflicting tendencies operating at the same time on the settler collective: one striving for indigenisation and national autonomy, the other aiming at neo-European replication and the establishment of a "civilised" pattern of life.[16] Indigenisation is driven by the crucial need to transform an historical

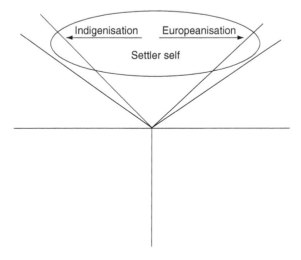

Figure 1.2   The settler collective

tie ("we came here") into a natural one ("the land made us").[17] Europeanisation consists in the attempt to sustain and reproduce European standards and way of life. Both trends remain fundamental features of settler projects. Historians of eighteenth-century British North America, for example, have faced for decades the apparent paradox of independence and "Americanisation" on the one hand, and recolonisation and "Anglicisation" on the other proceeding together, of a society becoming "more creole and more metropolitan" at once.[18] Similarly, the tension between the "frontier" thesis and Anglo-Saxon exceptionalism (one focusing on a particular circumstance, the other on the peculiar qualities of a special human material) also remained unresolved.[19] If one considers the inherent dynamism of the settler colonial situation, however, these oppositions are not irreconcilable: as both processes refer exclusively to the segment of the population system that is characterised by improvability, indigenisation and Europeanisation can be, and are, routinely compounded. The settler colonial idioms of "improvement" and "progress" refer to both.

While these tendencies are only ostensibly opposed, they operate in a context in which the settler colonial entity endeavours systematically to supersede its settler colonial features.[20] A completely Europeanised setting has ceased being settler colonial as much as a totally indigenised one has. This is another constitutive difference between the colonial and the settler colonial situation. A triumphant colonial society is a state of affairs where, as noted by Partha Chatterjee, change, the promised equality between coloniser and colonised, is forever postponed, where coloniser and colonised know and ultimately retain their respective places. On the contrary, a triumphant settler colonial circumstance, having ceased to be a dependency of a colonising metropole, having tamed the surrounding "wilderness", having extinguished indigenous autonomy, and having successfully integrated various migratory waves, has also ceased being settler colonial.[21] In other words, Europeanisation and indigenisation respond to the complementary needs of transforming the environment to suit the colonising project and of renewing the settler in order to suit the environment. These tendencies, of course, can be harmonised in a variety of ways, and the "changes in the land" inevitably correspond to the making of a "new man" (settler colonial traditions are particularly concerned with the possibility of regenerated manhood). Scholars of Europe overseas and its "simplification" have contested for decades whether continuity or discontinuity with European templates should be seen as dominant. Hartz's theory of "fragment extrication" focused on Europe and emphasised (fragmented) continuity; historical geographers disagreed and concentrated on land and market conditions in the new lands (and discontinuity). If one allows for the sustained copresence of both indigenisation and Europeanisation, however, the two approaches can be actually seen as mutually supporting and defining each other.[22]

Then again, neither indigenisation nor Europeanisation, despite recurring fantasies of ultimate supersession, is never complete, and a settler society is always, in Deriddean terms, a society "to come", characterised by the *promise* rather than the practice of a truly "settled" lifestyle.[23] Indigenisation and Europeanisation could then be seen as asindotic progressions: the line separating settler and indigenous must be approached but is never finally crossed, and the same goes for neo-European imitation, where sameness should be emphasised but difference is a necessary prerequisite of the absolute need to at once distinguish between settler self and indigenous and exogenous Others.[24] In the end, the indigenous remains always more genuinely indigenous, and "cultural cringes" linger on: "demisavages" and "horrible colonials" lurk behind all representations of regenerated frontier manhood (unshaved barbarians are a recurring concern of settler colonial imaginative traditions).

Settler projects thus express an unresolved tension between sameness and difference. Benedict Anderson has focused on the "spectre of comparisons" as it applies to the ways in which colonised peoples perceive their world: a double consciousness that compels them to see through the prism of a dominant culture.[25] In this way, the "spectre of comparisons" also haunts the way in which settlers see their world: comparisons highlighting the specific contradistinction separating indigenous and settler, contrasts with "home", of course, but also comparative references to other settlers and their projects (or with other modes of colonial practice). As a result, parallel to Australasian references to "Better Britonism", or Zionist images of redeemed Jewish life, for example, settler national projects are also often self-defined in opposition to corresponding exemplary settlerhoods (see, for example, a recurring Canadian insistence on

"orderly" frontiers vs. US "chaotic" conquest or New Zealand traditional representations of a humanitarian colonisation vs. Australian
destruction).[26] Settler colonialism is indeed a form of peer review-
ing: even when indigenous and settler agencies are the only ones
left contending on the ground, there is always an absent presence,
metropolitan or otherwise, that contributes to shaping the settler
colonial situation.[27]

Of course, settlers occupy the borderlands of their section. At one
end of the spectrum, they can be represented as collectives that
have "gone native", or, alternatively, they can be perceived as
inhabiting the exogenous margin of the settler segment of the population system. These are groups that have managed to retain a
"European" cultural specificity, a trait dialectically opposed to that
of more indigenising settler counterparts (depending on different
political sensitivities, these variants can be represented as either
positive or negative deviations).[28] In Quebec, the *habitant* is routinely represented as attached to both the soil and to "European"
traditions in opposition to the *coureur des bois*.[29] In Argentina,
gauchos are opposed to the Europeanising inclination of the liberal
elites; in Australia, "nomad" pastoral workers have been contrasted
against sober smallholders, and so on.[30] At any rate, settler projects
need to maintain an ongoing balance between indigenisation and
Europeanisation while embracing both, and this split is rarely
reconciled.[31] As noted by Henry Nash Smith in his classic reconstruction of Daniel Boone's historiographical career, this tension can
even exist within a single character: "the harbinger of civilization
and refinement", and someone perpetually escaping from it. "The
image of the Wild Western hero could serve either purpose," he
concluded.[32]

Indigenous Others

According to the representational regimes of settler colonial imaginative traditions, indigenous people are also ambiguously located:
they can be represented as "virtuous" and dignified, or "debased"
and savage (or both; indeed, each definition necessitates its dialectical counterpoint). The indigenous Others can be seen occupying the
left-hand section of this system. The movement that institutes the
settler colonial situation creates a further distinction between indigenous people that have been transformed by contact and those who
are awaiting this transformation.[33] True, indigenous people are rarely

represented as inherently virtuous, but sometimes they are (in these cases, however, it is their *potential* for morality that is especially emphasised). As John Comaroff and Alan Lester and David Lambert among others have explored in the case of early nineteenth-century South Africa, for example, missionary and settler perceptions can clash over the issue of an indigenous capacity to lead a regenerated lifestyle.[34] Nonetheless, beside not infrequent attempts to physically liquidate the indigenous presence, the general tendency in this context is to perceive the indigenous population as rapidly degrading and/or vanishing. The possibility of indigenous assimilation, though, as Jeffersonian images of "peaceable assimilation" continuously coexisting with genocidal impulses confirm, is habitually retained. Again, degradation and absorption are only apparently contradicting each other: as they both operate in the context of a progressive erasure of the indigenous presence (assimilating one part, and effacing the other in a variety of ways), they also refer to circumstances in which the settler colonial situation operates towards its ultimate supersession. In this context, fantasies of ultimately "emptying" in one way or another the indigenous section of the population system inevitably recur (Figure 1.3).[35]

At times, the indigenous community's very indigeneity is questioned (see below, "Transfer by Conceptual Displacement", p. 35). In these cases, they are perceived and treated as exogenous Others

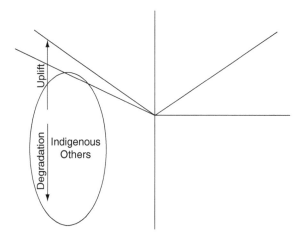

Figure 1.3   Indigenous Others

and become likely candidates for deportation (it is a recurrent phenomenon: black South Africans were thought to have entered the settler space after the Boer treks of the 1830s, and, in a different context, but in a similar fashion, Palestinians have also been represented as non-indigenous to Palestine; more generally, indigenous peoples – even Australian Aborigines – are frequently seen as "lost tribes" coming from somewhere else).[36] On the other hand, indigenous peoples can also be construed as putative settlers occupying a "higher" sector of the indigenous section of the population economy (e.g., representations of the "Aryan Maori" in New Zealand).[37] In this case, indigenous people are understood as awaiting closer association with the structures of the settler body politic (irrespective of whether this actually eventuates).

Exogenous Others

The exogenous Others that reside within the bounds of the settler entity can be seen as occupying a section on the right-hand side of the population system. They can also be represented either as "virtuous" or potentially so, or "debased" and hopelessly so. In the upper sector of the exogenous Others segment of the population system are the "probationary" settlers, waiting to be individually admitted into the settler body politic.[38] The main trend is towards a process of selective inclusion for individual exogenous Others that have entered or are entering the population economy, even though this is often quite controversial (on the other hand, access to migratory flows is often crucial in ensuring the very viability of the settler project). At the same time, selective inclusion is premised both on a categorisation that allows particular people to be considered for inclusion within the structures of the settler body politic *and* on a particular consciousness that allows specific migrants to embrace a settler colonial ethos. Selective inclusion necessitates collaboration. Integration and exclusion thus co-define each other. Nativist agitation in a number of settler settings, for example, moved from sustained attacks against Irish Catholicism in the earlier decades of the nineteenth century to attacking Asian labour in the later ones. This shift marks the 'whitening' of Irishness, but also underscores an ongoing settler need to pit indigenising settlers against exogenous (often racialised) alterities.

There are, however, recurring calls for deporting people that are construed as undesirable and exogenous (see, for example, repeated attempts to promote the "colonisation" elsewhere of emancipated African Americans in nineteenth-century United States, or the deportation of Queensland Kanak workers that inaugurated Australia as a federal entity).[39] Alternatively, the possibility of permanent segregation for these undesirables is also considered. As assimilatory selective inclusion (this includes variously constructed multicultural turns – "multicultural", after all, is a term that originated in settler Canada), expulsion, and segregation remain compatible management strategies, they all operate to ultimately empty the exogenous Others sector of the population system. More generally, as in the previous cases, these complementary strategies also contribute to settler colonialism's ongoing drive towards its own supersession (Figure 1.4).

Abject Others

In the lowest section of the population system dwell the abject Others: irredeemable, they are permanently excluded from the settler

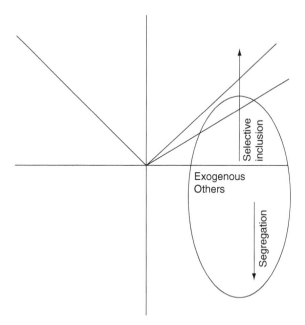

Figure 1.4 Exogenous Others

body politic, and have lost their indigenous or exogenous status. These people are disconnected from their land and communities, are the subject of segregative practices that are construed as enduring, and are principally characterised by restrained mobility (the absolute opposite of a settler capacity for unfettered mobility). Ongoing repression, of course, is one crucial element in the production of abject Otherness. However, even a recognition of native title, or a recognition of indigenous sovereignty in the context of renewed "treaty" traditions, as they discriminate between indigenous Others that retain entitlements and those who do not, is a crucial site for the constitution of abject Otherness.

A successful settler society is managing the orderly and progressive emptying of the indigenous and exogenous Others segments of the population economy and has permanently separated from the abject Others, drawing internal and external lines that cannot be crossed. If the settler collective epitomises a synthesis of indigenous and exogenous virtues, the abject Others typify a synthesis of indigenous and exogenous degeneracy – the two types remain dialectically linked (Figure 1.5).

A settler world

The original displacement of the settler collective also institutes an inside/outside dialectic. On the outside, as the indigenous/exogenous

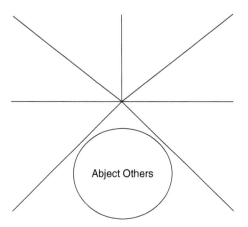

Figure 1.5   Abject Others

opposition becomes meaningless, the representational regimes of settler colonialism see either "improvable" or "non-improvable" people. From a variously defined notion of "home" (e.g., "England", "Britain", "Europe" – but there can be diasporic "homes", in the case of French Algeria, the north-western Mediterranean shore, in the case of Zionism as a settler colonial project, the "world Jewry"), settler migration flows directly into the settler segment of the population system, or, alternatively, migrants enter the improvable segment of the exogenous Others section. People needing reform (convicts, indentured and displaced persons, political prisoners, paupers, orphans, and others) would access the population system in this section, provided that they are deemed capable of eventual admission within the settler sector of the population economy. Beside "home", there is the "non-home" category, from which people may be allowed entry to the improvable section of the exogenous Others sector of the population system (although this is often quite a contentious issue, and different settler sensitivities may disagree on the improvability of specific groups). Exogenous Others that are perceived as unimprovable are permanently restricted entry: settler nativist agitation sees to it (Figure 1.6).[40]

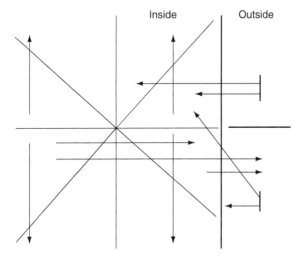

Figure 1.6 A settler colonial world

The internal–external dialectic operates to the right of the population system and indigenous people are prevented from establishing unmediated associations with external agencies. The settler polities stubbornly insist on a capacity to treat indigenous relations as an exclusively internal matter and have collectively opposed in 2007 the UN Universal Declaration on the Rights of Indigenous Peoples.[41] It is important to note that while, internally, the population economy takes a triangular shape, externally, settler colonial representational regimes remain stubbornly bilateral. On the outside, as Donald Denoon noted in relation to the long history of Australian eager involvement in overseas interventions, settlers inhabit a fundamentally colonial world.[42] Ronald Robinson's 1970s recognition of the settler as an "ideal prefabricated collaborator" of imperial endeavours could thus be recontextualised: the settler collaborates on the outside and, at the same time, asserts an independent sovereign capacity on the inside.[43] Appraising external subservience *as a function* of internal sovereign assertion can contribute to explaining, for example, the settler polities of the British Empire's commitment to it.[44]

Managing this population system and the processes that characterise it can be problematic. Indigenous and exogenous subjectivities/alterities and their internal but separate positioning must be administered in flexible ways.[45] Hybrid forms also structurally upset a settler population economy.[46] As one scholar has recently noted, "the success of *mestizaje* as a racial ideology" is the reason why a settler colonial paradigm remains inapplicable to Latin America (*mestizaje* as an official ideology, however, affects different Latin American countries differently: decidedly more Mexico and Brazil, than, for example, Bolivia or Argentina).[47] Hybrid forms disturb the triangular system of relationships inherent in the settler colonial situation, and ultimately reproduce a dual system where two constitutive categories are mixed without being subsumed.[48] In the end, as hybridity reproduces a constituent dual logic, it relates to colonial forms rather than settler colonial ones.[49] (On the contrary, settler colonial representational regimes need a triangular system of relationships: if the settler self is both indigenous *and* exogenous, it needs two dialectical counterpoints, not one – an indigenous and an exogenous one.)

If, in the context of a settler colonial population economy, hybrid life is a sexually transmitted disease, a triumphant settler entity has established a sovereign capacity to supervise indigenous and exogenous reproduction and is efficiently managing indigenous/exogenous mixing by suppressing its very possibility. Aboriginal people living "under the act", for example, needed officially sanctioned permission to marry in early twentieth-century Australia, and the 1897 Queensland *Aboriginal Protection and Restriction of the Sale of Opium Act* (which was a prototypical example of similar legislation elsewhere in Australia) envisaged complete governmental control over Aboriginal family life. Likewise, slave marriages in pre-Civil War United States were subjected to ongoing approval by the relevant slave owners.[50] Conversely, an anxious settler society expresses doubts regarding its ultimate capacity to patrol the borderlands of its population economy (self-assurance and anxiety, however, can and often coexist).[51] Hence, the recurrent strategic need to steal mixed children, and the determined and sustained attempt to repress indigenous/exogenous collective ethnicity, as epitomised, for example, by the historical experiences of the Métis in Canada and the Griqua people in South Africa.[52]

As explored by Wolfe in a seminal article dedicated to the various classificatory regimes involving indigenous people in Australia and the United States and blacks in the United States and Brazil, settler sovereign control over the population economy can manifest itself in several ways.[53] The "one-drop rule", for example (according to which any non-white ancestry makes an individual non-white), applies to African Americans, but not to indigenous people in Australia and the United States (Wolfe detected yet another pattern in Brazil's classificatory regimes).[54] And yet, even if the population economy management strategies applicable to indigenous and exogenous Others are ostensibly varied, as they both subsume racially mixed peoples in one or the other racial category, they both effectively deny the possibility of reproducing *mestizo* or mulatto existence (the legal status of Mulattoes in antebellum America, for example, was initially intermediate but was eventually reduced to that of "pure" blacks, and a colonial system came to resemble a settler colonial one).

The sustained compartmentalisation of the sectors accommodating indigenous and exogenous Others is all important to the management of a settler colonial population economy; *mestizo* and mulatto – even if they are to be repressed, indeed, exactly because they must be repressed – should remain the only possible hybrid categories.[55] (On the other hand, indigenous and exogenous Others mix; American indigenous scholar Jack Forbes, for example, recommended that we recover and appraise the inescapably triangular nature of ethnic relations in American society.)[56] In this context, the defining borders separating settler normativity and non-settler alterities can be reinforced or undermined at different times and for different purposes. Indeed, a selective capacity to draw lines and/or to erase them depending on opportunity and local circumstances constitutes a crucial marker of settler substantive sovereignty.

Inclusion and exclusion should thus be seen as operating concurrently.[57] Appraising fundamentally different political traditions in the United States and their emphasis on *either* inclusion or exclusion, Rogers M. Smith, for example, has critiqued "Tocquevillian" interpretations and their focus on liberal democratic traditions of political inclusion for neglecting stubborn legacies of racial, gender, and ethnic exclusion. (This neglect is performed in a variety of ways: by denying exclusion, interpreting it as an aberration, or a "tangential" tendency, and by outlining its eventual defeat or its marginal status.) On the contrary, Smith proposed that inclusion and exclusion be seen as coexisting in the context of a multiple-traditions political culture. This insight is relevant to understanding settler colonial forms. One result of this ambivalence/flexibility is that the borders separating settler and indigenous alterities can be undermined and reinforced concomitantly and without a need for consistency, as recently demonstrated in Australia, for example, by the simultaneous operation of the Northern Territory "intervention" (which in practice selectively suspends the *Racial Discrimination Act* [1975]) and the delivery of Prime Minister Kevin Rudd's 2008 apology. Settlers can be simultaneously attracted and disgusted; they often at once cherish and denigrate indigenous alterities.

In any case, the boundaries separating the indigenous and exogenous Others segments of the population system from contiguous sectors is that they must be internally porous and externally impermeable: one can get out but cannot get back in.[58] At the same time, while some boundaries must be understood as inherently temporary, for the same reason, irreducible residues must be understood as permanently excluded from access to the settler body politic. Perhaps the most salient feature of the population economies of settler colonialism is that whereas the tensions in force over the settler component lead "higher", those operating on the indigenous and exogenous Others lead inexorably "out".

Transfer and settler colonialism

The very possibility of a settler project – a collective sovereign displacement – is premised on what historian of the "Angloworld" James Belich has defined as "mass transfer", the capacity of shifting substantial clusters of peoples across oceans and mountain ranges.[59] On the other hand, as the settler colonial situation is primarily defined by an inherent drive towards supersession, the two non-settler/non-normative sectors of the population economy must be seen as disappearing in a variety of ways. Following and expanding on Palestinian scholar Nur Mashala's intuition that (Palestinian) "transfer" is the foundational category in Zionist thought, this section argues that all settler projects are foundationally premised on fantasies of ultimately "cleansing" the settler body politic of its (indigenous and exogenous) alterities.[60] The settler (mass) transfer – transfer is a more flexible term than, for example, removal – is thus mirrored dialectically by an array of other ones. This section lists a number of strategies that can be deployed *vis à vis* the indigenous population in order to enact a variety of transfers.

In the context of a settler colonial population economy, of course, a transferist imagination and practice applies to exogenous Others as well, as demonstrated, for example, by the deportation and dispersal following the British conquest of the entire Acadian population of what would become Nova Scotia (yet again, the Acadians could be represented as a community that had compromised itself by associating too closely with local indigenous people).[61] It is not surprising that the possibility of transferring people that can be construed as exogenous Others becomes especially tempting in the presence of unregulated migratory flows and other securitarian concerns. Moreover, the transfers of indigenous and exogenous Others are intimately related (in fact, transfer capabilities acquired in dealing with one group can be deployed in dealing with the other one).[62] The enactment of one transfer can facilitate, for example, conceiving the other, and calls for the "colonization" of freed African Americans in pre-Civil War United States were issued alongside demands for the removal of Indians. Nevertheless, this section focuses on transfer as applicable to indigenous people because exogenous Others, unlike their indigenous counterparts, do not challenge with their very presence the basic legitimacy of the settler entity (i.e., while the sustained presence of exogenous Others confirms the indigenisation of the settler collective, the presence of an indigenous residue dele gitimises it). In any case, despite their symmetrical positioning *vis à vis* settler normativity, the integration of exogenous Others is relatively less complicated than the integration of indigenous people. Belonging within the settler polity can be more easily organised for exogenous Others on the basis of a common exogenous origin and an emancipatory passage that follows displacement than, for indigenous Others, on the basis of a qualified dispensation granting rights that are premised on an original dispossession. It is no coincidence that settlers routinely fantasise about exchanging indigenous peoples with exogenous Others.[63]

As the historical experience of Palestinians confirms, transfer does not exclusively apply to bodies pushed across borders.[64] On the other hand, as I detail below, transfer does not apply exclusively to Palestinians either. The transferist approaches itemised here are obviously different from each other. Some operate discursively, others operate at the level of practice; indeed, some are way less offensive than others. At times, they complement each other and are deployed concomitantly; at times, they are premised on the successful enactment of previous transfers. Often different transfers are presented as alternative options (it is either one transfer *or* another, which pre-empts the possibility of avoiding transfer altogether), and as compassionate policy. Sometimes different transfers are antithetical and mutually exclusive, but they can also overlap and blur into each other. Indeed, different strategies can become activated at different times and in response to the settler project's relative power and specific necessities.[65] Moreover, different settler concerns recurrently propose different transfers targeting different aspects of indigenous life: settlers and their legislatures agitate for removal, missionaries for assimilation, the state operates by way of administrative transfers, and so on. However, as all these strategies aim to manipulate the population economy by discursively or practically emptying the indigenous sector of the population system (or sections of it), they share a transferist rationale. In the end, while the suppression of indigenous and exogenous alterities characterises both colonial and settler colonial formations, the former can be summarised as domination for the purpose of exploitation, the latter as domination for the purpose of transfer.

(A) **Necropolitical transfer:** when the indigenous communities are militarily liquidated.[66]

(B) **Ethnic transfer:** when indigenous communities are forcibly deported, either within or without the territory claimed or controlled by the settler entity. Wherever they end up, they cease being indigenous. Examples of this type of transfer are the forced removal of Cherokees from Georgia, and the expulsion of Palestinians from their homes during the Arab-Israeli conflict of 1948.[67] Settler colonial projects are specifically interested in turning indigenous peoples into refugees: refugees, even more so peoples that have been repeatedly forced to abandon their homes, are by definition indigenous to somewhere else – the very opposite of "Aboriginal".

This type of transfer can happen when indigenous people are moved into reservations *and* when they are moved out of them. The background and stated objectives of different policies can vary; there is a predictable and transferist insistence, however, on ensuring that indigenous people are serially mobilised.[68] Variously defined delusions of implementing "voluntary transfers" fit in with this type of transfer: after all, while the line separating voluntary and coerced migrations is traditionally a difficult one to draw, from a structural point of view, from the point of view of the population economy of a settler colonial circumstance, the distinction is largely irrelevant.

(C) **Transfer by conceptual displacement:** when indigenous peoples are not considered indigenous to the land and are therefore perceived as exogenous Others who have entered the settler space at some point in time and preferably after the arrival of the settler collective. A complementary corollary to this type of transfer is that local indigenous peoples can then be collapsed into an unspecified wider "native" category. Indigenous South Africans could therefore become "foreign natives" and "Africans". Similarly, Palestinians and Algerians could become "Arabs". As this wider category inhabits borderlands *outside* of the territory claimed by the settler entity, this type of transfer allows for the possibility of discursively displacing indigenous people to the exterior of the settler locale.

Transfer by conceptual displacement works equally in situations where indigenous people are perceived to be coming in from somewhere else and when they are perceived to be coming from nowhere in particular. Ubiquitous representations of indigenous people as pathologically mobile and "nomadic", constantly engaged in unpredictable and periodical migrations, "traversing" but not occupying the land, "roaming", "overrunning", "skulking", "wandering", and so on, fall within this category of transfer.[69]

(D) **Civilisational transfer:** when indigenous peoples in their supposed traditional form are represented as putative settlers. The already mentioned New Zealand tradition representing Maori as "Aryans" and French representations of the Algerian Kabyles emphasising, in contradistinction against local Arabs, their independence, sedentarism, secularism, and democratic social organisation are examples of this type of transfer. Alexis de Tocqueville, for example, celebrated the Kabyles by "Europeanising" them:

> Among the Kabyles, the form of property and the organization of government are as democratic as you can imagine; in Kabylia, the tribes are small, restless, less fanatical than the Arab tribes, but much fonder of their independence, which they will never surrender to anyone. Among the Kabyles, every man is involved in public affairs; the authority that governs them is weak, elections are always moving power from one to another. If you wanted to find a point of comparison in Europe [and Tocqueville certainly wanted], you might say that the inhabitants of Kabylia are like the Swiss of the small cantons of the Middle Ages.[70]

Civilisational transfer and transfer by conceptual displacement, however, interact. Charles Ageron, for example, notes how "the Kabyles were held to be descendants of the Gauls(!), the Romans, Christian Berbers of the Roman period or the German Vandals(!)."[71] The Kabyles were thus indigenous *unlike* the invading Arabs, and exogenous *like* the incoming French. Two types of transfer could thus be simultaneously operative in this context: the Arabs were not indigenous; the Kabyles could be represented as putative settlers (at least until they rebelled). In these cases, paradoxically, as one specific form of indigeneity is ostensibly celebrated, indigenous people cease to be perceived as indigenous at all. In Australia, during the first half of the twentieth century, as Russell McGregor has pointed out, "a significant strand of scientific opinion has held the Australian

Aboriginals to be racially akin to the Caucasians".[72] According to this type of transfer, the Europeans were not "returning" to Australia, but the Aborigines had once been "Europeans". Founder of the Israeli state Ben Gurion had fantasised in the 1910s and 1920s (i.e., *before* the beginning of militant Palestinian resistance) about Palestinian farmers being the descendants of Biblical Jews. Civilisational transfer was thus one way of immediately indigenise the settler on the one hand, and establishing the equivalence of settler and indigenous claims on the other.[73]

This is indeed a powerful form of transfer. Failing in that particular context to register Maori as indigenous, the New Zealand Federation Commissioners attending proceedings in federating Australia eventually recommended *against* federation on the basis of what they perceived as the colonies very questionable racial composition, a state of affairs that they deemed unsuitable to New Zealand standards of settlerness. At the end of the War of Algerian independence, a substantial number of collaborating Harkis were "repatriated" to France with the departing settlers.[74]

(E) Perception transfer: when indigenous peoples are disavowed in a variety of ways and their actual presence is not registered (perception transfer can happen, for example, when indigenous people are understood as part of the landscape). Examples of a systematic propensity to "empty" the landscape of its original inhabitants are ubiquitous: indigenous people are not seen, they lurk in thickets; ultimately, even if they were around, they may have been wiped out by a variety of what the Massachusetts Puritans called Providence's "wonderful preparation". Perception transfer is a crucial prerequisite to other forms of transfer; for example, it is crucial in allowing the successive activation of transfer by conceptual displacement. One of its consequences is that when really existing indigenous people enter the field of settler perception, they are deemed to have entered the settler space and can therefore be considered exogenous.

(F) Transfer by assimilation: when indigenous people are "uplifted" out of existence.[75] This transfer does not necessarily imply the displacement of indigenous people. The *language* of assimilation, however, inevitably refers to movement: assimilation "raises" indigenous

peoples (see Figure 1.3). A classic version of this type of transfer is envisaged in Canada's *Gradual Civilisation Act* of 1857 and
the subsequent *Gradual Enfranchisement Act* of 1869. These acts distinguished between "status Indian" and "Canadian citizen", and
allowed for conditional cooptation within the settler body politic for
indigenous persons that rejected their traditional communities and
"individualised" their land (in this case, transfer by assimilation was
accompanied by administrative transfer, see below).

The assimilation of indigenous people in settler contexts is indeed
a most complicated situation. Western Australia's *Natives (Citizenship
Rights) Act 1944*, for example, enabled Aboriginal people to apply for
a Certificate of Citizenship that would extend to successful applicants
the privileges and duties of a "natural born or naturalised subject
of His Majesty".[76] This two pronged characterisation of assimilation
epitomises the contradictions of a settler population economy: on
the one hand, indigenous people are "native born" by definition,
and this fact should not need administrative sanction; on the other
hand, not having been born anywhere else, they cannot logically
be the subject of any naturalisation process (only the settler collective, at once exogenous and indigenising, can be "native born" and
"naturalised" at the same time).

Assimilation is generally understood as a process whereby indigenous people end up conforming to variously constructed notions
of settler racial, cultural, or behavioural normativity.[77] The term
"assimilation", however, also means "absorption" (in some contexts
"absorption" is indeed interchangeable with "assimilation"): it is the
settler body politic that needs to be able to absorb the indigenous
people that have been transformed by assimilation (in some contexts, assimilation is referred to as "incorporation", which confirms
a bodily metaphor). But absorption and assimilation are not the
same: one focuses on the settler entity, the other on the indigenous
collective. One consequence of this unresolved ambiguity is that successful assimilation is never dependent on indigenous performance.
Another consequence is that assimilation policies in a settler society
respond to two quite different needs (as mentioned, settler colonial
projects often claim the sovereign right to manage the population
economy in contradictory ways – after all, it is the sovereign that
decides on the exception). The need to assimilate indigenous people can then coexist with the aim of reinstating an intractable and

unassimilable difference, which helps explaining why assimilation is never ultimately successful.[78]

Assimilation, however, can be accessory to other transfers. Discussions of assimilation have normally focused on its declared intent of ensuring the homogeneity of the social body, and its critics have generally contested whether this aim can justify imposition, or whether a homogeneous social body is even desirable. A crucial and generally neglected aspect of assimilation processes, however, is that they operate by imposing on the indigenous element of the population economy a number of exogenous traits. This is perhaps why the assimilation of indigenous people retains its appeal even in the face of centuries of systematic failure: on the one hand, indigenous assimilation operates as a necessary dialectical counterpoint to the indigenisation of the settler; on the other, even incomplete assimilation allows for the activation of various transfers by "repressive authenticity" (see transfer (H)). Indigenous autonomy can thus be effectively undermined for being too indigenous and not indigenous enough at once. More importantly, as assimilation allows indigenous people to be envisaged as only *temporarily* excluded, the ongoing possibility of an assimilation to come allows settler institutions to claim that they are *ultimately* representing all residents of the population economy.[79]

(G) Transfer by accounting: when indigenous people are counted out of existence.[80] This transfer includes instances when an administrative fixation with blood *quanta* enables predictions regarding the ultimate disappearance of indigenous people.[81] According to this type of transfer, a combination between indigenous and exogenous elements engenders an exclusively exogenous outcome. In this case, as in the previous one, the indigenisation of the settler is mirrored by a parallel exogenisation of the indigenous. It is significant that a shift from quantified descent to self-identified "ethnicity" in census gathering in Australia and New Zealand could be hailed as a victory of indigenous self-determination.[82]

Alternatively, the settler body politic can also claim an equally transferist sovereign right *not to count* indigenous people. Eighteenth- and nineteenth-century attempts to enumerate indigenous populations were an instrument of metropolitan and imperial endeavours to interpose an imperial agency between indigenous peoples and settler control. Settlers consistently resisted these efforts in a succession of colonial scenarios: in North America during the second half of the eighteenth century, in Spanish America during the Bourbon reforms, and in South Africa in the first half of the nineteenth century. It is indeed significant that both the United States and Australian constitutional texts explicitly ruled out the possibility of including indigenous peoples within the national census. In a different context, Arjun Appadurai has convincingly linked numbers – the creation of "enumerated communities" – with the development of colonial governance. Conversely, settler colonial governance at times relies on its sovereign capacity to preserve non-enumerated communities as a way to transfer them out of the developing political body.[83]

This type of transfer also includes the recurring underestimation of pre-contact indigenous populations. An inclination to discount indigenous people involves then the living and the dead.[84] At any rate, an inclination *not* to count indigenous peoples should not be seen as being a thing of the past or a trait limited to the consolidating settler polity. Widespread failure to register births as a way to make indigenous people disappear is a *current* problem in settler Australia and an issue that similarly affects other settler societies.[85] While international campaigns aimed at ensuring that every child is registered at birth normally target developing nations, in Australia this issue has failed to attract public awareness, or to be recognised as a problem (yet alone an indigenous problem).[86] Withholding birth certificates by making registration complex, unavailable in specific locations, or expensive, produces an indigenous class of *sans-papiers* that cannot attend school, work, vote, drive, travel, access social security benefits, open a bank account, and have a tax file number. It effectively turns indigenous peoples into refugees in their own countries (see transfer (B)).

(H) Transfer by means of "repressive authenticity": when, as Patrick Wolfe has noted, "authentic" indigeneity is "constructed as a frozen precontact essence, a quantity of such radical historical instability that its primary effect is to provide a formula for disqualification".[87] A selective acknowledgement of "authentic" indigenous claims allows, for example, targeting the ways in which entitlements can be transmitted across generations. While serving in the settler colony of South Australia, future perpetrator of colonial massacres in Jamaica Edward John Eyre fantasised about an Aboriginal sovereignty that rested exclusively on the truly "authentic" Aboriginal elders he had personally encountered. Explicitly articulating an inherently temporary indigenous sovereignty, he did not allow for the possibility that these elders could ever be succeeded. He was thus recognising an indigenous sovereignty in order to deny it.[88]

This type of transfer quickly establishes a situation in which a lack of recognition ensures that really existing indigenous people and their grievances are seen as illegitimately occupying the indigenous section of the population system.[89] Their perceived illegitimacy can be then imaginatively "rectified": as "unauthentic" indigenous peoples cannot occupy the indigenous sector of the population system, they are perceived as usurpers and can conceptually be transferred "elsewhere".

(I) **Narrative transfer (I):** when indigenous people are represented as hopelessly backward, as unchanging specimen of a primitive form of humanity inhabiting pockets of past surrounded by contemporaneity. A more sympathetic version of this type of transfer includes indigenous people being compared with and imagined as "freedom loving" ancient Germans or Britons. Either way, this transfer focuses on indigenous continuity with "the past". While these pockets can be understood as the narrative equivalent of indigenous territorial reserves, this type of narrative transfer establishes a situation in which really existing people are transferred "elsewhen". The indigenous sector of the population economy is thereby discursively emptied.[90]

(J) **Narrative transfer (II):** when a "tide of history" rationale is invoked to deny legitimacy to ongoing indigenous presences and grievances.[91] This transfer focuses on "fatal impacts", on indigenous discontinuity with the past, and typically expresses regret for the *inevitable* "vanishing" of indigenous people. If they have *had* their last stand, if their defeat is irretrievably located in the past, their activism in the present is perceived as illegitimate.[92] An emphasis on an unbridgeable discontinuity between indigenous past and postcolonial present, between an indigenous golden age and contemporary decadence, can then be used to dismiss an indigenous insurgency that must no longer subsist. Indigenous survival is thus transferred away, foreclosed.

In the context of this type of transfer, settler discourse can at times recognise the historical reality of indigenous violent dispossession and genocide. It is now an established Australian convention, for example, that "the traditional custodians of the land we meet on today" should be publicly recognised. These original custodians, it is implied, are long gone – they are not really existing people with really existing grievances. No one thinks of recognising the "still unsurrendered sovereignty" of really existing Aboriginal communities and their "even now unextinguished title to land". It is well-meaning; however, in this case, an acknowledgment of an original custodianship actually contributes to ruling out the *ongoing* possibility of indigenous autonomy and self-determination. Emphasising the gap between past and present, original custodianship apotropaically chases (i.e., transfers) the spectre of indigenous actionable proprietorship away. Conversely, in post-1984 Aotearoa/New Zealand, it is Treaty relationships and associated patterns of judicial litigation that chase the need to chase that spectre away. However, even if they constitute antithetical approaches, both apotropaic denial and Treaty practice are premised on emphasising the distance between past and present.

(K) Narrative transfer (III): when a radical discontinuity within the settler body politic is emphasised, and references to its "postcolonial" status are made. Highlighting an intractable discontinuity between a colonial past and a postcolonial present is thus part of a settler colonial transferist attitude whereby really existing indigenous people and their unextinguished grievances are seen as illegitimately occupying the indigenous sector of a postcolonial population system (indeed, in these cases a postcolonial condition is invoked precisely to unilaterally deny the very existence of a settler colonial system of relationships). Narrative transfer is then deployed as an instrument of denial.

(L) Narrative transfer (IV): when "settlers are also indigenous peoples" claims are made. This transfer focuses on settler continuity, and emphasises how the settler ethnogenesis happened on the land. In this case, even the acknowledgement of indigenous prior occupancy enables a type of transfer that ultimately establishes a moral equivalence between conflicting claims – while indigenous people just happened to have arrived earlier, both groups have successfully indigenised.[93]

A corollary to this transfer is an "indigenous people are also settlers" type of discourse. In this version, indigenous people, just like the settler collective, are shown to entertain an historical relation to the land.[94] This version of narrative transfer can also sustain the moral equivalence between settler and indigenous claims (indigenous people, again, have merely arrived earlier, but both groups settled and pioneered the land).

Both versions of this narrative transfer constitute a crucial passage in an attempt to deny a particular ontological connection linking indigenous peoples to their land. Either way, as the inherent difference between settler and indigenous relationship to the land is erased, indigenous people as distinct from settlers are transferred away. (Moreover, narrative transfers (I) and (IV) emphasise unbroken continuities; narrative transfers (II) and (III) emphasise intractable discontinuities: there is a narrative transfer available for all situations. And of course, narrative transfers can complement each other and be deployed concomitantly as required.)

(M) Multicultural transfer: when indigenous autonomy is collapsed within exogenous alterity. In this case, settler normativity is retained even if the divide between indigenous and exogenous alterities is unilaterally erased and indigenous people are discursively transferred into a different category (e.g., the "multicultural" nation).[95]

(N) Bicultural transfer: when a bicultural compact is implemented or is given renewed constitutional validity, as in the case, for example, of Aotearoa/New Zealand's Waitangi process. Settler normativity is retained even if the divide between indigenous and settler communities is effaced and subsumed within a wider binational unit. As insightfully noted by New Zealand critical theory scholar Stephen Turner, indigenous peoples are then required to perform their indigeneity according to officially sanctioned protocol, cease being indigenous *per se*, and end up performing a compulsory type of indigeneity for the sake of the settler state.[96]

(O) Transfer by coerced lifestyle change: when it is the indigenous way of life and social and political organisation that is transferred away. Enforced sedentarisation, for example, may look like the absence of transfer, but efforts to immobilise indigenous people necessarily imply a degree of displacement. Besides, this type of transfer is conducive to other transfers. While transfer by sedentarisation is premised on a previous "nomadisation" of indigenous peoples (see transfer (C)), it enables the possibility of initiating transfer by assimilation and transfer by repressive authenticity (transfers (F) and (H)).

The individualisation of communal indigenous tenure had devastating consequences for indigenous cohesion in the United States and New Zealand (even if it was less effective in Canada). In this case, it was a specifically indigenous customary way of allocating, transferring, and recognising property rights that was transferred away.[97] A further version of this type of transfer is when indigenous ecosystems become targeted. In this instance, it is indigenous traditional forms of economic activity, not bodies, that are transferred away.

(P) Administrative transfer: when the administrative borders of the settler polity are redrawn and indigenous people lose entitlements they had retained in the context of previous arrangements (e.g., the Bantustans that were established during South Africa's apartheid). In this case, as the settler entity retains the sovereign capacity to draw and enforce administrative boundaries, it is rights – not bodies – that are transferred, and indigenous peoples become the subject of a transfer that does not necessarily displace them physically. The institution of territorial reserves often fits in with this type of transfer, but administrative transfer can also take the form of a shift in the individual and collective legal capacities of specific indigenous constituencies.[98] The case of "exempted" Aborigines and "competent" Indians can be mentioned in this context.[99] Settlers insist on their capacity to define who is an indigenous person and who isn't, and this capacity constitutes a marker of their control over the population economy. Privileging a definition of indigeneity that is patrilineally transmitted, for example, can allow the possibility of transferring indigenous women and their children away from their tribal membership and entitlements.

(Q) Diplomatic transfer: when indigenous peoples are constrained within sovereign or semi-sovereign political entities (e.g., the Palestinian Authority that would have emerged as a result of the Oslo process). In this case, as a territorial section of the settler controlled locale is excised from the settler body politic, indigenous peoples are transferred outside of the settler entity's population economy. This phenomenon is not infrequent and variously informs a number of decolonisation processes: de Gaulle had in mind demographic considerations that involved France proper when he opted to allow for the discontinuation of French rule in Algeria. The settler dominated Federation of Rhodesia and Nyasaland was disassembled for similar reasons.

(R) Non-diplomatic transfer: when the settler entity retains paramount control but ostensibly relinquishes responsibility for a specific area (e.g., post-disengagement Gaza). In this case, as in the previous one, a territorial section of the settler controlled locale is seemingly excised from the settler body politic, and indigenous peoples are transferred outside of the settler entity's population economy. Israel, however, retained exclusive control of the Gaza population registry despite an ostensible withdrawal; settler sovereign control of the population economy was never relinquished.

(S) Indigenous incarceration/criminalisation/institutionalisation: when indigenous peoples are forcibly institutionalised in one way or another. At times, indigeneity is collapsed with criminal behaviour, and incarceration, of course, transfers indigenous people away from their communities and land. Criminalisation, however, is also crucial to the disavowal of the inherently political character of indigenous demands. As indigenous people are collectively reclassified as something else (e.g., a criminal class), the indigenous sector of the population system is emptied and discursively transferred to another domain.

However, similar transfers are also activated when indigenous peoples are reclassified as "the poor", or when indigenous people are infantilised as "natural, simple, naive, preliterate, and devoid of self-consciousness" children.[100] In the Canadian system of residential schools, transfers (F) and (S) can be seen as operating concurrently.

Treating the indigenous "problem" as a welfare matter is also a transferist reflex. Calls to "close the (socioeconomic) gap" between indigenous and non-indigenous constituencies are premised on indigenous dysfunction, not sovereign entitlement. As indigenous rights become settler generosity, indigenous sovereign capabilities are transferred away. Both denunciations of "welfare dependency" and defences of indigenous welfare can thus be seen as transferist responses.[101]

(T) **Transfer by settler indigenisation:** when settler groups claim *current* indigenous status, as epitomised, for example, by the (New York) Upstate Citizens for Equality organisation's slogan: "[b]orn in the USA: We Are Native American".[102] Similar claims are routinely issued in other settler societies as well. Attempts to establish the "New Zealanders" as an ethnic category, instances of Afrikaner groups collectively seeking indigenous minority status in post-Apartheid South Africa, and Asian immigrants demanding recognition of their "native" status in Hawaii are examples of this type of transfer. As the indigenous segment of the population system is discursively invaded by settler constituencies claiming their indigeneity, indigenous specific alterity becomes effaced.[103]

Sometimes settler indigenisation includes the appropriation of indigenous cultural attributes or even the very language of indigenous resistance.[104] Opposition against native title, for example, is recurrently based on a powerful mobilising set of images including "traditional" (settler) lifestyles, and deep and long-standing, "ancestral" (settler) connection to place. On the other hand, hostility against the possibility of positive discrimination favouring indigenous constituencies (which may include recognition of indigenous sovereignty) is persistently framed within the idiom of racial equality. Historian Geoffrey Blainey's response to the Australian High Court's recognition that native title may have survived (where it had not been explicitly extinguished), for example, included a populist call for "land rights for all".[105]

Transfers (T) and (L) are often used conjointly. However, they remain crucially distinct: in one case, the past is used as a legitimating factor, in the other, the focus is entirely on the present, and the possibility that the past be used as a foundation for legitimating claims is rejected.

(U) **Transfer by performance:** when settlers – indeed often the very epitomes of regenerated settlerhood – dress up as natives.[106] Examples of this type of transfer include the Boston Tea Party, when American patriots dressed as Indians led the disturbances, and elite Israeli *Mistaravim* army teams (a unit of Israeli soldiers who operate in hostile environments dressed up as Arabs).[107] All Blacks non-Maori performers of the Maori Haka before Rugby Union international matches, and Native American mascots identifying sporting teams could also be mentioned in this context.[108]

This transfer can operate literally as disguise and at the cultural level. The Jindyworobak cultural movement in 1930s Australia, for example, insisted on the need to draw inspiration from the Australian land and its genius. This inspiration, they assumed, would unite Australians and Aborigines into a single cultural brotherhood. While in *Playing Indian*, Philip J. Deloria has focused on the role of performing Indianness in enabling the construction of settler self and identity formation, in *Going Native*, Shari M. Huhndorf links going native with primitivism, ambivalent feelings about modernity, and the need to obscure a violent conquest (and resolve recurring anxieties pertaining to the nation's founding).[109] The "transfer" effect of these performances, however, should also be emphasised. Playing indigenous, even when aided by the display of "traditional" dress, customs, and ceremonies, and even when there is a genuine attempt to involve actual indigenous peoples, is never entirely convincing. It is important to note, however, that the soliloquy between more and less indigenising settlers does not need indigenous people.[110] As settlers *occupy* native identities, indigenous people are transferred away.[111]

(V) **Transfer by name confiscation:** when settlers confiscate the very term that identifies indigenous peoples. Naming, of course, is about and produces entitlement (it is no coincidence that often compensation in the form of cultural redress involves officially "returning" indigenous names to landmarks and geographical features), but name appropriation is an equally powerful dispossessory tool. Donald Denoon has noted this recurring phenomenon (he was writing on "Australasia" and referring collectively to Australia, New Zealand, and New Caledonia): "Despite differences between the situations and the peoples, each settler society gave a collective name to the original people, then told them to forget it as they appropriated that term and re-named the Indigenes". Similarly, *"Canadien"* had initially been associated with Indians, but was eventually appropriated by French Canadians, and many states in the United States are identified by indigenous group designations. In the case of the New Zealand of the "Maoriland" period (1880–1914), the name was appropriated twice.[112] This does not happen naturally; outlining these processes, Denoon detects a deliberate act of suppression: "In each case the earlier usage, being inconsistent with emerging social forms, was first abandoned and then suppressed."[113] In this context, "emerging social forms" means the progressive entrenchment of a settler colonial project.

The power of this type of transfer should not be underestimated: the long-term viability of the settler project is ultimately compromised when settlers fail to indigenise their collective label. French *Pied Noir* left French Algeria, not an Algerian France. A possible alternative is to change the country's name, as, for example, Israel was able to establish after 1948. It can go the other way as well, and very few Rhodesians remain in Zimbabwe.[114]

(W) Transfer by racialisation: when "blackness" and "whiteness" are seen as categories fundamentally defining the social body in accordance to what Charles W. Mills has authoritatively described as the "racial contract".[115] The racial contract categorises indigenous peoples as something else (e.g., non-white colonised people), effaces their indigeneity, and blocks out the indigenous/exogenous dynamic that is intrinsic to the settler colonial situation. The recoding of indigenous people as racially different thus constitutes a form of transfer, one result of a desire to exchange indigenous Others with exogenous ones.[116]

As this transfer obliterates the distinction between colonialism and settler colonialism and allows settler colonialism to disappear behind other forms of colonial expropriation, the ideological labour performed by this type of transfer should not be underestimated.[117] Quite significantly, however, both the racist ideologies that insist on the dichotomy between white and non-whites and their adversaries transfer indigeneity away: it is unsurprising that the relationship between indigenous activism in settler locales and civil rights agendas has been a contrasted one.[118]

(X) **Transfer by executive termination:** when indigenous alterity, its very name, is administratively terminated. In 1638, at the conclusion of the Pequot War, the Treaty of Hartford stipulated that the surviving Indians "shall no more be called Pequots but Narragansetts and Mohegans".[119] To foreclose federal involvement, in 1880 the Rhode Island state legislature declared the Narragansett people "extinct".[120] In 1899, an Imperial act redefined the Ainu of Japan as "former Aborigines". In this case, "Aborigines" – literally, people who have no other origin – became "former Aborigines" without moving: a logical impossibility (Ainu people resisted this transfer in a variety of ways and in June 2008 a parliamentary resolution finally and officially acknowledged their indigenous status). After the Second World War, the US Congress went on a termination spree and dissolved dozens of indigenous tribes. Similarly, indigenous Tasmanians were not officially recognised for decades.

(Y) **The transfer of settlers:** when settlers move into secluded enclaves in the attempt to establish a population economy that is characterised by no indigenous presence (even if it is frequently imagined, however, this course of action is rarely undertaken). This transfer has a long history, especially as far as metropolitan efforts to manage settler frontiers are concerned. Imperial and colonising polities have recurrently attempted to enforce the rigorous separation of indigenous and settler spaces and at times transferring settlers seemed more viable than transferring indigenous people. "Protectorates of Aborigines" were established as branches of government in the settler colonies to this end (they were supposed to check the "harmful" effects of contact with "civilisation" and to enable the activation of transfer (F)).[121] British imperial authorities even partitioned North America in 1763, and declaratively attempted to prevent settler trespass.

On the other hand, it should be emphasised that the possibility of transferring settlers, the possibility of imagining a settlerless locale beyond what in Australian traditions are known as the "boundaries of location", crucially enables indigenous transfer. As it establishes the acceptability of population transfers and confirms the need for rigorous spatial separation, thinking about removing settlers or preventing them from entering indigenous areas is ultimately functional to the establishment of corresponding indigenousless spaces. Israeli settlers, for example, were transferred from Gaza in 2005 in the explicit attempt to sustain the ongoing transfer of Palestinians else where and in the context of an unashamedly transferist ideology and practice. As recurring Afrikaner calls to establish separate white homelands in South Africa also demonstrate, the transfer of settlers is a current phenomenon.

(Z) Transfer by indigenous/national "reconciliation": when reconciliation is officially sanctioned and the indigenous section of the population system disappears into the "Reconciled Nation" category. Apart from the obvious positive effects that a genuine reconciliation process entails, especially if one considers the alternatives, reconciliation processes can also be seen as contributing to the extinction of otherwise irreducible forms of indigenous alterity. Besides, a triumphant settler society must be a fully reconciled one, and apologies and Reconciliation are indeed a powerful act of relegitimation and settler self-supersession.[122]

In "Making and Unmaking of Strangers", Zygmunt Bauman notes that all societies "produce strangers". He then contends that the

> typical modern strangers were the waste of the state's ordering zeal. What the modern strangers did not fit was the vision of order. When you draw dividing lines and set apart the so divided, everything that blurs the lines and spans the divisions undermines the work and mangles its products. [...] The strangers exhaled uncertainty where certainty and clarity should have ruled. In the harmonious, rational order about to be built there was no room-there could be no room-for neither-nors, for the sitting astride, for the cognitively ambivalent. The order-building was a war of attrition waged against the strangers and the strange.[123]

In Bauman's account, two main strategies to carry out the elimination of strangers are available:

> [i]n this war (to borrow Levi-Strauss's concepts) two alternative, but also complementary strategies were intermittently deployed. One was *antropophagic*: annihilating the strangers by *devouring* them and then metabolically transforming them into a tissue indistinguishable from one's own. This was the strategy of

assimilation-making the different similar: the smothering of cultural or linguistic distinctions, forbidding all traditions and loy-
alties except those meant to feed the conformity of the new and
all embracing order, promoting and enforcing one and only measure of conformity. The other strategy was *anthropoemic*: *vomiting*
the strangers, banishing them from the limits of the orderly world
and barring them from all communication with those inside. This
was the strategy of exclusion-confining the strangers within the
visible walls of the ghettos or behind the invisible, yet no less tan-
gible prohibitions of *commensality*, *connubium*, and *commercium*,
expelling the strangers beyond the frontiers of the managed and
manageable territory; or, when neither of the two measures was
feasible-destroying the strangers physically.[124]

In a modernist context, the stranger's presence was understood as
inherently temporary, but in a postmodern predicament, strangers
are here to stay: in "our postmodern part of the world the age of
anthropophagic and *antropoemic* strategies is over", he concludes.[125]
Bauman's analysis does not specifically address the constitutive
difference between indigenous and exogenous strangeness in a settler
context (and in doing so, by collapsing indigenous and exogenous
alterities, he may actually contribute to one type of discursive
transfer). Nevertheless, his study applies to both settler colonial
modernities and settler colonial postmodernities: *anthropophagic* or
antropoemic strategies are now (largely) anachronistic. And yet, even
if indigenous and exogenous alterities are now predominantly construed as enduring, as the list of available transfer strategies suggests, transfer remains a fundamental attribute of a settler colonial
population economy.

In *The Tropics of Empire*, Nicolás Wey Gómez has recently explored
the intellectual prehistory of European colonial traditions. He traced
the medieval trajectory of tripartite Aristotelian political theory and
followed its eventual transit into colonial practice and ideology.
According to Aristotle's theory, Greeks, as opposed to both the northern Barbarians (audacious, but lacking prudence and resolve) and
Asians (endowed with great intellectual capacities, but lacking in
strength and spiritedness), are the only ones truly capable of self-
determination. While this set of ideas was instrumental in justifying
the enslavement of African and Indian colonised people (a topic that

Wey Gómez explores at length), a tripartite vision of the world, as I have argued in this chapter, is also relevant to settler colonial formations and their population economies.[126] As a settler population economy is focused on transfer rather than the subjugation of indigenous people, it was the other side of Aristotle's political theory that was instrumental to the specific requirements of an alternative colonial form. Wey Gómez's book is subtitled *Why Columbus Sailed South to the Indies*. But if Columbus sailed south in the very colonial expectation to encounter people he could justifiably enslave, one could argue that settlers in the main "remove" to temperate areas in the expectation that the people they would encounter can be displaced.

On the other hand, as already noted in the introduction, settler invasion "is a structure not an event" – no matter how much it tries, the settler colonial situation cannot ultimately supersede itself.[127] Despite settler delusions of final transformation, save for indigenous genocide, mass deportations, or a settler counter-exodus that empties the population system of its settler component, a triangular system of relationships and its population economy remain unavoidable. Can a non-transferist approach to the population economy of settler polities be theorised? Can a way out of the settler colonial situation be envisaged beyond the elimination of its indigenous or exogenous elements? Even if a triangular structure of relationships should be understood as enduring, what could change is the content of these relationships and, most crucially, the type of agency that is charged with its governance. In other words, what could change is the implicit settler sovereign entitlement that underpins the settler colonial situation and the management of its population economy. Calls for the recognition and enactment of indigenous sovereignties have characterised the activities of what has in recent decades become a true indigenous international.[128] Shifting the very ability to manage the population economy away from the settler collective, the recognition of indigenous forms of sovereignty in a variety of settler polities would constitute a genuinely non-transferist move.

2
Sovereignty

In this chapter, I outline a special type of sovereign entitlement that is claimed by a specific class of settlers: those who have come to stay, those who will not return "home".[1] It is an *animus manendi* that distinguishes the settler from the other colonists – as the very word "settler" implies, it is the *intention* to stay (as opposed to the sojourners' intention to return) that contributes the crucial differentiating trait. Thomas Jefferson, for example, supported "extending the right of suffrage (or in other words the rights of a citizen) to all who had *a permanent intention of living in the country*". "Take what circumstances you please as evidence of this", he added: "either having resided a certain time, or having a family, or having property, any or all of them."[2] *Animus manendi* is thus manifested by residency, suitable reproduction, and possession.[3]

In this chapter, I also argue that while settlers see themselves as founders of political orders, they also interpret their collective efforts in terms of an inherent sovereign claim that travels with them and is ultimately, if not immediately, autonomous from the colonising metropole. The idea that residents of a colonial polity would enjoy special rights has a very long lineage, and even precedes the inception of clearly recognisable colonial relationships. Normally, sovereignty is understood as one basic criterion defining a political space, and a territory is defined in its unity as the extension of a particular sovereignty and jurisdiction. As a growing literature confirms, however, the relationship between sovereignty and territory is indeed a complex one.[4] In this chapter, I focus on the corporate nature of settler political entities and suggest that a settler sovereignty should be understood in pluralistic terms – a concept contiguous with self-government and suzerainty – and not as primarily concerned with establishing state institutions. A focus on political power rather than state sovereignty, it is argued, enables an exploration of settler colonialism's self-constituting capacity and its inclination to privilege isopolitical relations between colonising metropoles and settler colonial peripheries (an isopolity is a particular constitutional arrangement between political entities where citizens of one constituent polity are automatically accorded rights in another).[5] Often operating on a different plane, settler understandings of a localised corporate sovereignty can thus coexist beside, within, and in conjunction with colonial, imperial, national, and even postcolonial sovereignties.

Settler colonial political traditions in a multiplicity of locales shared a particular cluster of ideas pertaining to the foundation of new societies: if sovereignty can be seen as the relationship between people, power, and space over time, this chapter argues that a settler sovereignty is characterised by an exclusive interpretation of settler peoplehood, a specific understanding of sovereign capacities and their location, and by the conviction that the settler colonial setting is charged with a special regenerative nature. Of course, this approach does not deny the actual messiness of "settlement" and associated processes. Most of the colonists who moved to the New Worlds did so individually, without a conscious determination to establish a new, ideal, society, and with no specific understanding of their inherent sovereignty. However, ideas about entitlements emanating from residing individually and collectively in a special place travelled too, were available, or eventually became available (at any rate, settler colonial orders could also be instituted *following* alternative colonial foundations). Placing an emphasis on a number of previously neglected factors that contributed to the consolidation of settler colonial transnational imaginaries (and selectively recuperating lines of historical inquiry that were eventually abandoned), the first section of this chapter emphasises the need to explore this untidiness by developing a new analytical frame. The second section sketches the ways in which self-constituted settler colonial sovereignties can articulate their operation within and without developing colonial and imperial sovereignties.

An ancient and corporate foundation

The idea that individuals permanently residing outside of Europe should enjoy particular rights – entitlements that are explicitly framed in the language of special *sovereign* rights – has a very ancient origin. Aristocratic families settling in Sardinia on behalf of the Pisan Republic, for example, stubbornly insisted on their sovereign prerogative to remain citizens and *at the same time* exercise their personal domination over the territory they were administering (and its people).[6] While Belgian historian Charles Verlinden convincingly demonstrated that the development of colonial relations in the Atlantic world was historically continuous with pre-modern Mediterranean arenas, claiming special exemptions against a sovereign power on the assumption that European settlers living in a colonial locale must enjoy exceptional rights is as old as colonialism. Genoese colonists only accepted to permanently settle in the Cape Verde Islands in the 1460s after "great liberties and franchises" had been granted to them. They claimed that since the islands were so distant from Portugal, colonists should be exempt from paying tithe or other tribute. They also demanded that feudal obligations not be extended to newly settled domains, a long-lasting and recurring demand of settler colonial discourse.[7] Later, it was in the British Caribbean that a revendication of the pre-eminent sovereignty of colonials within their domains was articulated by the local legislatures.[8] In all these cases, it is not a reference to ancient rights or to unsurrendered personal freedoms that is invoked in order to assert autonomy from obligations; it is, on the contrary, *an entitlement that emanates from residency in a special locale*. It is at the same time a "blue-water" rationale for (settler) colonial autonomy that rejects the possibility of reproducing "Old World" relations in a separate setting. Both ideas would enjoy remarkable currency.

However, a settler sovereign claim should be seen as based on *a particular lifestyle* as well as on residency in a special locale (of course, as one is premised on the other, the two remain intimately linked). Advocating separation from Virginia after the Revolution, settlers from the "western districts" emphasised in a memorial both *difference from*, and *complementarity with*, what they perceived as constitutively dissimilar circumstances:

> Our nearest seaports will be among you, your readiest resources for effectual succour in case of any invasion will be to us: the fruits of our industry and temperance will be enjoyed by you, and *the simplicity of our manners* will furnish you with profitable lessons. In recompense for these services you will furnish our rustic inhabitants with examples of civility and politeness and supply us with conveniences which are without the reach of our labour.[9]

Another petition referred to the "Inconveniences, Dangers, & Difficulties, which Language itself wants Words to express & describe". Settlers had to endure; on the contrary, the petitioners claimed that the "Rest of their Countrymen [were] softened by Ease, enervated by Affluence and Luxurious Plenty & unaccostumed to Fatigues, Hardships, Difficulties or Dangers".[10] A conciliatory tone should not deceive: an assertion of a right that is based on uncorrupted "simplicity of manners", in this case, amounts to the proclamation of a separate, inherent, and irreducible sovereignty that arises from embracing a particular lifestyle.

The possibility that colonies would immediately establish their independence had always been an established assumption of reflections dedicated to the founding of new societies. Hobbes, for example, had explicitly considered this possibility in *Leviathan* (1651). That this could happen was just one of the possible arrangements.

> The procreation, or children of a Commonwealth, are those we call plantations, or colonies; which are numbers of men sent out from the Commonwealth, under a conductor or governor, to inhabit a foreign country, either formerly void of inhabitants, or made void then by war. And when a colony is settled, they are either a Commonwealth of themselves, discharged of their subjection to their sovereign that sent them (as hath been done by many Commonwealths of ancient time), in which case the Commonwealth from which they went was called their metropolis, or mother, and requires no more of them than fathers require of the children whom they emancipate and make free from their

domestic government, which is honour and friendship; or else they remain united to their metropolis, as were the colonies of the people of Rome; and then they are no Commonwealths themselves, but provinces, and parts of the Commonwealth that sent them. So that the right of colonies, saving honour and league with their metropolis, dependeth wholly on their license, or letters, by which their sovereign authorized them to plant.[11]

Generally accepted narratives of colonial expansion followed by settlement, the gradual development *in situ* of an identity that is distinct from the metropole's, and, eventually, by a settler assertion of independence should then be integrated with an understanding of a settler sovereignty that is never relinquished and travels with the settler collective.[12]

The Pizarroist movement in 1540s Spanish America is another early example of a settler assertion of a distinct sovereignty, a right to self-government that is invoked against metropolitan attempts to exercise direct power and, specifically, to interpose the imperial agency between indigenous peoples and settlers (as noted, the need to autonomously control the local population economy is a recurring and specific demand of settler concerns).[13] *Annales* historian Marc Ferro calls this phenomenon "colonist-independence", notices its unbroken continuity from sixteenth-century Spanish America to 1970s Rhodesia, and describes it as the "most advanced stage of white colonial expansion".[14] The enduring resilience and recurrence of these rhetorical stances suggest that Louis Hartz's insight regarding the fragments being both *traditional* and *prenational* political bodies may have retained some analytical cogency: an historiography that routinely assumes that settler colonial forms are inherently constitutive of modernity should also be integrated with an appraisal of settler colonialism's parallel escape from it.[15]

Conversely, a failure to allow for the transfer of sovereign prerogatives can have disastrous consequences for the settler enterprise. The collapse of English Puritan attempts in Providence Island (1625–1630) and Scottish efforts in Darien (1698–1699, 1699–1700), for example, confirms that settler efforts prefer sovereign autonomy over colonial subordination. The investors of the Providence Island Company (the cream of Puritan society) had remained in England and retained control of the whole enterprise throughout the colony's short history (Puritan Massachusetts would indeed be premised on an entirely different model). Effective power remained in England, and while communication remained difficult and governance inflexible, an insistence on a corporate monopoly of shipping and labour shortages severely hindered growth. Most importantly, as the colony had also been founded in the pursuit of privateering opportunities, the colonists were required to contribute to the colony's defences. The usual relationship in which it is the community of settlers that vocally demands the protection of the colonising metropole was in this case fundamentally upturned, and it was the settlers that were contributing to the imperial effort, not vice versa. The colony failed to prosper or even consolidate and was eventually abandoned. Similarly, those in charge of the Darien venture in what is today Panama (all the councillors, except one) did not even dismount the ships. In this case, as ultimate power (and sorely needed provisions) remained aboard, no transfer of any sovereign prerogative was ever initiated.[16]

On the contrary, Francis Jennings's analysis of the *Invasion of America* convincingly outlines a localised, stubborn, punctilious, resilient, and ultimately effective determination to sustain a variety of local sovereignties against metropolitan interference and against each other. He highlights the "feudal" nature of the original colonisation of the Americas: as "in feudal times" the sovereign's "authority rose and fell proportionately to its distance from the scene of operations".[17] However, in the context of research aimed at recovering a specific genealogy of settler colonial dispositions and despite an obvious circumstantial incapacity to institute meaningful direct metropolitan control, it is not the feudal nature of the relationships between local European settlers and a distant sovereign that should be emphasised, but, on the contrary, the specific nature of a self-governing capacity that is acquired via a *voluntary movement* to a separate location. Settler projects are recurrently born in a vacuum of empire that is intentionally sought, and in a displacement that is associated with a determination to establish unique political settings (of course, a settler project is actually premised on a double vacuum, and conditional loyalty *vis à vis* the metropolitan sovereign is also necessarily accompanied by a systematic disavowal of indigenous sovereignties). Only an outward movement allows an assertion of a separate sovereignty that does not require a revolutionary break:

it is not a leftover from transplanted political traditions, it is the beginning of a distinct political tradition and its sovereignty.

This tradition and sovereignty operated within a system of corporate governance that made settler endeavours particularly strong. It was the City of London as a *corporate* collective entity constituted in "The Society of the Governor and Assistants, London, of the New Plantation in Ulster, within the Realm of Ireland", also known as "The Honourable The Irish Society", that undertook to settle what it would call Londonderry. Jonathan Bardon's reconstruction of this beginning outlines an unmistakably corporate endeavour:

> On 17 December 1613 at a court of Common Council, with great pomp and ceremony, a draw was held for the twelve proportions of the Londonderry plantation. [...] The fifty-five London Companies, regularly levied for contributions to the enterprise, arranged themselves into twelve associations, the Goldsmiths, for example, joining with the Cordwainers, Paint-stainers and Armourers. By the luck of the draw, taken by the City swordbearer, the Grocers, the Fishmongers and the Goldsmiths got fertile proportions, while the Drapers and the Skinners were left with land that was poorer and more inaccessible.[18]

Similarly, the Massachusetts Bay Company retained a corporate system of governance even after it ceased being a joint-stock venture and became a landed body politic endowed with a written constitution (it had not yet left England, but, as it will be claimed below in relation to a capacity for self-reification, settler colonialism is routinely imagined *before* it is practiced).[19] The "settlers of 1820" relocated to the Cape Colony in accordance with a remarkably articulated system of corporate organisation that allowed for a flexible capacity to accommodate for self-funded groups of independent settlers and clusters of settlers-to-be, people that had not migrated independently but needed the involvement of some interested landlord.[20] The list of settler colonial endeavours characterised by a corporate foundation is indeed extensive, and involves projects operating in a variety of frontiers at quite different times, including 1730s Georgia, 1810s Red River Colony, 1830s South Australia, 1840s New Zealand, and, more recently, the Western Australia of the Group Settlement scheme and pre-state Israel.[21] These are widely differing enterprises, taking place at various times, under remarkably diverse political circumstances, in dissimilar locales, and in response to often diverging impulses. This variety confirms a pattern of corporate sovereign action.

Of course, an emphasis of corporate non-state foundational imprintings is not a historiographical novelty, especially in the context of the historiography of the colonial foundations of what would become the United States. Reflecting typologically on early experiences in the colonisation of North America, L. D. Scisco had detected in 1903 a widespread pattern of corporate "union of proprietorship with jurisdiction" (he based his definition of "plantation" type colony on this amalgamation), and Carter Goodrich and Sol Davison's pioneering 1930s work on working-class participation in the "Westward Movement" described a multitude of associations, societies, cooperative endeavours, schemes, and subscriptions, all constituted for the purpose of settler migration.[22] In their global appraisal of settler colonial forms in the twentieth century, Caroline Elkins and Susan Pedersen emphasised the role of the state in promoting settler projects and a related settler capacity to control local institutions and inform its activities.[23] Alternatively, beside references to expanding colonial/imperial polities, the role of individual initiative in the "opening" of frontiers and in compelling settlement processes has been repeatedly emphasised.[24] The point is not to deny these elements' importance; after all, individualist acquisitiveness can only be understood in relation to collective acquisitiveness. These, however, were not the only factors involved, and the history of settler displacements should be seen as fundamentally characterised by non-state corporate forms.[25]

On the other hand, in the global analysis of settler colonial forms, a corporate foundation should be understood as *corporatist* as well as corporate: it is a corporate effort for the purpose of settlement and not an enterprise exclusively or primarily aimed at accruing returns on capital investment.[26] The political traditions of settler colonial endeavour often express a determined resolve to subordinate market forces. The British South Africa Company, which had autonomously settled the Rhodesias without direct British administration, never paid dividends to its shareholders. Afrikaner *Volkskapitalisme*, as it was developed in the context of 1930s South Africa, espoused the idea that the entire settler social body should benefit from a flourishing economy.[27] Cooperative schemes and populist agitation against monopolies and "money power" fit in with this tendency. A focus on the global expansion of capitalist relations has produced an historical literature that overlooks a long-lasting determination to produce social bodies where capitalism is at the service of settlement and not vice versa.[28] An account of an ongoing drive to *escape* market forces should accompany established interpretative patterns centred on "imperialism" and "settler capitalism"; the two movements could then be understood as coexisting, even if operating in mutual tension (conversely, but it makes sense, this escape is mirrored by ongoing and parallel attempts to force indigenous people to *enter* the wage economy).

An historiography of settler colonial phenomena that has focused on the dynamics of imperial and capitalist expansion, state activity, and individual initiative should therefore be integrated with the understanding of a localised corporate foundation.[29] HBO TV series *Deadwood* recently reflected on the contested self-constitution of a settler community. Series I tells the story of the establishment of a foundational sovereignty; Series II recounts its complicated and conflicted subsumption/cooptation within an external territorial polity; and Series III relates the story of a mining monopsony's challenge against the local body politic.[30] Such analytical sharpness is often beyond the reach of traditional historical approaches.

Self-constitution, isopolity

In *The Psychology of Apartheid*, Peter Lambley noted a peculiar Afrikaner capacity for self-reification.[31] This, however, was not a unique case, and the ability to will a collective identity and its institutions into existence characterises in one way or another all settler projects. Jacqueline Rose presents a similar argument in *The Question of Zion*.[32] Outlining the rationale for the original Puritan Massachusetts experiment of the early 1630s, John Winthrop's *Modell of Christian Charity*, for example, insists on an inherent settler sovereignty *and* on a self-constituting law-making capacity: "Thus stands the case between God and us. Wee are entered into Covenant with him for this worke [that is, constructing the 'city on the hill']. Wee have taken out a Commission. *The Lord hath given us leave to drawe our own articles* [...]."[33] While settler communities routinely express the notion of an inherent self-governing capacity, this ability is generally perceived as emanating from *within* the community of settlers (this is, after all, the meaning of a covenant, and settler political forms often operate by way of an explicit or implicit covenant that organises the political life of the local settler entity).[34]

At the same time, this capacity is recurrently understood in ongoing tension with external colonising agencies (i.e., metropolitan, but also federal, provincial, or state ones): settler discourse recurrently resents distant sovereigns – when they interfere because they do, when they do not because they neglect their duties. Alexis de Tocqueville knew that the self-governing nature of the communities he was describing was probably the most important feature of his subject and begun his examination by focusing on the *local* institutions of American political culture.[35] Indeed, as well as emanating from a *particular location* and a *specific lifestyle*, a settler sovereign capacity is therefore also seen as deriving from an appropriate *dimension* of the body politic. The Anti-Federalists, for example, believed that only small communities organised as self-governing polities would uphold a genuine form of (settler) popular sovereignty. On this point, the Federalists concurred (even if they disagreed on whether an unrestrained popular sovereignty would be a sensible thing). In *Unruly Americans and the Origins of the Constitutions*, Woody Holton outlined an antidemocratic passage (i.e., a move against the settler/farmer democracies of the 1780s in the United States) and concluded that the establishment of huge electoral districts was an all-important safeguard "against popular influence", even if "the one that was least visible in the Constitution".[36]

The history of colonial settlement in backcountry North America is characterised by a pattern of self-constituting local jurisdictions contesting the established claims of seaboard centres of power. This insurgency can only be understood if the perception of an inherent sovereign capacity is taken into account.[37] When future president Theodore Roosevelt noted in his *Winning of the West* that "the mountaineers ignored the doctrine of State Sovereignty", what he really meant was that they actively *disregarded it in exchange for another* (i.e., the doctrine of squatter sovereignty, variously espousing the "natural" right to move into "vacant" territory *and* self-govern).[38]

In 1772, the Watauga Association constituted the first independent settler body politic beyond the Appalachian Mountains, when, in the words of early twentieth-century historian George Henry

Alden, a government was "formed by absolutely no authority than that of the people directly concerned".[39] In typically settler colonial fashion, the Association drew up a written covenant undertaken by a number of individuals pledging mutual support. The Watauga Compact outlined the means by which local settlers could "regulate" political life, organise their community, and maintain local control.[40] This polity settled judicial disputes, organised the militia, and negotiated with Indians, establishing a comprehensive system of settler governance. Crucially, it asserted settler autonomy against exogenous Others and enforced settler control over indigenous policy – both essential prerequisite markers of substantive settler sovereignty.

Similarly, and not far away, the Cumberland Pact established another self-constituted (and radically democratic) settler polity: it enfranchised all freemen over 20 years of age, stipulated that elections could be called at any time, and that all men had to serve in the self-constituted militia. As North Carolina was deemed unable to defend the local community, establishing a militia – the exercise of a self-defensive capacity – crucially underpinned the settler self-constitution. The State of Frankland/Franklin eventually declared independence in what can be seen as a settler manifesto:

> We unanimously agree that our lives, liberties and property can be more secure and our happiness much better propagated by our *separation* and consequently that it is our duty and inalienable right to form ourselves into a new and independent state.[41]

"Separation" here is key: on the one hand, it is at the origin of the settler project, the moment when a collective body "moves out" in order to bring into effect an autonomous political will; on the other hand, it is also its outcome, the moment when a sovereign polity begins implementing actual jurisdiction (hence, as it underscores separation in both senses, a settler preference for a "blue water" type of disconnection from the colonising core).

Settlers in backcountry North America recurrently articulated this logic. A petition noted that Virginia and Pennsylvania were "separated by a vast, extensive and almost impassable Tract of Mountains, by Nature itself formed and pointed out as a Boundary between this

Country & those below it".[42] Another source also emphasises a "blue water" turned "green mountains" rationale for settler independence:

> When we consider our remote situation [...] we cannot but reflect that such a distance renders our Interest incompatible; for when any part of a State lies so remote from its Capital that their produce cannot reach the market, the Connection ceases, & from thence proceeds a different Interest & consequently a Coolness.[43]

In a self-fulfilling way, and in accordance with a self-evident circular logic, separation is thus the product of separation.[44] But this is not an exclusively American phenomenon. Similar words would be reproduced, for example, in Piet Retief's 1837 Afrikaner "manifesto":

> We despair of saving the colony from those evils which threaten it by the turbulent and dishonest conduct of vagrants, who are allowed to infest the country in every part; nor do we see any prospect of peace and happiness for our children in a country thus distracted by internal commotions [...]. We solemnly declare that *we quit this colony with a desire to lead a more quiet life* than we have heretofore done [...]. We make known that when we shall have framed a code of laws for our future guidance, copies shall be forwarded to the [Cape] colony for the general information [...].[45]

The dialectical opposition between "turbulence", "vagrancy", and "commotion" on the one hand, and a cluster of images comprising happiness, appropriate familial relations, and peace on the other – an opposition crucially centred around the inside/outside dichotomy – produce a determination to "remove". It is only on the outside that regenerated life becomes possible. The manifesto outlines in fact a settler political entity that understands itself as endowed with an inherent law-making capacity emanating form the very possibility of moving collectively across space, and a polity that, by declaring its intention to merely notify the colonial sovereign of its self-constitution and substantive jurisdiction, explicitly denies any subordination to it.[46] In this way, a settler project constitutes a political body that wills itself into existence by imagining its movement to an unspecified location.

The very Jeffersonian itinerary from "unsettled" domain to various degrees of territorial status and eventual statehood within the United States, as outlined by the Northwestern ordinance of 1787 and its 1784 predecessor, is premised on a perception of (and a consequent accommodation with) a settler sovereign capacity. In a letter to Madison, Jefferson argued that Virginia should immediately relinquish its claims to the recently settled Kentucky region (and cede it to the Union) in order to avoid what he perceived as the very concrete possibility that local settlers would establish an independent polity *outside* of the American republic.[47] Settlers may, he considered,

> separate themselves and be joined by all our settlements beyond the Alleghany, if they are the first movers; whereas if we draw the line, those at Kentucky having their end will not interest themselves for the people of Indiana, Greenbrier, etc., who will, of course, be left to our management [...]. Should we not be the first movers, and the Indianans and Kentuckyians take themselves off and claim to the Alleghany, I am afraid Congress would secretly wish them well.[48]

The recognition of a settler autonomous capacity and a consequent need to accommodate it is a passage that would be repeated numerous times in consolidating settler contexts elsewhere, a stance that would similarly shape developments way beyond the limits of the future United States.[49] However, if Jefferson's plan for the West was indeed a pre-emptive move designed to defuse the issue of settler independence, his articulation explicitly recognised that the settlers carried a foundational sovereign entitlement, and that settlement is born in settler independence. Elsewhere and afterwards, it often went without saying.[50]

Jefferson and Edward Gibbon Wakefield – the Wakefield who had been behind the Durham Report – thus share a similar assessment of settler capabilities (they, however, propose diametrically opposed blueprints for the organisation of settler neo-Europes, one promoting a "dispersed" and egalitarian society, and the latter espousing the need to ensure "concentration" and the reproduction of appropriate hierarchical relations – imaginative coherence, after all, does not imply political convergence).[51] Then again, episodes of utter settler self-reification are actually extreme cases: settler collectives

rarely need an outright assertion of their ultimate sovereign independence. Historian Peter Onuf, for example, concluded that "Vermont
alone had truly created itself", which in fact means that only
Vermont *needed* to truly create itself.[52] As settler colonial political
traditions focus on the self-governance of the local community, and
as imperial and national structures rarely affect settler control over
local matters, colonial and settler colonial sovereignties can routinely accommodate each other (this, in turn, contributes to their
mimetism and to making settler colonial political traditions less
immediately recognisable). Corporate self-constituted structures can
accommodate a variety of sovereign claims.

If a settler sovereignty can be understood as distinct and operating
in conjunction with other colonial, national, and imperial sovereignties, traditional interpretations of expanding colonial sovereign
orders may need modification.[53] Patricia Seed's *Ceremonies of Possession* is a perceptive analysis of the rituals of colonial possession
the different European empires developed and performed in order
to assert their respective prerogatives in the New World.[54] However, besides the *colonial* rites of possession and the colonial/imperial
sovereignties they represent in distinctive national and cultural
styles, a *settler colonial* sovereignty can also be asserted through the
performance of specific rituals and ceremonies. In their inherent dissimilarity, and even if they routinely overlap (settler colonial regimes,
after all, often supersede previous foundational colonial arrangements), colonial and settler colonial possessions require different
performances. The latter are manifested, for example, by the production of surveying plats and other deeds conveying real estate
(an essential instrument allowing the transfer of real estate across
generations), and especially by ploughing (which can, in Lockean
terms, sustain a claim), by the collective performance of familial
rites sanctioned by a locally constituted church and congregation
(especially births, weddings, and burials: the establishment of normative familial relations is a crucial marker of a successful settler
project), and by a capacity to transform the landscape (clear fields
and pastures, erect fences, buildings, and other improvements).

The localised enactment of judicial practices also constitutes a crucial rite of settler possession. Damen Ward has, for example, recently
drawn attention to a number of forums that articulated settler
autonomous political discourse and claims in early New Zealand: the
public meeting, an institution that was extensively and effectively

used to lobby the government (or to articulate settler opposition); constitutionalist language, which in the context of colonial political life could be used to advocate settler local control over indigenous peoples and to contest governmental involvement; and juries, whose political significance was crucial in the development and enforcement of localised settler power against governmental exogenous interference.[55] Most importantly, however, substantive settler possession is manifested by the exercise of autonomous control over indigenous and exogenous Others: keeping both at bay, or selectively distributing the right to reside within the bounds of the settler polity (the capacity of exercising an exclusive authority over the local population economy, as I have argued in Chapter 1, remains the ultimate and non-negotiable limit of a settler radical sovereignty).

However, even if the "ceremonies of possession" performed by colonialism and settler colonialism can be conceptualised as discrete, colonial and settler colonial sovereignties are not mutually exclusive, or the result of a zero-sum game. On the contrary, colonial and settler colonial sovereignties can be conceptualised as *distinct and concomitant.* If they can be concurrent, however, if sovereignty in a settler colonial context can be seen as "an act of co-creation", the articulation of these distinct sovereign forms needs to be explored.[56]

There are several possibilities beside the Jeffersonian/Wakefieldian compact whereby settler sovereignties operate *within* a specific system of national and imperial control. Settler colonial political projects, for example, can operate *parallel* to someone else's sovereign claim, and, as settlers programmatically seek areas lacking substantive jurisdiction, this can frequently happen. Historian of American conceptions of freedom Eric Foner, for example, has noticed how settlers in North America routinely disregarded the boundaries of the different imperial colonial sovereignties. In this context, "American freedom" included the right to settle anywhere they thought fit.

> National [and imperial] boundaries made little difference to [settler] expansion; in Florida, Louisiana, Texas and other areas, American settlers rushed in to claim land under the jurisdiction of Spain, France, Mexico, and Indian tribes, confident that American sovereignty would soon follow in their wake.[57]

And yet, as well as the powerful and self-fulfilling expectation that the national sovereignty of the United States would territorially catch up with their movement, it is likely that it was a specific understanding of their inherent sovereignty that allowed settlers to accommodate their claims within the internationally recognised limits of Spanish, French, Mexican, or Indian nominal jurisdictions. Settlers knew that their self-governing capacity was indeed compatible with the imperial, national, or indigenous sovereignties in which they were operating. The fact that future US President Andrew Jackson even at one point swore allegiance to the king of Spain should not necessarily be seen as "opportunism"; rather, it could be seen as an expression of a settler sovereignty that could subsist besides (indeed, above) Spain's imperial and internationally recognised sovereign claim.[58] In any case, again, this was a global phenomenon that went beyond North America, and settlers preceded the establishment of colonial sovereignties elsewhere as well: in New Zealand, where the New Zealand Company constituted a settler government before the formal extension of British nominal authority, in Fiji, Hawaii, and elsewhere.

Settlers can also *subvert* recognised sovereign orders, as they eventually did in Texas, or *establish* entirely new ones (as the Mormons initially attempted after a final resettlement in what would become Utah, or in the case of the Boer Republics). Alternatively, settlers can accommodate their claim *beneath* an already consolidated or consolidating alien sovereign domain, as in the case of the many communities of Europeans establishing "colonies" in various Latin American countries (where they often ended up constituting a "state within the state").[59] The Welsh settler colony of Chubut, Patagonia, was established in 1865, well before the Argentinean occupation of the region in the 1870s. The local community was able to protect its language and customs, and it was only in the 1910s that the Argentinean government was finally able to exercise its effective sovereignty in the region by imposing its legislative authority and by forcing Indian and Welsh children to attend federal schools.[60] The reverse is also possible, and at times it is the community of settlers that is invited to fill a "void", or to redress what it is perceived as a racial, colonising, and civilisational deficit, as in the case, for example, of Paraguay's dealings with German and Australian experiments in regenerative colony building in the 1880s and 1890s.[61] This "invitation" is only possible in a context where different sovereign claims are understood as compatible – indeed functional – to the colonising or national project. Communities of Germans and other northern Europeans migrating collectively were able to settle almost everywhere in the settler and would-be settler world, in Australia and the Americas. Ukrainians were welcome to resettle in Canada, and Zionist settlement, of course, was facilitated in the context of the post-Balfour declaration "surrogate" colonisation of Palestine.[62]

Finally, settler projects can also operate as *a function* of enabling colonial regimes, as in the cases of the Japanese settlers in Korea and Formosa, the French *Pied Noir* in Algeria, the Italian settlers in Libya, the Portuguese in Mozambique and Angola, and the Israeli settlers in post-1967 West Bank and Gaza.

The settler and the national or imperial sovereignties can then articulate their respective operations in a multiplicity of ways within a spectrum of relationships characterised by unfettered settler control at one extreme and the comprehensive subordination of the settler collective at the other. There can be a situation where settler and state sovereignties coincide, where a settler legislature exercises unfettered control. Alternatively, an isopolitical relationship can be instituted, uniting colonising metropole and settler periphery, where separation is accompanied by the selective allocation of rights to settlers transferring from the metropole. There can also be settler subsumption within national and imperial structures, a situation where the border between "migrant" and "settler" becomes blurred, and sympolitical connection between colonising metropole and periphery (a sympolity is an institutional arrangement where there is no separation between colonising metropole and settler locale), a situation where it is the distinction between colonial and settler colonial forms that becomes indistinct (of course, these articulations often blur into each other, and are recurrently tested and subject to change depending of shifting balances of power).

While in the latter instance, the settler endeavour is weakened by dependence on a metropolitan determination to underwrite its survival (even if settler lobbies and political agitation are crucial factors in shaping colonial policy, that determination may not last), utter failure to operate within an imperial or national sovereignty can also have disastrous consequences for the settler endeavour, as devastating as the already mentioned failure to transfer any sovereign capacity. It can expose the settler community to alternative claims, deprive it of protection against indigenous and exogenous activities, and starve it of the capacity to attract capital and new settlers. As both operating within a constraining colonial framework and entirely outside of it can be fatal, it is isopolitical arrangements that are best suited to serve the settler colonial endeavour. Settler colonial political traditions thus prefer to think in isopolitical ways and routinely imagine a *single political community across separate jurisdictions*. Jefferson, for example, coherently endeavoured to protect the rights of the little republics he envisaged being founded in the newly settled and would-be settled areas. These rights would indeed amount to the establishment of isopolitical relations, a prospect that the Federalists were unwilling to entertain (debate surrounding the possibility of enabling Congressional vetoes over state legislation had prompted Madison to decry the "evil of imperia in imperio", the "absurdity of a sovereignty within a sovereignty", as good a definition as any of an isopolitical bond).[63]

In another context, James Belich has perceptively described an isopolitical relationship by underscoring what he has defined as "recolonisation" on the one hand, and the Anglo-settler perception of co-owning the metropolitan cores and their imperial possessions on the other.[64] The Dominions' role, he noted,

> was quite distinct from that of the subject colonies; they were more similar to Kent than to Kenya. The concepts "British Empire" and "British Commonwealth" conceal a virtual nation, an ephemeral second United States, Britain-plus-Dominions, whose Dominion citizens considered themselves co-owners of London, the Empire, and British-ness in general.[65]

Similarly, Marilyn Lake's work on the 1908 Australian visit of the US Pacific fleet identified an isopolitical moment: when imagining a new kind of fraternal community of white men (i.e., "a perpetual concord of brotherhood") becomes possible as an alternative against the prospect of a multi-racial and *colonial* British empire.[66] This was a transnational isopolitical moment, but, as Carl Berger has suggested for Canada, developing settler isopolitical nationalisms and imperial commitment continuously co-defined each other in reciprocal tension for a very long time.[67]

Albert Venn Dicey, founding academic at the London School of Economics, even explicitly called in 1897 for the establishment of an "isopolity" of the Anglo-Saxons (he interpreted it as "common citizenship"), an entity that would unite Britain and its settler dominions with the United States. Quite significantly, he did not perceive his proposal as entailing major change; indeed, he argued, isopolitical relations should be merely formalised in order to mirror already existing ones. Of course, as he was thinking about an imagined community of white settler men, he took care to exclude indigenous peoples from the bounds of the proposed isopolity.[68] The prospect of isopolitical arrangements between Britain and the British neo-Europes, however, had been for decades a crucial part of the imperial debate. John Robert Seeley, among others, also an advocate of an isopolitical union, had been acutely aware of United States-based settler expertise in establishing and managing isopolitical relations. In his opinion, the British Empire should do "what the United States does so easily, that is hold together in a federal union countries very remote from each other".[69] Decades later, Australian Prime Minister Robert Menzies's 1950s notion of a Britishness stretching from "Cape York to Invercargill" was also an expression of an isopolitical separation that is, paradoxically, underpinned by identity.[70] Indeed, rather than being an anachronism, isopolitical sensitivities would be constantly reconfigured in different settings and survive even the emergence and consolidation of a globalised international system of sovereign states after the Second World War.

An historical literature interested in the formation and consolidation of state, imperial, or national institutions has ignored settler colonialism's preference for isopolitical ties. Settler discourse resents sympolitical relations, the dominating, disabling interference of metropoles impinging on settler self-governing capacities (especially as it interferes with settler exclusive control over indigenous and exogenous Others – indigenous policy, land, labour, and trade on the one hand, and immigration on the other). At the 1911 British Imperial Conference, where the settler colonies were determined to maintain their control even if they might support a uniform definition of Britishness, South African Minister of Education F. S. Malan concluded that "under a uniform naturalization policy, an individual might be able to circumvent local law by appealing to the imperial standard". In this case, the principle of (settler colonial) responsible government would be overturned. The settler control of the population economy was ultimately incompatible with British imperial (sympolitical) citizenship, and the latter was never realised.[71] Of course, settler colonial forms can emerge victorious but can also lose. The history of American independence, when settler and national sovereignties became coterminous, is also the history of a metropolitan attempt to disestablish isopolitical relations and replace them with sympolitical ones that backfired. Conversely, the history of Algerian independence, when it was the anti-colonial and national sovereignties that became coterminous, is also the history of a settler attempt to establish isopolitical relations that backfired. After all, the *Pied Noir* leadership staged coups in Algiers, not Paris.

Recovering and exploring settler colonialism's isopolitical propensity can help a better framing of settler colonial sovereign forms. Firstly, accounting for an isopolitical imagination can help an understanding of how settler colonial forms are transferred from one context to another. If it is *one* isopolitical entity operating across a number of jurisdictions, institutions, policies, expectations, political languages, and patterns of reference can be seamlessly transmitted. Secondly, investigating an isopolitical imagination highlights a situation in which the settler "archive" of the European imagination is shared in multiple directions: from metropole to settler periphery, from settler periphery to metropole, and from settler frontier to settler frontier.[72]

The sovereignty claimed by settler collectives does not focus on the state and insists on the law-making corporate capacity of the local community, on its self-constituting ability, on its competence to control the local population economy, and on a subordination to the colonising metropole that is premised on a conditional type of loyalty.[73] Lauren Benton has recently emphasised that imperial sovereignty was not initially concerned with territory. As "subjects could be located anywhere, and the tie between sovereign and subject was defined as a legal relationship, legal authority was not bound territorially", she concludes.[74] Yet, by linking it to territory in unprecedented and territorialising ways (see Chapter 3), the settlers developed alternative forms of sovereignty.[75] Indeed, Ken MacMillan has convincingly argued that the very development of imperial notions of sovereignty and the legal apparatuses supporting them was a response to the challenges brought forward by the need to manage the communities of European settlers inhabiting imperial peripheries.[76] The ultimate consolidation of imperial sovereignty can thus be interpreted as a response to a multiplicity of assertions of settler sovereignty, not vice versa. The two forms should be seen as opposed and yet tied in a dialectical relationship.

Imperial sovereignties could be challenged or accommodated, but settlers knew they were asserting *their own* as they moved across space. Enduring political claims have characterised the long-term development of settler polities, and their recurrence demonstrates the connectedness of a global phenomenon. While colonial and settler colonial sovereign forms interact and operate in tension and/or in collaboration with each other, a resilient settler sovereign capacity makes them inherently distinct: the expansion of settler colonial sovereignties cannot be collapsed within the expansion of colonial and imperial sovereignty.

There is a growing scholarship dedicated to the development of corporate sovereign forms in colonial settings. Philip J. Stern's work on the British East India Company refers to a historiography that has traditionally recognised the Company's quasi-sovereign character:

> the Company, we are told even by its best historians, was "a state within a state", with "semi-sovereign status" or a "delegated sovereignty"; a sort of "department of state" with "quasi-governmental powers"; and a "fledgling version" of its "metropolitan sire".[77]

While Stern pushes this argument forward, insisting that the East India Company should be seen as a "a body politic on its own terms", and as "an independent form of polity and political community", Stern also links this particular sovereignty to early modern understandings of sovereignty, when "national territorial states did not have a monopoly on political power", and where "sovereignty was composite, incomplete, hybrid, layered, and overlapping".[78] In the same article, Stern quotes Joyce Lee Malcolm's conclusion that seventeenth-century Englishmen "were thoroughly confused about sovereignty, knew they were, but found the ambiguity tolerable".[79] The particular corporate sovereign detailed by Stern in the case of the East India Company could assist an analysis of settler colonial sovereign forms as well. Inheriting and perpetuating a long history of autonomous corporate endeavour, settlers are generally *ambivalent* about sovereignty, know they are, and find this ambiguity advantageous.

Theorising a settler colonial corporate understanding of sovereignty is especially important because this sensitivity contributed significantly to shaping the institutions of the settler states.[80] This was the case where settlers were able to retain substantive control over their domain, but also where settlers had to confine their activity within the bounds of consolidating imperial and national institutions. In a convincing analysis of the origins of the United States Constitution, for example, Woody Holton has argued that those who opposed the document establishing the federal institutions of the United States, and those who actually led the unsuccessful rebellions, influenced significantly and in a multiplicity of ways its shape, timing, and content.[81] The United States federal establishment that would successfully contest settler control over local, territorial and state institutions is shown as emerging from a struggle where what has been here defined as a settler colonial understanding of a sovereign capacity was able to infiltrate it. The Jeffersonian and Jacksonian settler colonial "moments" of the following decades would not be explicable without reference to a capacity to impress a specific reading of colonisation and associated processes. And yet, a settler sovereignty is localised and transcolonial at once, as the establishment of an array of white-settler polities in a number of sites of colonial expansion during the nineteenth and twentieth centuries demonstrates. The "settler revolution" remains a global phenomenon, and settlers were able to recurrently impose their sovereignty well beyond the limits of the consolidating United States.[82]

3
Consciousness

In this chapter, I focus on the way settler perceive their predicament and on a number of paranoiac dispositions characterising the settler colonial situation. This chapter also explores the possibility of a Lacanian (imaginary–symbolic–real) interpretation of settler colonial phenomena. First, there is an imaginary spectacle, an ordered community working hard and living peacefully *Little House in the Prairie*-style. Then, there is the symbolic and ideological backdrop: a moral and regenerative world that supposedly epitomises settler traditions (e.g., the "frontier", the "outback", the "backblocks", and so on). Finally, there is the real: expanding capitalist orders associated with the need to resettle a growing number of people.

Focusing in particular on Australia as an exemplary settler colonial setting, but referring to other locales as well, this chapter also suggests that "settler society" is in itself a fantasy emanating from a painful perception of growing contradictions and social strife, where the prospect of settler migration literally operates as a displacement of tension, and where the longing for a classless, stationary, and *settled* body politic can find expression. Settler projects are inevitably premised on the traumatic, that is, *violent*, replacement and/or displacement of indigenous Others. However, for reasons that will be outlined below, settler colonialism also needs to disavow any foundational violence. The outbreak, intensity, and duration of a number of comparable "history wars" in the historiographies and public discourse of settler societies can thus be interpreted as one result of the resilience of particular foundational traumas *and* their disavowal. Beside disavowal as a defensive mechanism and the ways in which it influences relations with indigenous Others (first section), this chapter also focuses on two more psychoanalytical processes characterising the settler colonial situation: primal scene and screen memory (second section).[1]

Two factors may make this approach to the study of settler colonial phenomena especially rewarding. On the one hand, "settlement" is typically imagined *before* it is practiced (a settler migration can be construed as a pre-emptive act, a displacement where tensions arising from economic and social transformation are channelled on the outside). On the other hand, as fantasies of settler regenerated life precede the practical act of settling on the land, the sometimes painful conflict between fantasy and reality is bound to produce a number of defensive formations. For these reasons, "the settler archive of the European imagination" has a tendency to operate by way of disavowal and repression.[2] As the repressive character of sources makes a focus on what is concealed more interesting than an analysis of what is explicitly articulated (and as archival and documentary sources remain inherently unsatisfactory), an historical analysis of settler colonial forms and identity requires a specific attention to practice as a clue to consciousness. Jacqueline Rose concluded in *States of Fantasy* that there is "no way of understanding political identities and destinies without letting fantasy into the frame".[3] An appraisal of the imagination and psychology of settler colonialism is therefore needed.

Disavowal, non-encounter

There is an established interpretative tradition relating to colonial phenomena and their psychoanalytic dimension. In his theoretical outline of colonial phenomena, Jürgen Osterhammel, for example, refers a number of foundational texts in order to define colonialism as an environment where the colonisers *as well as* the colonised suffer personality deformations, and where there is a need to see "statements by colonizers" as expressions of social pathology as well as ideology.[4] This interpretative tradition, however, does not focus specifically on the psychoanalysis of *settler* colonialism and generally subsumes settler colonial forms within colonial phenomena at large.[5] On the contrary, settler collectives are traumatised societies *par excellence*, where indigenous genocide and/or displacement interact with other traumatic experiences (in the case of Australia, for example, a concentrationarian past; more generally, the dislocations of migration). Of course, perpetrator trauma should also be included in this context, leading to stubborn and lingering anxieties over settler legitimacy and belonging. Even when trauma is effectively repressed, and in Australia, for example, it *was* effectively repressed for a long time, trauma remains in a latent state and can emerge in varied forms.[6]

In addition to an inevitable original founding violence, one should also emphasise that settler collectives are also *escaping* from violence. In this context, a "secure future" in a new land is recurrently and dialectically opposed to an "uncertain prospect" in an old one, and a determination to produce a *settled* political body is routinely expressed in formulations of *settler* colonial political traditions. That is, a settler society is commonly articulated as a circumstance primarily characterised by the absolute or relative lack of violence; it is a fantasy of communities devoid of disturbances or dislocations, and a situation where the transplanted settler collective would get back a *jouissance* that was historically taken away. As "settler society" can thus be seen as a fantasy where a perception of a constant struggle is juxtaposed against an ideal of "peace" that can never be reached, settler projects embrace and reject violence *at the same time*.[7] The settler colonial situation is thus a circumstance where the tension between contradictory impulses produces long-lasting psychic conflicts and a number of associated psychopathologies.[8]

Political theory has often assumed that *all* political orders are based on an initial law-establishing violent inception.[9] However, settler colonial regimes occupy a peculiar position in this context because their violent foundation must be disavowed: a recurring narcissistic drive demanding that a settler society be represented as an ideal political body makes this inescapable.[10] In the case of settler colonial contexts, and in contradiction with other political entities, a Freudian type of ego-ideal formation is also at play, where the narcissistic idealisation of the ego and identification with the parents ("the motherland") come together in representations of the settler entity as both an ideal society *and* as truer and uncorrupted version of the original social body. As a result, a stress on identification with the mother country produces neo-English mimicry through anaclitic types of object-choice (i.e., Euroepanisation), and identification with universal republicanism would produce an alternative type of ego-ideal formation (i.e., indigenisation). The two processes, however, overlap, and American patriots fought for their Saxon rights of freeborn Englishmen, while nineteenth-century Australian nationalists asserted their difference in the face of metropolitan condescension and associated self-loathing.

Recurring narratives emphasising an immaculate origin notwithstanding, the concept of a founding violence is especially cogent with regard to the foundation of settler political orders, where the founding collective is primarily characterised by military and reproductive capability, and where the initial nucleus of a settler society is an expression of a sovereignty that is above all marked by a violent self-defensive capacity.[11] The circle of wagons/the Trekboers' laager are thus settler heterotopias located in an indefinite site on the frontier and a transitory bulwark for the exercise of a polity reduced to its bare minimum.[12] Consequently, even when settler colonial narratives celebrate anti-indigenous violence, they do so by representing a defensive battle ensuring the continued survival of the settler community and never as founding violence *per se*. Instances of celebratory myths of settler survival include Orangist celebrations of the Battle of the Boyne, Afrikaner renditions of the battle of Red River, and Israeli narratives of the War of 1948 (less-known military episodes occupying similar positions in local settler narrative mythologies include the battle of the Muddy Flat of 1854 outside Shanghai, the repression of the Kanak insurgency in 1878 New Caledonia, and "victory" in the Second Matabele War in 1890s Rhodesia).[13]

At the same time, settler political traditions often emphasise characteristics that are deeply entrenched in Western political cultures. Expressing a widespread notion, for example, Condorcet identified the "family settled upon the soil" as the basic building unit of the state, and Comte insisted that the "prime human revolution [is the] passage from nomadic life to sedentary state".[14] In another context, anthropologist Ana María Alonso perceptively outlined a "sedentarist metaphysics" resulting in "a vision of territorial displacement as pathological, as a loss of moral bearings that makes the uprooted the antithesis of 'honest citizens' ".[15] If this is relevant for much of Western civilisation, where wandering Jews and nomadic Gypsies, for example, are classically pathologised in various ways, it is more emphatically so as regards settler body politics, where the need to emphasise settler fixity encourages the perception of indigenous and exogenous Others as "unsettled", and where projections of a nomadic state are used as a strategy to draw different circles of inclusion and exclusion and to deny entitlements in a settler polity (it is not only about withholding the possibility of access to rights; representing unsettledness, as I have suggested, is also a crucial discursive ingredient in a number of transfers). As a result, derogatory images implying an enhanced degree of mobility are consistently and recurrently projected onto indigenous people and their lifestyles (projection, after all, is a crucial defensive mechanism). In turn, this dynamic allows a typically settler colonial inversion, where indigenous people are nomadified and settlers can perform their indigenisation and express their nativism. Accordingly, for example, victorious Afrikaners declared a Zulu leader the "the ruling prince of the emigrant Zulus" and defined Zulus as "newcomers", and the Israeli Supreme Court insisted that displaced Palestinians during and immediately after the 1948 Arab-Israeli War be defined as "wanderers": men who wander "freely and without permit within the defense lines of the state and within the offensive lines of the enemy".[16]

A remarkable instance of systematically disavowed violence in a settler colonial context is represented by Tocqueville's *Democracy in America* (undoubtedly one foundational text of settler political traditions).[17] Scholarly reflection on *Democracy in America* has focused on "America" and "democracy"; Tocqueville's text, however, especially in the light of his later attempts to promote a settler colonial project in Algeria, can also be seen as a general exploration of settler colonial political formations. As his account focuses on the encounter between a settler community (the bearer of democratic ideals) and the exceptional geography it settles (a scenario that facilitates the establishment of an agrarian society of equals), Tocqueville narrates the unique combination between a land that is unframed by social relations (a "wilderness" waiting to be cultivated) and a settler collective (which is also assumed to be divested of any prior social determination). Tocqueville thus describes a people without history in a place without history, a recurring trope in many settler colonial formations.

However, images of settler democratic citizenship and polity are only made possible by a comprehensive disavowal of the presence and sovereignty of indigenous groups, and his notes on the violence against indigenous people, along with observations on slavery (this is telling, as they both define the indigenous and exogenous limits of the settler democracy), are cast to the margin of *Democracy in America* in an appendix. The ongoing currency of this narrative (and of its inherent disavowal of indigenous presences) should not be underestimated, as it shaped Turnerian notions of "frontier" democracy, for example, and, by way of analogy and identification (also a crucial psychoanalytical mechanism), the development of the other settler entities as well.

Ayse Deniz Temiz's outline of Tocqueville's account, for example, notices that the "transition from the state of nature to the social state is incomparably smoother in Tocqueville's exceptional case" (as opposed to the Hobbesian transfer of power to the sovereign, or Rousseau's social contract, for example), and that

> the state of law does not rule out the natural state, but emerges alongside it. For the law does not arise as a collective response to a conflict which it takes upon itself to dissipate, rather it emerges spontaneously, so to say, as supplement to a conflict-free natural state.[18]

Only a sustained disavowal of *any* founding violence allows a seamless process of settler territorialisation. True, at times, settler political traditions cannot possibly lay claim to a "quiet land", and a celebration of frontier violence becomes a feature of national mythologies. In these instances, however, a quiet and peaceful idyll and disavowal re-emerge *after* the "closing" of the troubled frontier, the cessation of hostility, and *after* the establishment of a purportedly settled/settler order.

Since Tocqueville defines ownership of land as the condition for settler democracy, and its allocation as the basis for the egalitarian community, settler citizenship is seen as conditioned on *property of* – and *residency on* – the land. The settler citizen is therefore territorialised in unprecedented ways (hence the pivotal importance of the term "settler", which implies a marked degree of fixation). The relationship between territorialisation and ego formation has already been authoritatively explored, and Freud even referred to "foreign internal territory" in order to describe the "relation between the repressed and the ego".[19] However, more than other political regimes (and in particular *colonial* regimes, where transient colonials do not commit to remaining in any specific place, and as it dispenses with the labour of colonised Others), a *settler* colonial project is predominantly about territory. At the same time, the territorialisation of the settler community is ultimately premised on a parallel and necessary deterritorialisation (i.e., the transfer) of indigenous outsiders.[20] There is no way to avoid a traumatic outcome.

Disavowal of all founding violence, however, cannot allay anxiety. Recurrent representations of "quiet country" and "peaceful settlement" notwithstanding, settlers fear revenge. Jonathan Bardon's reconstruction of Ulster life after the early seventeenth-century plantation of communities of British settlers exemplifies a number of inherent settler fears and their neurotic transformation (similar anxieties would be reproduced, to mention a few cases, in 1860s Queensland, 1950s Algeria, 1970s Rhodesia, and the West Bank of the Second Intifada):

> On the lonely settlements by the Sperrins or Glenveagh the baying of a wolf at the moon must have sent a chill down the spine of many a colonist who had never heard the sound before. The fear of woodkerne lurking in the thickets was better founded. The greatest threat, however, was the smouldering resentment of the native Irish who worked and farmed with the settlers.[21]

Bardon quotes a 1628 warning that "it is fered that they will Rise upon a Sudden and Cutt the Throts of the poore dispersed Brittish", but similar anxieties about indiscriminate indigenous violence are relevant to most settler colonial circumstances; indeed, ongoing concerns with existential threats and a paranoid fear of ultimate decolonisation can be seen as a constituent feature of the settler colonial situation.[22] (Besides a fear of indigenous revenge, other neurosis-generating settler anxieties include paranoid fears about degenerative manifestations in the settler social body, apprehensions about the debilitating results of climate, remoteness, geopolitical position, racial contamination, inappropriate demographic balances, and concerns about the possibility that the land will ultimately turn against the settler project.)[23]

More generally, however, as well as denying any founding violence, disavowal is also directed at disallowing the very existence and persistence of indigenous presence and claims. Sources frequently refer to indigenous people as "shadows", and the recurring construction of various mythologies portraying dying races and "vanishing" Indians should be referred to a specific settler need to ultimately disavow the indigenous presence (and thus enact a crucial type of transfer).[24] Summarising a remarkably widespread notion, author of *National Life and Character: A Forecast* Charles Pearson called indigenous peoples an "evanescent" race.[25] While, as already noted, a settler gaze is characterised by a tendency to depopulate the country of indigenous peoples in representations and especially in recollections (i.e., in rationalisations that follow successful settler colonisation), settler projects are recurrently born in a perception of "emptiness".[26] It borders on wishful thinking, and it is a mode of perception that informs the whole history of settler colonial endeavours. From his ship, Captain Cook had *assumed* that Australia would be mainly uninhabited, but even more informed twentieth-century representations of locales earmarked for settlement activity also share a distorted perception. The 1930s travel literature depicting fascist Italy's African "Empire", for example, insisted on an extraordinarily empty landscape (as it was decidedly more imagined than practiced, Italian colonialism provides a privileged point of view in the exploration of the imagination of colonialism).[27] Israeli poet and journalist Haim Gouri's 1967 perception of the newly conquered West Bank similarly epitomises the incapacity to register an indigenous presence:

> It seemed to me I'd died and was waking up, resurrected [...]. All that I loved was cast at my feet, *stunningly ownerless*, landscapes revealed as in a dream. The old Land of Israel, the homeland of my youth, the other half of my cleft country. And their land, the land of *the unseen ones*, hiding behind their walls.[28]

Indeed, claims that areas to be annexed and opened up for colonisation are "vacant" are a constituent part of a settler colonial ideology. For example, an 1834 motion advocating the annexation of Natal argued that "the country had been visited by the tyrant Chaka, who, like a typhoon, had swept away the inhabitants, leaving it *entirely depopulated* and *in a state of nature*."[29] The perception of a "state of nature" and the appraisal of a vacuous/defective indigenous authority are recurring components in the articulation of a settler project: the Ulster plantation was initiated after the Irish leadership had left for the continent in 1607, and, as mentioned, the New England Puritans saw the Indian killing plague in terms of a "wonderful preparation".[30] Instances relating to this pattern of reference, however, are persistent throughout the history of settler colonial forms, and include Israel Zangwill's well-known slogan identifying "a land without people for a people without a land", as good a definition as any of settler colonialism's ability to disavow.

Accordingly, the land must be represented as a blank slate, or, in the words of Karen Kupperman, "a stage tableau, with the arrival of the Europeans as the rising of the curtain and the beginning of the action".[31] Explorer-surveyor Thomas Mitchell (the fact that exploring and surveying are collapsed is significant – surveying is a crucial ceremony of settler possession) travelled through what would become Victoria, Australia, in 1838.[32] He was quite pleased:

> Every day we passed over land which for natural fertility and beauty could scarcely be surpassed; over streams of unfailing abundance and plains covered with the richest pasturage. Stately trees and majestic mountains adorned the ever-varying scenery of this region, the most southern of all Australia and the best.[33]

It was an empty landscape, and the indigenous inhabitants remained a presence only detected by reference to "camp-smoke", or to the "camp litter" that was left behind (and yet Mitchell crucially relied on Aboriginal people for information and support). As a result, the potential for colonisation was quite obvious: this territory, "still for the most part in a state of nature, presents a fair *blank sheet for any geographical arrangement* whether of county divisions, lines of communication, or sites of towns".[34] His perception epitomises what we can understand as settler gaze: on the one hand, Mitchell's vision could dismiss the Aboriginal presence; on the other hand, he could *see* a whole settler body politic "to come", inclusive of its constituent institutions, the towns, the administrative units they would represent, and their interaction (even its contradictions – hence his recommendation that "the partial or narrow views of the first settlers" be countered with wise central planning). Accordingly, as a settler polity to come was projected onto the visual field, really existing indigenous presences were being discursively dislodged.

Ultimately, the disavowal of both a founding violence and of indigenous presences systematically informs settler perception.[35] Accordingly, the only encounter that is registered is between man and land.[36] However, while an encounter that is premised on a foundational disavowal can be better described as a non-encounter, there is another factor that enables a comprehensive disavowal: first encounters between indigenous peoples and settlers, founders of political orders who have come to stay, are actually quite rare. Indigenous peoples first meet with traders, explorers, captives, missionaries, castaways, and other agents of colonial expansion, even anthropologists – rarely with settlers. Indeed, as already noted, settler colonial orders often replace previous colonial regimes, denouncing (and disavowing) previously established and mutually constructed plural "middle ground" traditions.[37] Representing encounters between different societies was a crucial step in the process of finally discarding the idiom of European discovery and conquest, and associated narratives involving the march of civilisation against savagery and wilderness. While the literature on *colonial* encounters is large and sophisticated, with attention now placed on agency and constructed meaning, exploring the settler colonial encounter and dealing with both disavowal and infrequency, has been especially complex.[38]

As non-historical approaches sometime display an analytical sharpness that is seldom within the reach of traditional historical narratives, a fictional reconstruction can perhaps better frame an encounter that is more imagined than practiced. Ray Bradbury's classic science fiction interpretation of settler colonialism insightfully captures how, in a settler philosophical perspective, the indigenous Other ultimately does not exist: it is either a being that, literally, cannot be touched, or a life form whose identity and appearance invariably assumes the shape that the coloniser is willing to project (in Bradbury's account, there are two categories of indigenous Martians).[39] It is thus an encounter characterised by either a lack of perception, or an awareness that is systematically distorted by wishful thinking. A passage from the *Martian Chronicles* reconstructs the impossible dialogue between an indigenous Martian (of the first type) and a settler. They chance on each other accidentally:

'I can see through you!' said Tomás [the settler].

'And I through you!' said the [indigenous] Martian, stepping back.

Tomás felt his own body and, feeling the warmth, was reassured. I am real, he thought.

The Martian touched his own nose and lips. '*I* have flesh', he said, half aloud. '*I* am alive'.

Tomás stared at the stranger. 'And if *I* am real, then *you* must be dead'.

'No, you!'

'A Ghost'

'A phantom!'[40]

Indigenous person and settler occupy the same locale but have never met; the place, their places, is/are charged with irreconcilable meanings. Later, *The Martian Chronicles* reconstructs the meeting between another indigenous Martian (of the second type) and an elderly settler:

Who is this [the indigenous Martian], he [the settler] thought, in need of love as much as we? Who is he and what is he, that, out of loneliness, he comes into the alien camp and assumes the voice and face of memory and stands among us, accepted and happy at last? From what mountain, what cave, what small last race of people remaining on this world when the rockets came from Earth? The old man shook his head. There was no way to know. This, to all purposes, was Tom [his dead son].[41]

Afterwards in the same chapter, settler man and indigenous Martian exchange a dialogue that emphasises the impossibility of a relationship going beyond an apparently compatible need to project images and, on the other hand, to mirror them:

'You are Tom, you were Tom, weren't you? You aren't joking with an old man; you are not really Lavinia Spaulding [another settler's daughter]?'

'I'm not anyone, I'm just myself; wherever I am, I am something, and now I am something you can't help'.[42]

An unbending logic of exclusion becomes operative in Bradbury's account: for settlers, indigenous people are ghosts, even luminous spheres; they are spirits without a body. In settler renditions, indigenous people frequently appear elusive, insubstantial, apathetic, aimless, and impermanent: a relationship, even a negative one, is impossible, and everything indigenous can thus be reduced to reminiscence (a conceptual move, indeed a narrative transfer that restricts an actually existing indigenous presence to temporary and instable pockets of past surrounded by future). For settlers, the Martian country is being born right at the moment of settlement, with villages built with California redwood and Oregon pine. Before settlement and terraformation, it was nothing: pure space, a setting devoid of meaning, and the stage tableau where the curtain had not yet risen.

As the settler colonial encounter can be better understood as a non-encounter, the specific circumstances of the settler colonial situation contribute to making mutually constructed meaning problematic. When the settlers occupy the land, indigenous peoples are unwillingly transformed into neighbours and, therefore, into intruders. A neighbour, as Slavoj Žižek recently noted quoting Freud, is "primarily a thing, a traumatic intruder, someone whose different way of life (or, rather, way of *jouissance* materialised in its social practices and rituals) disturbs us".[43] A settler state of mind is relevant to understanding the stubborn and recurring perception that sees indigenous peoples entering the settler space when obviously and historically the opposite is the case. Frantz Fanon, addressing a specific conflict emanating from an indigenous insurgency against settler domination, pointed out a lack of mutual constitution, and concluded that "it is the settler who has brought the native into existence and who perpetuates his existence."[44] The settler colonial non-encounter is a fundamentally asymmetrical dynamic; a systemic lack of reciprocity should be emphasised.

Primal scene, screen memory

The disavowal of a foundational violence and indigenous presences leads to another Freudian notion, that of the primal scene.

Temiz's insightful unpacking of the primal scene as it applies to exogenous Others entering the settler space is relevant to settler colonial dispositions towards indigenous people as well:

The primal scene is the moment of inception of the subject's memory, which coincides with the moment when the illusion of a perfect origin, as a state of plenitude without conflicts, is disturbed for the first time by the acknowledgement of the other's presence. This painful acknowledgement of the other that undermines the sovereignty of the subject, however, often takes place alongside a disavowal, a split consciousness and denial of the other's presence on the blank slate of the self's memory. Thus simultaneously recognized and negated, the other becomes a fetish for the self, namely that which the self approaches as its limit, without ever acknowledging it as its corollary, a full-fledged subject. The subject's condition for recognizing the other as fetish is to deny him/her agency or the capacity for change by pinning him/her down with a fixed image.[45]

Both indigenous and exogenous Others are thus a fetish for the inherently ambivalent indigenising/Europeanising settler self. In the case of the settler non-encounter with the indigenous person, however, especially if we understand the pervasive and ubiquitous relevance of a settler libidinal investment on the notion of "virgin land" (and take into account the inherently ambivalent nature of "motherland" in settler discourse), the notion of primal scene acquires a non-metaphorical quality ("primal scene" usually refers to the sexual intercourse between the parents as experienced by the child as an act of violence on the part of the father). The painful discovery of indigenous Others can thus produce aggressiveness beyond disavowal.

Moreover, as indigenous people ostensibly enjoy a prior and meaningful relationship with the land, their presence painfully upsets a settler libidinal economy focusing on "unspoilt", "untouched" circumstances, and "providential gifts". Francis Jennings famously concluded in *The Invasion of America* that the land "was more like a widow than a virgin".[46] This constituted a paradigmatic breakthrough that finally acknowledged Indian history and land management practices. The fact is, however, that the land could more

frequently be described as a married woman engaged in a fulfill-
ing and ongoing relationship, and an 1897 report on the possibility
of directing Jewish migration to Palestine, for example, honestly
concluded (in a pre-Zionist/non-Zionist way) that "the bride is beau-
tiful, but she is married to another man".[47] While aggressiveness
and disavowal should be considered as closely related manifestations
emanating from a fixation with the fantasy of an *exclusive* relationship with the (mother)land, the sustained resilience of *terra nullius*
in the face of manifest indigenous attachment to land should thus
be associated with a number of repressive impulses (as well as with a
self-serving settler inclination to dismiss alternative claims to land).

   Locke's notion that "in the beginning all the world was America"
also confirms an explicit link between primal scene and settler society
(i.e., that it is "settlement" that supersedes the state of nature, and
that original settler appropriation, for example, an enclosure, is an
act that defines and precedes the inception of historical processes).[48]
While Locke's approach already expressed a long-lasting notion that
settlers are natural men engaged in building a settled life in an ahis-
torical locale, recurring representations of settler original idylls insist
on an immaculate foundational setting devoid of disturbing indigenous (or exogenous) Others. Again, the foundational experience of
the settler colonisation of Ulster can constitute a point of reference.
The Montgomery manuscripts reconstruct the Scottish settler colony
of Donaghadee and depict a newly recuperated "Golden peaceable
age" (again, as mentioned, settlers see themselves as "returning"):

> Now every body minded their trades, and the plough, and the
> spade, building and setting fruit trees, &c, in orchards and gardens,
> and by ditching in their grounds. The old women spun, and the
> young girls plyed their nimble fingers at knitting – and every body
> was innocently busy. Now the Golden peaceable age renewed, no
> strife, contention, querulous lawyers, or Scottish or Irish feuds,
> between clans and families, and sirnames, disturbing the tranquil-
> ity of those times; and the towns and temples were erected, with
> other great works done (even in troublesome years).[49]

It is significant that being "innocently busy", an absence of "strife" or
"contention", and appropriate gendered productive order in another
place are all crucial tropes in settler representations of colonising

endeavours. An anxious reaction to disconcerting and disorienting developments produces a drive to think about a pacified world that can only be achieved via a voluntary displacement.

Ultimately, the fact that these images coexist with ongoing (explicit, latent, or intermittently surfacing) apprehension may actually suggest the activation of a splitting of the ego-like process, where two antithetical psychical attitudes coexist side by side without communicating, one taking reality into consideration, the other disavowing it.[50] The humanitarian denunciation of violence in settler colonies, which functions as a dialectical counterpoint to disavowal, may confirm the existence of a traumatic circumstance where a judgement of condemnation (as opposed to repression) is deployed as a defensive mechanism.[51] A notable example of humanitarian denunciation of settler genocidal violence is Benjamin Franklin's condemnation of the Paxton Boys and their brutality. (It is telling, however, that Franklin's lamentation actually culminates in discursive transfer: he finally wishes the Indians were elsewhere, safer with "the ancient Heathens", the "cruel Turks", even the "Popish Spaniards", or the "Negroes of Africa". The Paxton Boys, on the other hand, were busy with other transfers: threatening, killing and driving out while dressed as Indians – it was a dialogue between transfers.)[52]

Indeed, even if they constitute ostensibly divergent stances, disavowal and condemnation, amnesia and nostalgia, what Terry Eagleton has described as "the terrible twins [...] the inability to remember and the incapacity to do anything else", are intimately connected and represent a spectrum of possible stances *vis à vis* settler colonialism's inherently violent drive.[53] The notion of the primal scene also allows a better understanding of the already mentioned peculiar inversion mechanism by which indigenous people are seen as entering the settler space, and disturbing an otherwise serene, unperturbed circumstance *after* the beginning of the colonisation process, after settlement.[54] Since the trauma induced by the settler discovery of their presence *follows* the moment of inception of the settler memory, indigenous Others are inexorably destined to be confirmed as the "peoples without history" of Western intellectual traditions.

Narratives of settler colonisation emphasising notions of *peaceful* settlement (i.e., the "vanishing Indian" trope in the United States, the Canadian myth of essentially nonviolent dealings, representations of

Australia as the "quiet" continent), however, often resemble another Freudian form, screen memory: an inaccurate reconstruction that obscures what really happened (being one compromise formation, however, screen memories can also reveal it). In an article reconstructing a 1906 anthropological expedition to German East Africa, Andrew Zimmerman has analysed an instance of screen memory developing in a colonial setting (screen memories, of course, characterise both colonial and settler colonial phenomena, even if they hide different things). According to Zimmerman's outline of Freud's argument, screen memories emerge from

> compromises between an unconscious recognition of the importance of an experience and an equally unconscious desire not to recognize the experience at all [that is, the importance of colonisation is emphasised on the one hand, while indigenous destruction is repressed on the other]. Freud illustrates how displacement and condensation play roles in screen memories, as they do in the dream work. He shows also how unimportant details from the remembered situation may stand in for the important, but still unconscious elements that motivated the memory in the first place.[55]

Not surprisingly, as screen memories display a focus on particulars of relatively little significance as a way to foreclose analysis of a traumatic past, they can be especially interesting for what they reveal in the act of concealment. Examples of screen memories in a settler colonial context include an obsession with marking the sites of initial exploration, and nostalgic and idealised reconstructions of settler pasts, an attitude epitomised by what historian Inga Clendinnen has called "smoke rising from slab huts" narratives.[56]

If screen memories characterise settler reconstructions of the colonising past, more generally, a conflictual relation with history is typical of a settler consciousness.[57] Historiographer Eviatar Zerubavel convincingly notes how disregarding histories that precede the arrival of the "first" settlers is one essential feature of the politics of memory in settler colonial contexts. *Time Maps* defines this tendency as "mnemonic myopia", and refers, for example, to Israeli national-religious histories celebrating in an anti-Zionist way the Hasidic pilgrims from Belarus of 1777 rather than the first pioneer settlement of 1882.[58] However, while myopia is unsurprising as regards settler denial of indigenous pasts, it is also a recurrent feature of the settler memory of *all* alternative pasts. Jay Gitlin's critique of US historiographical orthodoxies, for example, also emphasises a mnemonic myopia-like phenomenon:

> The standard practice seems to be as follows: Discuss various imperial "intrusions" at the beginning; let the "Great War for Empire" (1756–1763) serve as a sort of clearinghouse event – we remove the French and prefigure the irrelevance of the British, then come back to the Spanish briefly in time for Texas and the Mexican War.[59]

Mnemonic myopia, moreover, may also affect a perception of the country itself. Geographer Paul Carter, for example, insightfully concluded in *The Road to Botany Bay* that "the country did not precede the traveler", and that, in fact, it was "the offspring of his intention".[60] Again, while this seems convincing as regards a variety of sensibilities, it may be especially valid for settlers, people that have come to stay and have a specific emotional investment in denying all alternative entitlements. Louis Hartz's intuition that "fragment extrication", the founding of a new society, produces a circumstance where the "past is excluded" and the "future shrinks" may have thus retained analytical cogency.[61]

The point here is not that reconstructions of the past that operate like screen memories are dishonest, consciously concealing, or inherently untruthful. An awareness of compromises between repressed elements and defensive mechanisms, however, should be an essential part of the interpretation and reinterpretation of settler colonial sources and their historiographies. For example, in the same way as an awareness of what is progressively concealed in successive renditions of the same dream reveals the repressive nature of defensive mechanisms, an historiography of Australian history demonstrates how Aboriginal history was progressively excised from received narratives.[62] In the process, the attention that nineteenth-century scholarship dedicated to Aboriginal people was eventually replaced with sustained repression by the mid-twentieth century (a condemnation phase then began in the 1970s).[63] Examples of variously repressed or displaced memories in an Australian historiographical context include the myth of the "Quiet Continent" concealing a number of bitter land wars and associated brutality (Raymond Evans calls Queensland "arguably one of the most violent places on earth during the global spread of Western capitalism in the nineteenth century"), the notion of an egalitarian "Australian Legend" concealing a remarkably gendered history, the perception of a non-sectarian body politics concealing traditions of Catholic exclusion, celebrations of Australian larrikinism concealing political subservience, representations of a classless society concealing a stratified social body, and narratives of successful multicultural integration concealing trauma, poverty, and ongoing exclusion.[64]

While disavowal allows the ostensibly contradictory dyad represented by settler "invader" and "peaceful" settler to coexist, resistance against acknowledging trauma should not be surprising. In the case of Australia, the *Bringing them Home Report* issued by Human Rights and Equal Opportunities Commission in 1998 had an inherently cathartic charge. The practice it was promoting, however, was progressively abandoned and replaced by the notion of a "practical reconciliation", a construction that was not practical and did not induce reconciliation (formulations of "practical reconciliation" could be interpreted by referring to what psychoanalysis understands as defusion of instincts: one demanding that the Aboriginal problem be ultimately dealt with, the other promoting a fantasy where ultimate reconciliation can be unilaterally declared in act of wish fulfilment). While elsewhere – in South Africa, or Peru, for example – the local "Truth and Reconciliation" commissions were able to more effectively approach traumatic histories (it is interesting to note, however, that the scope of their mandate was explicitly framed in ways that would not cover the legacies of colonial and settler colonial pasts), in Australia work on the stolen generations has characteristically unleashed a number of defensive mechanisms: "children were not stolen" (denial); "it was for their own good" (rationalisation); "those were the times" (intellectualisation).[65] In a similar fashion, an historiography of the Aboriginal experience that had consolidated since the 1970s eventually generated paranoiac imaginings of a conspiracy to fabricate "unauthentic" pasts.[66]

Public and official expressions of regret for past injustice were eventually issued in a multiplicity of jurisdictions. This has been especially controversial as regards the memory of settler colonisation, where a reluctance to express an apology was often paralleled by a parossistic

determination to apologise (considering Australian debates surrounding the possibility of an apology, Haydie Gooder and Jane M. Jacobs
have even sceptically and ironically referred to the "sorry people").[67]
Recent debate pertaining to legislative proposals demanding that the
"positive role" of colonisation be recognised in French history curric-
ula (with a specific reference to the *settler* colonisation in Algeria), as
supported by returned settlers and their lobbies, is a case in point.[68]
An apology would have a cathartic charge, and would acknowledge
the existence of a traumatic past over and against a number of deeply
entrenched mnemonic traces. Yet again, defensive and/or paranoiac
stances cannot be effectively met with rational argument (this is what
many participants to the many "history wars" of the 1990s and 2000
have attempted). As denialists have not reasoned themselves into
denial, they cannot be reasoned out of it. Something else is needed.

While the very idea of settling the land is an act that is inevitably
premised on the perception of "empty land", a settler inclination
to disavow any indigenous presence is crucially located in Western
hermeneutic traditions. Plato, for example, refers to the relationship
between body and soul as "colonisation": *katoikizein* (specifically:
the act of settling a colony).[69] For Plato, the soul descends into an
inanimate body like settlers begin inhabiting a place. This founding
metaphor has important consequences for an analysis of settler dispositions. First, as far as settlers are concerned, they are the first real
inhabitants of the place they settle (a seventeenth-century English
colonist to Ireland epitomised this notion by concluding that "we
rather than they [are] the prime occupants, and [they are] only
Sojourners in the land").[70] Secondly, if colonisation and settlement
are an appropriate metaphor to describe the relationship between
soul and body, the reverse is also true, and the soul's proprietary
command over bodily matters that is typical of Western explanatory
systems is mirrored by a settler determination to possess and dominate place. Most importantly, confirming a powerful drive towards
disavowal, there are no indigenous people in Plato's metaphor; settler colonisers see no indigenous person as they proceed to inhabit
the land.

When denial becomes impossible, when indigenous presences
successfully challenge settler colonialism's defensive mechanisms, a
particular version of what Albert Memmi described in his influential
1960s exploration of colonial phenomena as the "Nero complex"

(and what Dirk Moses defined as settler colonialism's "genocidal moments") may become activated.[71] Memmi argued that

> accepting the reality of being a colonizer means agreeing to be a non legitimate privileged person, that is, a usurper. To be sure, a usurper claims his place and, if need be, will defend it by every means at his disposal. This amounts to saying that at the very time of his triumph, he admits that what triumphs in him is an image which he condemns. His true victory will therefore never be upon him: now he need only record it in the laws and morals. For this he would have to convince the others, if not himself. In other words, to possess victory completely he needs to absolve himself of it and the conditions under which it was attained. This explains his strenuous insistence, strange for a victor, on apparently futile matters. He endeavors to falsify history, he rewrites laws, he would extinguish memories – anything to succeed in transforming his usurpation into legitimacy. [...]

> Moreover, the more the usurped is downtrodden, the more the usurper triumphs and, thereafter, confirms his guilt and establishes his self-condemnation. Thus, the momentum of this mechanism for defense propels itself and worsens as it continues to move. This self-defeating process pushes the usurper to go one step further; to wish the disappearance of the usurped, whose very existence causes him to take the role of usurper, and whose heavier and heavier oppression makes him more and more an oppressor himself.[72]

One important feature of the Nero complex (a trait that Memmi did not explore as he assumed that colonialism ultimately needed the labour of the colonised and did not consider that settler collectives often carry out a localised "conquest of labour" that renders the indigenous person superfluous) is that aggressive instincts turned towards the outside world remain active even if the indigenous presence is finally liquidated. There is no solution; even indigenous disappearance and demographic takeover cannot dissipate settler aggressiveness: behind every settler, inevitably, lurks the "unsettler".[73]

4
Narrative

Settler colonialism has been resistant to decolonisation. Some settler polities decolonised later, some tentatively, some not at all.[1] And yet, as underscored, for example, by the 2007 UN declaration on the Rights of Indigenous Peoples and by its careful assertion of an indigenous right to self-determination that must be respectful of the sovereignty of existing states, there is a need to focus on the possibility of post-settler colonial futures in a not-yet post-settler colonial world.[2] Considering the at times irresistible trajectory of decolonisation processes during a number of crucial decades in the twentieth century, the resilience of settler colonialism requires explanation.

In their theoretical definition of settler colonialism Anna Johnston and Alan Lawson have perceptively noted an intractable doubleness/ambiguity: the "typical settler narrative", they argue, "has a doubled goal. It is concerned to act out the suppression or effacement of the indigene; it is also concerned to perform the concomitant indigenization of the settler".[3] As I have outlined in Chapter 3, these aims are sustained by a number of intertwined and mutually supporting defensive mechanisms: disavowal of founding violence and of indigenous people, which contribute to and are sustained by a settler colonial form of "primal scene", allowing for further disavowal and for the production and reproduction of screen memories (these, in turn, further sustain the other two). On this basis, in this chapter I suggest that an appraisal of a narrative deficit (and, specifically, an exploration of the structural differences separating colonial and settler colonial narrative forms) can contribute to explaining particularly contested traditions of decolonisation in settler polities. The first section deals with what is here defined as the settler narrative form, a particular way of understanding and organising historical change in settler colonial political traditions; the second section explores the specific difficulty of telling the end of the settler colonial story.

Colonial narratives, settler colonial narratives

Narratives and their availability matter. Narratives are a fundamental part of everyday life, and their construction constitutes an act that allows nations, communities, and individuals to make sense of the world. Crafting stories helps making sense.[4] An argument highlighting the importance of narratives in the development of feelings of ethnicity has been made, for example, by Anthony D. Smith, when he identified "this quartet of myths, memories, values and symbols", and the "characteristic forms or styles and genres of certain historical configurations" as the "core" of ethnicity.[5] However, as settler colonialism is immediately premised on a foundational and historically situated movement (settlers move in from elsewhere at a particular point in time), there is a specific need to focus on the way different narratives and their availability inform political life in settler societies (moreover, as mentioned, settler colonialism's inherently dynamic character also renders the issue of narrative particularly relevant). On the other hand, a sustained scholarly activity on the literatures of colonialism (and, of course, postcolonialism) has not yet explored the specific differences separating colonial and settler colonial storytelling (indeed, the very distinction between colonial and settler colonial phenomena, as I have argued in the introductory chapter, has so far also eluded sustained theoretical definition). In this section I argue that colonial and settler colonial narrative forms should be seen as a distinct and that that the stories we tell regarding these two phenomena are structurally different, even antithetical.[6] These narrative forms interact, overlap, and interpenetrate, and yet, as they remain analytically distinct, they should be seen as two structurally different types.

Colonial narratives normally have a circular form; they represent an *Odyssey* consisting of an outward movement followed by interaction with exotic and colonised Others in foreign surroundings, and by a final return to an original locale (interaction, of course, can take many different forms, from being captive at one end of the spectrum to dispensing wanton genocidal destruction at the other end).[7] We should attend to the ongoing relevance of a circular narrative structure. As Mary Beard recently put in a *Sunday Times* review of Alberto Manguel's *Homer: Iliad and Odyssey* (she was quoting critic Harold Bloom), "Everyone who reads and writes in the West is still a son or daughter of Homer."[8] This is particularly so, I would argue, with regards to colonialism. Emma Christopher, Cassandra Pybus, and Markus Rediker have noted how colonial narratives are foundationally shaped by a multiplicity of "middle passages", an expression originally designating "bottom line of a trading triangle, between the 'outward passage' from Europe to Africa and the 'homeward passage' from the Americas back to Europe".[9] These authors are specifically interested in retrieving the experience of enslaved colonised people and in the possibility of deploying this category to the understanding of other forced migrations. Coherently, they note this term's limiting Eurocentrism and develop the "middle passage" as a foundational interpretative category – as "not merely a maritime phrase to describe one part of an oceanic voyage", but as "the structuring link between expropriation in one geographic setting and exploitation in another".[10] And yet, I would argue that the "middle passage" retains an exceptional constitutive cogency as it applies to colonising Europeans as well. After all, in the context of the narrative structure of colonialism, "colonialism" can also be seen as a middle passage, as what happens in between an outward and a homeward journey. A Dutch proverb, referred to in one of the essays contained in their collection neatly confirms colonialism's narrative circularity (and a characteristically colonial binary encoding separating "home" and "colony" – a separation that settler colonialism inevitably complicates by collapsing settler "home" and colonial locale): "He who does not take Amsterdam with him to Batavia will not bring Batavia back with him to Amsterdam".[11]

On the contrary, there is no middle passage for settler colonising Europeans. In their case, no return is envisaged. Far from being the bottom line of a triangular movement, in the words of Ralph Waldo Emerson, but this was an extremely widespread notion, the oceanic crossing is a Lethean passage over which settlers "have had an opportunity to forget the Old World".[12] If there is no possibility of returning, if it is not an *Odyssey*, as settlers come to stay, the narrative generally associated with settler colonial enterprises rather resembles an *Aeneid*, where the settler coloniser moves forward along a story line that cannot be turned back (or, similarly, an *Anabasis* replicating the story of Xenophon's "marching republic" – "Anabasis", after all, is literally the act of travelling from the coast to the interior of a country, a movement that is implicit in typical settler colonial narratives of travel, penetration into the interior, settlement, endurance, and success). We should also attend to the ongoing consequence of this narrative structure because, if it is true that we are sons and daughters of Homer, it is also true that, as he did with Dante, Virgil is still taking us by the hand.[13] Indeed, more than any other text, the *Aeneid* provides a specific foundational reference for settler colonial endeavours. "Aborigines", after all, are the original inhabitant of *any* country (those who are there *ab origine*, at the beginning). The original Aborigines, however, were the people of Latium at the time when Aeneas and his companions arrived and settled in Italy.[14]

Animus revertendi as opposed to *animus manendi* (as mentioned, the intention to return in specific contradistinction to the intention to remain) thus sustain structurally distinct, circular and linear, narrative forms.[15] If colonial personnel return and can be likened to what Benedict Anderson calls "secular pilgrims", sojourners who travel back and forth, settler migration remains an act of non-discovery (i.e., the non-encounter outlined in Chapter 3).[16] The archetypal voyage of discovery is Ulysses's – but discovery is necessarily about going *and* coming back. Discovery, by definition, ultimately requires a circular narrative structure (there is a consolidated literature interpreting travel narratives as colonial texts).[17] Ulysses returns: he engages with many peoples in a multiplicity of places but never thinks of settling as an option. Besides, his urge to return is also due to a need to avenge those who doubted his eventual homecoming; unlike the settler, he slaughters at home. Aeneas – who has nothing left behind – also will not settle anywhere, focused as he is – with a force and an intensity that also resembles a "return" – on his final destination.

On the contrary, settlers do not discover: they carry their sovereignty and lifestyles with them. At times, they even relocate with their neighbours. As they move towards what amounts to a representation of their world, as they transform the land into their image, they settle another place without really moving.[18] Significantly, unlike Ulysses, who returns to something from which he had been temporarily detached, settlers construe their very movement forward as a "return" to something that was irretrievably lost: a return to the land, but also a return to an Edenic condition (now, *this* is a return), to a Golden Age of unsurrendered freedoms (or, in the case of Zionist settlers, a return to Palestine). In any case, settlers do not report back; Aeneas does not report back.

Moreover, whereas colonisers see themselves in a middle passage between home and home, between departure and return, the settler collective inhabits a third narrative phase, a segment that succeeds both the "Old World" and a period of displacement in the wilderness, a "frontier" phase made up in succession by entrance into a district, battling the land, community building, and, eventually, by the "closing in" of the frontier. Quite naturally, inhabiting structurally different narrative spaces influences the way in which colonisers and settler colonisers interpret their respective enterprises. The possibility of multiple middle passages allows a flexibility that settlers do not have, and defeat and relapse do not necessarily imply the failure of a colonial ideology. On the contrary, the settler colonial story locates the consolidating settler collective in history's latter days, hence a stubborn, recurring and inherent anxiety at the prospect of defeat or compromise.[19] (On the other hand, the very fact that the settler polities are perceived as inhabiting a narrative space that cannot be followed by a subsequent passage crucially contributes to blocking out indigenous peoples' struggles for a post settler colonial future – "what could these people possibly want"?).

Colonial and settler colonialism emerge, again, as structurally distinct formations. The colonial situation can be seen as characterised primarily by a circular narrative structure and by an ideology insisting on an intractable dichotomy permanently separating coloniser and colonised. Settler colonialism, on the contrary, can be seen as characterised by a linear narrative structure (and, as I have argued in Chapter 1, by a triangular system of relationships comprising three different agencies). And again: the colonial situation reproduces cycles of opposition between civility and barbarism (i.e., despite the ubiquitous underlying trope of civilisation's victory over savagery); colonialism immobilises relationships and establishes a pattern of repetition. In marked contrast, settler colonialism mobilises peoples in the teleological expectation of irreversible transformation. Colonial and settler colonial master narratives thus mirror each other: individual settlers have an intention to stay and operate in a system that supersedes itself; colonists have an intention to return and operate within a system that reproduces itself. One can instinctively think of neo-colonialism but there is no such thing as neo-settler colonialism.

Anthropologist Deborah Bird Rose's understanding of a Western settler narrative form, as opposed to an Australian Aboriginal one, refers, for example, to a white Australian settler palindrome in which all time is seen as developing towards the birth of Christ and then towards his second coming. A palindrome

> thus articulates the view that a plan of history exists, that history moves from an early (proto- or pre-) configuration through disjunction/transfiguration to the realised or fulfilled configuration [...]. The violence by which those on the pre-zero side of the frontier are forced to give way to those arriving from the post-zero side is asserted to exist within a moment that is about to be overcome. The metaphor of right and left hands is useful for describing life during this explosive moment. The right hand of conquest can be conceptualised as beneficent in its claims: productivity, growth, and civilisation are announced as beneficial actions in places where they purportedly had not existed before. The left hand, by contrast, has the task of erasing specific life. Indigenous peoples, their cultures, their practices of time, their sources of power, and their systems of ecological knowledge and responsibility will all be wiped out and most of the erasure will be literal, not metaphorical. This creates the tabula rasa upon which the right hand will inscribe its civilisation.[20]

In another context, but in a way epitomising a similar type of reasoning, Arthur Bird's 1889 description of the United States efficiently expressed both a settler colonial project's unboundedness and a settler palindromic narrative structure (and settler colonialism's orientational metaphors):

> the United States of America, – bounded on the north by the North Pole; on the South by the Antarctic Region; on the east by the first chapter of the Book of Genesis and on the west by the Day of Judgement.[21]

However, while a settler colonial narrative form should be seen as opposed to an indigenous one, as Rose demonstrates, a settler colonial palindrome is also structurally incompatible with the circular nature of the colonial narrative form. What is crucial in the context of an exploration of colonial and settler colonial narrative structures and their different modes of operation is that whereas a colonial ideology would understand "progress" as characterised by indigenous fixation and permanent subordination, a settler sensibility envisages a particular set of narrative refrains and a specific understanding of history where "progress" is typically understood as a measure of indigenous displacement (i.e., transfer) and ultimate erasure. "Progress" remains, but acquires an inherently dissimilar meaning: colonialism and settler colonialism are progressing towards very different places.

The fact that settler narratives resemble a palindrome, however, does not necessarily mean that they must invariably be seen as "progressing" (even if narratives of settler colonial endeavour recurrently praise the advent of settler modernity). Settler colonial narrative orders often display a special narrative form emphasising decline from settler colonial to inordinately non-settler, a narrative order opposed to the traditional "rough frontier to civilised settled life" paradigm (after all, a palindrome is by definition a sequence that retains its meaning even if it is read backwards). Historian of the American West John Mack Faragher, for example, detects instances of declensionist narratives in US historiography:

> [i]n a time-honored protocol of western social thought, the prescriptive "good community" is located in some past time, is seen to have suffered irretrievable declension, and is imaginatively reconstructed in order to critique the dislocation and anomie of contemporary life. In his influential history of eighteenth-century Dedham, Massachusetts, for example, Kenneth Lockridge asserts that American communalism atrophied when New Englanders "abandoned the web of relationships created by residence in the villages" for settlement in the open country, thereby surrendering to "the incoherence of individual opportunism". His perspective is part of a powerful interpretation, first promoted by the Puritans themselves, that reads American history as decline,

from *Gemeinschaft* to *Gesellschaft*, community to individualism, meaning to incoherence.[22]

In any case, whether they envisage a progressive movement or identify a degenerative tendency, settler narrative structures remain powerful, reproducible, and mobilisable whether in relation to reconstructions of the past or imaginings of the future, as recently confirmed by the remarkable successes of settler re-enactments TV series like *The Colony* (2004) and *Outback House* (2005) in Australia, *Frontier House* (2002) in the United States, *Pioneer Quest* (2000) in Canada, and, in a slightly different format, *Kid Nation* (2007), where 40 kids aged 8–15 spent 40 days in a nineteenth-century New Mexico ghost town while re-enacting foundational rituals.[23] Science fiction also routinely imagines the future as an extension of a settler colonial past.[24] Comparing the legacies of slavery and conquest – the colonial and the settler colonial – Patricia Nelson Limerick has emphasised settler colonialism's ongoing narrative currency (and colonialism's narrative demise): "an element of regret for 'what we did to the Indians' had entered the picture", she noted, "but the dominant feature of conquest remained 'adventure.' Children happily played 'cowboys and Indians,' but stopped short of 'masters and slaves' ".[25]

Of course, this narrative availability matters beyond reconstructions of the past and imagining the future. The ongoing activation of settler narrative refrains and their impact in shaping perception and political action should be emphasised as it applies to current situations as well. In the context of developing sensitivities regarding the conflict in the Middle East, for example, a narrative convergence related to a settler colonial enterprise can contribute to explaining US support for Israeli policies in the Occupied Territories.[26] Ultimately, the settler narrative form is especially foundational and powerful in a multiplicity of contexts because it responds, reproduces and engages with one of the fundamental Western stories: Exodus. The basic narrative of journeying to the Promised Land involves promise, servitude, liberation, migration, and the establishment of a new homeland; all tropes that specifically inform settler colonial projects on a multiplicity of levels.[27]

And yet, *exactly* because this story is compelling, telling its end remains extraordinarily complex. Albert Camus, who knew how to tell a story and knew about settler colonialism, tried.[28] *The First*

Man (incomplete, published posthumously, and autobiographical) explores the settler colonial condition and hypothesises its end (he was writing during the war of Algerian independence, and had planned to write "the history of the end of a world").[29] In one crucial moment of self discovery, the main protagonist reflects on the country of his birth and the country he has rediscovered while searching without success for his past (a Lethean passage is a Lethean passage – all memory is erased):

> But after all there was only the mystery of poverty that creates beings without names and without a past [...]. The Mahón people [Spaniards from the Balearic island of Minorca] of the Sahel, the Alsatians on the high plateaus, with this immense island between sand and sea, which the enormous silence was now beginning to envelop: the silence of anonymity; it enveloped blood and courage and work and instinct, it was at once cruel and compassionate. And he [i.e., Camus] wandering through the night of the years in the land of oblivion where each one is the first man, where he had to bring himself up [...] and he was sixteen, then he was twenty, and no one had spoken to him, and he had to learn by himself, to grow alone [...] like all the men born in this country who, one by one, try to learn to live without roots and without faith, and today all of them are threatened with eternal anonymity and the loss of the only consecrated traces of their passage on this earth.[30]

The stories settlers tell themselves and about themselves are crucial to an exploration of settler colonial subjectivities. In Camus's reconstruction, every settler is a "first man" and, therefore, settler manhood (as opposed to metropolitan manhood, for example, but also to indigenous manhood – that is, settler manhood as opposed to exogenous *and* indigenous alterity at once) is a truer form of manhood: a manhood that grows in isolation and is self-constituted, volitional, self-imposed (indigenous manhood, on the other hand, is no manhood at all: his "all the men born in this country" entirely disavows the colonised Arabs – they remain invisible and are transferred away).[31] French President Nicolas Sarkozy's November 2009 proposal that Camus be reburied at the Panthéon, France's national collection of great heroes, was met with controversy. Critics pointed out that Camus had been an individualist who consistently refused honours, others noted that the writer would have never agreed with Sarkozy's politics and leadership. The incongruence of adding to the Panthéon someone who understood his capacity to write as primarily premised on *not* being French was not mentioned.

On the other hand, in Camus' rendition settler life without history is tragically followed by the prospect of death without history. A settler fixation with permanence finds an outlet in anxieties about eternal anonymity. Aeneas's "empire without end" turns out to be an empire that can and indeed will be forgotten. This realisation induces in the end a "Nero complex" type of response. During his search, the protagonist meets a settler who tells him about his own father, "a real settler". After receiving the order to evacuate, the settler had methodically destroyed the fields, uprooted the vines, and poisoned the land. "And when a young captain, informed by who knows who, arrived and demanded an explanation, he said to him, 'Young man, since what we made here is a crime, it has to be wiped out' ".[32] For Camus, the end of the settler colonial story is indeed the end of everything.

Telling the end of the settler colonial story

In this section I discuss the possibility of decolonising settler colonial forms. The discontinuation of a colonial regime always remains within colonialism's cultural horizon; on the contrary, the discontinuation of a settler colonial circumstance remains unthinkable beyond, as I have argued in Chapter 1, supersession: a final assimilation/destruction of autonomous indigenous subjectivities, an ultimate assertion of an independent settler polity, or even, as mentioned, a successful process of indigenous/national reconciliation. In a recent essay entitled "The Settler Contract", Carole Pateman has noted the ongoing impossibility of settler decolonisation (unless what she describes as an original "settler contract" is undone). The power of the settler contract, she argued, where the settlers are "the natural figures of the thought experiment in the texts of political theory come to life", has meant that, even if the "process of decolonization and national self-determination that began after the Second World War has swept away all but tiny remnants of the colonies of the European powers", the "Native peoples of the two new Worlds [i.e., North America and Australia], living within the boundaries of the states constructed from the plantation of settlers, have never been seen as candidates for sovereignty".[33]

How can this resilience be explained? This section argues that in the case of *settler* colonial contexts a specific narrative form produces a situation in which there is no intuitive narrative of settler colonial decolonisation, and that a narrative gap contributes crucially to the invisibility of anti-colonial struggles in settler colonial contexts.[34] As insightfully pointed out by historian of British imperialism and decolonisation Roger Louis, the scramble for colonies that started at the end of the nineteenth century had ultimately produced colonial polities that could be turned over to successor states in a symmetrical process of counter-scramble.[35] In this sense, he remarked, imperial expansion and decolonisation mirror each other. However, if decolonisation is generally understood as a transaction whereby a colonial state is transformed into a self-governing territorial successor polity, problems inevitably arise when the (settler) colonising state *is* the self-governing territorial successor polity.[36] Besides, decolonisation's traditional focus on external relations and sovereign independence or autonomous self rule against a variety of imperial metropolitan centres inevitably obscures the position of settler colonised indigenous constituencies.[37] If decolonisation is an exercise in devolution, colonialism itself is an exercise in state-formation (the classic example is the British East India Company's surreptitious shift from commercial monopoly to constituted territorial polity). Settler colonialism, on the other hand, is primarily characterised by indigenous deterritorialisation accompanied by a sustained denial of any state-making capability for indigenous peoples. Thus, in a settler colonial context sovereignty needs to be negotiated *within* a polity rather than *between* polities; the decolonisation of settler colonial formations was bound to be complicated.

Complicated, of course, does not mean unnecessary. Broadly speaking, one can detect three approaches to settler decolonisation: settler evacuation, the promotion of various processes of indigenous reconciliation, and denial associated with an explicit rejection of the possibility of reforming the settler body politic (of course, while these three possibilities are conceptually distinct and are here addressed separately for analytical purposes, it should be emphasised that they routinely overlap and intertwine in complex ways).

Even if they had come to stay, at times, settlers depart. This is so especially when their sovereignty had been subsumed sympolitically within the operation of a metropolitan colonising endeavour (see Chapter 2). In these cases, as the settler project is premised on an enabling colonial order, the discontinuation of a colonial regime spells the discontinuation of the settler colonial one. While settlers want to stay, even more, they want a colonial and settler colonial world to remain in place. As Frantz Fanon perceptively prophetised, "the settler, from the moment the colonial context disappears, has no longer an interest in remaining or in co-existing".[38] The settlers don't necessarily go together and at once. There are varied patterns of settler departure, and even examples of accommodation with nationalist movements taking over at the moment of decolonisation. Of course, the reverse process is also possible and at times it is the community of settlers that is eventually expelled by nationalist forces. Soon after taking control of Libya in the late 1960s, Colonel Gaddafi threw out the remaining Italian community. In a dense commemorative calendar and in a split fashion that underlines an inherent distinction between colonial and settler colonial regimes, Libya celebrates "Independence Day" to mark the end of a colonial sovereignty, and "Evacuation of Fascist Settlers Day" to symbolise an ultimate break with a settler colonial past.[39] In this case, two systemically different regimes require distinct markers to celebrate their separate conclusion.

Quite significantly, however, where decolonisation takes the form of a settler collective exodus, as happened in Algeria, Libya, Kenya, Angola, Mozambique, North and South Rhodesia/Zimbabwe, South West Africa/Namibia, and more recently, in the Gaza Strip (evacuation of Israeli settlers, but not yet of colonial control), the decolonisation of territory is not matched, even symbolically, by an attempt to build decolonised relationships. Indeed, in these cases, settler departure conceptually mirrors and reinforces settler colonialism's inherent exclusivism, and confirms a "winner takes all" settler colonial frame of mind that demands that settler sovereignties entirely replace indigenous ones (or vice versa). By denying the very possibility of a relation between coloniser and colonised after the discontinuation of a settler colonial regime, settler departure thus produces a circumstance where decolonisation cannot be construed as a relationship between formally (yet not substantively) equal subjects.

Settler departure confirms a settler state of mind insisting that settler colonialism can only come to an end when either one of the
indigenous or exogenous elements finally disappears (a palindrome,
after al, allows for either one of these exits).

If settler colonialism in locales where the population economy
consisted of variously defined white minorities could not afford
decolonisation, in white settler nations it was settler exodus that
was never an option. In these cases, once the physical disappearance
of indigenous peoples had also become a non-viable option, other
strategies were developed. Throughout the 1970s and 1980s many of
these polities were facing contradictions arising from their encompassing a number of unreconciled "nations within".[40] In response,
the white settler nations initiated a number of political processes
envisaging a variously defined post-settler compact, were thus initiated. Projects of national or indigenous reconciliation developed
in dramatically different political circumstances and produced varied
results; and yet, despite their diversity, these initiatives collectively
represent a possible type of post-settler institutional endeavour (especially if it is intended as a process whereby it is the settler entity
that *reconciles* itself with indigenous survival and sovereignty).[41]
Nonetheless, even partially reforming the settler structures of the
body politic, usually under the impulse of judicially led reforms
endorsing constitutional and legislative transformation, has proved
painstakingly difficult, has encountered increasing opposition, and
in some jurisdictions eventually came to a standstill (or was even
reversed).

Beside settler exodus and a variety of political processes aimed at
establishing post-settler compacts, a third type of situation has also
occurred, where a sustained denial of the settler colonial character of
the polity has been upheld (this was so in Israel and in the United
States, for example). While in these polities the relative invisibility
of imperial and settler colonising endeavours has remained conven-
tional, the prospect of enacting post-settler decolonising passages
vis à vis indigenous peoples has remained unlikely. This invisibility
could be sustained via two related strategies of denial, one focusing on anti-colonial struggles leading to settler independence, and
the other emphasising experiences of subaltern migration. On the
one hand, as Alan Lawson insightfully pointed out, a focus on settler independence allows a "strategic disavowal of the colonising

act" (and a concomitant transformation of "invaders" into "peaceful settlers"):

> In the foundations of [settler] cultural nationalism, then, we can identify one vector of difference (the difference between colonizing subject and colonized subject: settler-Indigene) being replaced by another (the difference between colonizing subject and imperial centre: settler-imperium) in a strategic disavowal of the colonizing act. The national is what replaces the indigenous and in doing so conceals its participation in colonization by nominating a new colonized subject – the colonizer or invader-settler.[42]

On the other hand, and contributing towards a similar pattern of disavowal, the colonising settler can disappear behind the subaltern migrant. Settler societies – societies that are premised on an original sovereign settler foundation – can then be recoded as postcolonial migrant societies. The migrant blocks out the "settler", independence (the "post") occludes the "colonial", and the "settler colonial" is thoroughly concealed.

Detecting settler colonialism and its operation, of course, is not enough, and the decolonisation of settler colonial forms needs to be imagined before it is practiced. This has proved especially challenging, and, as Iris Marion Young has remarked, an "institutional imagination" of an entirely new character has to be developed.[43] If settler colonialism is by definition an ambivalent circumstance where, in a triangular system of relationships, the settler is colonised and colonising at once, decolonisation necessarily requires at least *two* moments: the moment of settler independence on the one hand and the moment of indigenous self-determination on the other. The first moment is easily conceptualised – we instinctively *know* about the 4th of July (even if, as I have argued in Chapter 2, a settler sovereign assertion travels with the settler since the beginning). The second passage is yet to be formulated.

In the end, the two sovereignties – the settler and the indigenous one – are generally perceived as inherently incompatible and mutually exclusive in the context of a zero sum game, and "decolonisation" in settler contexts is further complicated by the fact that one decolonisation (settler independence) inevitably constitutes an effective acceleration of colonising practices at the other end (i.e., further indigenous loss of autonomy).[44] Settler independence can thus be construed as an example of what Bird Rose has in another context defined as "deep colonising": a predicament where the very institutions that should operate towards a supersession of colonial contingencies are actually contributing to reinforcing their operative registers.[45]

Moreover, as James Tully has also remarked, if it is devised as an exercise in *settler* nation building, even well meaning processes of indigenous and national reconciliation, or the incorporation of indigenous governance structures within the settler polity, ultimately contribute to the erasure of variously defined indigenous sovereignties and therefore to the reproduction of settler colonising practices. Tully defines these practices as "extinction by accommodation" (as noted in Chapter 1, accommodating stances can crucially sustain a number of highly effective types of indigenous transfer).[46] In the end, the positioning of indigenous sovereignty in the context of settler political orders remains a most challenging undertaking, and establishing a workable post-settler practice can be testing even in the context of comparatively more sustained attempts to establish a shared indigenous/settler sovereignty.[47]

It should be noted, however, that not all settler stories are equally powerful and that there are alternative, very commanding, equally available, and equally mobilisable narrative structures. Again, narrative does matter. Some settler regimes could be discontinued because, among other reasons, the story of the end of settler exclusive political ascendancy was easier to tell. The end of the settler colonial story could be told, for example, as the end of ethnic and racial discrimination and the attainment of civil and constitutional rights. Recognising the crucial importance of the demise of apartheid South Africa (in the context of an analysis that otherwise stresses the continuities between colonial and postcolonial African political orders), Mahmood Mamdani, for example, has noted that for

> the first time in the history of African decolonization, a settler minority has relinquished exclusive political power without an outright political defeat. I am not arguing that this minority has given up its interests, only that it has consented to exploring ways of defending these interests other than a monopoly over political power and the rights of citizenship [...].[48]

This process, he concluded,

> has set the political trajectory of the African continent on a course
> radically different from that of the Americas. The Americas is the
> continent of settler independence. The South African transition
> means that nowhere on this continent has a settler minority suc-
> ceeded in declaring and sustaining the independence of a settler
> colony.[49]

Beyond Africa, in the white settler nations, telling the story of
an end to attacks on indigenous substantive autonomy, a move
that demands abandoning a cluster of narrative structures, remains
a much complicated process, especially if one considers that the
powerful narrative of an extension of civic rights to indigenous constituencies had already been deployed in the context of forced and
less coerced assimilation campaigns aiming at enacting a specific type
of indigenous transfer.

And yet, even if the story of what a post-settler colonial passage to come, of what should happen next, has been impossible to
tell beyond envisaging a final disappearance of all settler colonial
residues from the settler body politic, the story of what happened in
the past *could* change. It is significant that all processes of constitutional rearrangement involving indigenous constituencies in settler
nations have necessitated a significant revision of traditional historical narratives and a comprehensive reinterpretation of national
and/or regional pasts. Indeed, the role of historians in contributing to
institutional and judicial readjustment has in some cases been deci-
sive, and historians and other academics involved in the production
of indigenous and national histories in settler societies have in some
cases made history by literally (re)writing it.[50] Inevitably, as historical revisions challenged entrenched foundational narratives, these
revisionisms have often engendered a number of denialist responses.
Reacting to these revisions, as outlined in Chapter 3, a defensive type
of settler historical discourse also materialised.

It is also significant that these constitutional rearrangements typically promote historiographies where an evolving partnership *in the
present* would find confirmation in specific representations of pre-
or non-settler colonial pasts. In the process, narratives representing a two-step sequence constituted by an original and irrevocable

indigenous dispossession followed by a phase of multicultural inclusion (a periodisation that focuses on exogenous Others and "transfers" indigenous peoples away) have been comprehensively challenged by decades of scholarly recuperation of indigenous agency.[51] In a reforming Aotearoa/New Zealand during the 1980s and 1990s a historiographical upgrading of ostensibly discontinued traditions of partnership underpinned a general process aimed at establishing "treaty" practices as a way to address historical grievances.[52] While in the context of a discussion of Aotearoa/New Zealand's attempts to judicially "rectify" the past W. H. Oliver has even talked about a "retrospective utopia", as insightfully pointed out in a recent article by Bain Attwood, a similar inscription of "treaty" traditions was also initiated in an Australian historiographical context by Henry Reynolds with *The Law of The Land*.[53] He saw Reynolds's intent as similar to what Eric Hobsbawm has referred to as the "invention" of a tradition (specifically, a moral tradition of colonial if not settler colonial respect for indigenous title and rights), and quoted Mark Mckenna's remark that *The Law of the Land* "uncovered what Australia's history 'might have been' – a history of 'perpetual possibility' – rather than a history of what was" – as good a definition as any of the construction of a tradition.[54] While the Australian government promoted legislation in the spirit of this "invented" tradition in the early 1990s, this tradition could be subsequently forgotten, as demonstrated by subsequent Aboriginal policies under John Howard (or partially reinstated, as suggested by newly elected Prime Minister Kevin Rudd's February 2008 parliamentary apology).

Elsewhere, history-writing and public debate surrounding indigenous politics also decisively informed each other. South Africa's transition to post-apartheid also produced a dramatically changing historiographical landscape, where the historiography of the northern frontier witnessed a remarkable acceleration, possibly because it provided an exemplary original multiethnic, hybrid, and "open" (and previously neglected) frontier setting. Nigel Penn significantly noted in his historiographical outline that "the widespread acceptance of the election results of 1994 has begun a process of the rolling back, or opening, of frontiers everywhere". He then concluded that it "is possible that an 'open' frontier situation, as existed in the northern frontier zone for so long, will be seen as being the more typical South African scenario after all".[55] In North America a renewed historiographical tradition and an emphasis on frontier exchange and on a long lasting "middle ground" also revolutionised received understandings of colonial and Western history and underpinned developing relations between Indian nations and settler polities.[56]

These trajectories confirm that history and academic discourse, and the narratives that are produced and reproduced in a variety of contexts are crucial in all processes of indigenous reconciliation in settler polities. However, the historiographical shifts that have underpinned these processes have generally produced a situation where non-settler colonial pasts were upgraded and retroactively mobilised in order to sustain the possibility of post-settler compacts. The problem is that both an emphasis on the "middle ground" (a complex system of intercultural arrangements that is established when indigenous people retain the power to enforce indigenous practices on newcomers) *as well as* the alternative stance of deploying an anti-colonial rhetoric that does not distinguish between colonial and settler colonial forms, risk bypassing the issue of settler colonialism and focus on something else. The "middle ground" sustains the fantasy of "returning" to a noncolonial past, the anticolonial rhetoric sustains the prospect of possibly moving "forward" to a noncolonial future; neither stance, however, actually addresses the specificities of the settler colonial situation – its mimetic character is confirmed. On the contrary, an anti-settler colonial imagination and rhetoric are needed.

In the end, the reforming settler polities of the 1980s and 1990s share historiographical discussions where a settler colonial past is evaded rather than finally addressed.[57] Emphasising complex traditions of settler-indigenous partnership has thus been easier than insisting on the need to decolonise settler colonial sovereignties and radically reform the settler colonial polities. A widespread disinclination to enact substantive decolonising ruptures resulted in a tendency to avoid disturbing foundational structures, including foundational narratives of origin and settlement and their linear structure. Ultimately, the acknowledgment that "settlement" establishes legitimacies without extinguishing indigenous ones, and that indigenous sovereignties need to be accommodated in a decolonising, post-settler move, has remained elusive.

This impasse can be referred to a lack of a suitable narrative of settler decolonisation. The structural difference between colonial and settler colonial narrative forms does have an impact on the ways in which the decolonisation of settler colonial forms can be conceptualised. In *The Invention of Decolonization* Todd Sheperd has recently argued that decolonisation was "invented" in the context of the Algerian War. The notion that the independence of formerly colonised territories is inevitable – "the certainty that 'decolonization' was a stage in the forward march of history, of the Hegelian 'linear History with a capital H' " – had rendered decolonization "wholly consistent with a narrative of progress", he noted. It was a complete turnaround: "[n]o longer the exception among European overseas possessions, Algeria now became the emblematic example".[58] As the "invention" of decolonisation that he reconstructs is premised on a deliberate repression of the settler colonial fact, a repression that he is able to extensively document, Shepard's argument paradoxically confirms that it is in settler colonial contexts that decolonisation is most difficult. Decolonisation could be "invented" in Algeria only after the comprehensive denial of a history of settler colonialism and a settler colonial reality had been enacted. In turn, that denial required two related displacements: the settlers had to be physically transferred to France (the transfer of settlers), and Algerians had to be the subject of administrative transfer (from citizens of the French Republic to citizens of postcolonial Algeria). The Algerian "solution" to the colonial problem was thus premised on the effective repression of the settler colonial one.

Indeed, *there is* an acceptable narrative of decolonisation for the formerly colonised Third World, centred around nation-building and economic development (irrespective of whether this actually happens – it very rarely does). This format of postcolonial history can be described either as a progressive narrative of independence and nation-building (i.e., there is *some fit* between this narrative and reality) or as a more sobering denunciation of neo-colonialism and state failure (i.e., there is *no fit* between this narrative and reality). Either way, getting out of the colonies could be represented as a "forward" movement (a circular narrative form, after all, allows one to proceed forward even when going back). Conversely, in settler colonial contexts withdrawing from colonial practices of indigenous dispossession can be only perceived as a "backward" movement signalling the demise of original settler claims and their legitimacies. Lacking the possibility of a clearly defined decolonising moment (i.e., the moment in which it is *settler* colonialism that is discontinued), settler colonial contexts retained the policy objectives, if not the methods, of their settler colonising pasts. The drive towards further extinction and/or assimilation of indigenous law, tenure, autonomy, and identity was retained.

On the other hand, outlining sustained Native American attempts to negotiate indigenous sovereignty within and without the structures of the United States "liberal democratic settler state", Kevin Bruyneel has recently argued for a "third space" of indigenous sovereignty. He described it as an ambiguous and ambivalent sovereign space, a form of indigenous sovereignty that is compatible with a settler sovereignty and yet functioning beside its operational registers. His account of the evolution of Native American political discourse emphasises how the mobilising rhetoric of anti-colonialism was unsuitable for the specific conditions of settler-colonised peoples. Neither "a rights-equality framework" nor "a nationalist-decolonization framework" could work. On the contrary, indigenous militancy formulated "self-determination and tribal sovereignty" as an expression "postcolonial nationhood":

> The claim for postcolonial nationhood adhered fully to neither a civil rights framework for defining equality nor a third world decolonization framework for defining anti-colonial sovereignty. Instead it located itself across the boundaries and through the gaps of colonial [i.e., *settler* colonial] imposition, in the third space, where indigenous political life fights to claim its modern status on its own terms.[59]

A black-white binary could not sustain indigenous attempts to negotiate a third space of sovereignty and the prospect of equality was also inadequate. This strategic distinction, however, is not accidental; it results from the very fact that being colonised is structurally different from being *settler*-colonised. Settler decolonisation requires an imagination that is alternative from traditional accounts of decolonising passages.

In the context of a settler colonial mentality, the very presence of indigenous peoples is normally unsettling, but an acknowledgement of indigenous sovereignty, even a "sovereignty without the mechanisms of statehood", is even more so, and this difficulty is compounded by a narrative deficit.[60] As long as there are no available narratives of settler decolonisation, a general narrative identifying indigenous dispossession and loss of collective autonomy as "progress" is bound to remain paradigmatic, and settler colonisation, a colonising act where settlers envisage no return, still tells a story of either total victory or total failure.

Discontinuing settler colonial forms requires conceptual frames and supporting narratives of reconciliation that have yet to be fully developed and narrated.[61] There are by now substantial histories of the various settler societies, and, for example, in the case of Australia, a recent apology for past injustice (an apology regarding the Indian Residential School System was also offered in the Canadian House of Commons in June 2008). There is, however, no compelling or intuitively acceptable story about what should happen *next*. If decolonisation implies by definition a degree of restoration/devolution of political sovereignty, taking responsibility for a painful history is bound to be better than a denial of responsibility, but it certainly does not amount to the *relinquishment* of responsibility for a post-settler future. (Besides, as it was construed as the moment in which a settler society finally acts to overcome one last remaining colonial residue, Rudd's apology reproduced a typically settler narrative structure – after all, fantasies of a way forward out of the settler colonial situation, supersession, are an inherent trait of settler colonial narrative structures.)[62]

Fanon emphasised the compartmentalising immobility of the colonial world:

> A world divided into compartments, a motionless, Manichaeistic world [...] this is the colonial world. The native is being hemmed in; apartheid is simply one form of the division into compartments, of the colonial world. The first thing the native learns is to stay in his place, and not to go beyond certain limits.[63]

According to Fanon, this immobility can only end when the colonised decides to put an end to the history of colonisation – the history of pillage – and to bring into existence the history of the nation – the history of decolonisation. On the contrary, settler colonialism *transfers*. If decolonisation must be a reclamation of mobility (the reverse of constrained and subjected immobility), settler decolonisation must be an ultimate rejection of any transfer (the opposite of a coerced and subjected mobility),

If the settler sovereignty (or, in the words of Carole Pateman, the original "settler contract") and the population economy that this sovereignty underpins remain undisturbed, when and if indigenous communities are acknowledged, acquire a degree of substantive self-determination, are able to access native title, receive an apology and possibly some compensation (all necessary elements of any genuinely post-settler compact), the public generally perceives a sovereignty that is inherently subversive of settler/national foundations.[64] The "S" word can be a scary one. Former Australian Prime Minister John Howard effectively epitomised this concept when he dismissively emphasised that "a nation cannot make a treaty with itself".[65] What he meant is that a *settler* nation cannot make a treaty with its non-settler components. Then again, this is exactly the point: a post-settler nation, even if the precise meaning of such a compact is yet to be determined, could.

Notes

Introduction: The Settler Colonial Situation

1. Karl Marx and Friederich Engels, *The Communist Manifesto*, p. 39.
2. Quoted in Moses I. Finley, "Colonies", p. 186.
3. Charles Darwin, *Voyage of the Beagle*, pp. 110–111.
4. The reverse is also true: the interpretative categories that are developed to make sense of settler colonial settings are not always applicable to colonial and postcolonial environments. This argument is put forward, for example, by Paulomi Chakraborty in "Framing 'Always Indigenize' beyond the Settler-Colony".
5. Mahmood Mamdani, "When Does a Settler Become a Native?".
6. James Belich, "The Rise of the Angloworld", p. 53.
7. The scholarly literature dedicated to ethnic difference and associated conflicts has rarely drawn the analytic distinction between settlers and other migrants and often uses these terms interchangeably. For an example of this failure, see Stanley L. Engerman and Jacob Metzer (eds), *Land Rights, Ethno-Nationality and Sovereignty in History*. Framing theoretically their collection of essays, these authors conclude that people move in the expectation of material gain, which seems incontestable but is somewhat inoperative: mass displacements have rarely been spurred by the individual and collective expectation of material loss.
8. Georges Balandier, "The Colonial Situation", p. 54.
9. An international conference marking the 50th anniversary of this article's initial publication and a special issue of an academic journal confirm this longevity. See Frederick Cooper, "Decolonizing Situations: The Rise, Fall, and Rise of Colonial Studies". Fifty years later, settler colonialism remained out of sight.
10. Jürgen Osterhammel, *Colonialism*, pp. 16–17.
11. A. G. Hopkins, "Back to the Future", p. 215.
12. D. K. Fieldhouse, *The Colonial Empires*, pp. 11–12.
13. A constitutive distinction between these two groups is a long-lasting feature of reflections on colonialism. Puritan administrator of Massachusetts William Bradford, for example, already lamented in the 1630s that there were "many in this land, who without either patent or license, order or government, live, trade, and truck, not with any intent to plant, but rather to forage the country, and get what they can, whether by right or wrong, and then be gone". Quoted in Adam J. Hirsch, "The Collision of Military Cultures in Seventeenth-Century New England", p. 1195.
14. Thomas Paine noted that "the parent country of America" was "Europe, and not England": that colonisation was an all European feat made sense – indeed, it made *Common Sense*. Thomas Paine, *Common Sense*, p. 84.

15. Separating "internal" and "external" colonialisms, however, erases the distinction between metropoles and settler societies. By treating the "Old" and "New" Worlds as essentially alike, this move thus effaces settler colonialism as it ostensibly recognises its difference from colonialism.

16. See Ronald J. Horvath, "A Definition of Colonialism"; Moses I. Finley, "Colonies"; George M. Fredrickson, "Colonialism and Racism", pp. 216–235, especially p. 221; and Jürgen Osterhammel, *Colonialism*, especially p. 7.

17. For an organised reading of the literature on settler colonialism, see, for example, Udo Krautwurst, "What is Settler Colonialism?", especially pp. 59–60. Krautwurst downplays the distinction between colonial and settler colonial phenomena on the basis of the intuition that every colonist is "a *potential* permanent resident or settler" and that settler societies "are simultaneously colonial societies and vice versa" (pp. 58, 63). Sure, colonial and settler colonial forms inevitably interpenetrate each other, but why should this imply that they cannot be considered as distinct?

18. For examples of this interpretative tradition, see Catherine Hall, *Civilising Subjects*; and Ann Laura Stoler and Frederick Cooper, "Between Metropole and Colony" (Stoler and Cooper explicitly argue, p. 4, that metropole and colony should be appraised within a "single analytical field"). Amy Kaplan and Donald E. Pease's *Cultures of United States Imperialism* also analysed internal and external US colonialisms within the same frame and saw them as co-determining each other and dialectically related.

19. Louis Hartz, "A Theory of the Development of the New Societies". Hartz's conclusions were comprehensively criticised; and yet, his critics generally shared with Hartz the perception of a simplified Europe (they crucially disagreed, however, on the causes of this phenomenon). Of course, if it is about the reproduction of fragmented or otherwise derivative European forms, settler colonialism as a distinctive "situation" disappears. For criticism of Hartz's thesis, see, for example, Cole Harris, "The Simplification of Europe Overseas".

20. Arghiri Emmanuel, "White–Settler Colonialism and the Myth of Investment Imperialism", p. 40.

21. Donald Denoon, "Understanding Settler Societies", p. 511. See also Donald Denoon, *Settler Capitalism*.

22. See David Prochaska, *Making Algeria French*, pp. 9, 7.

23. Alan Lawson, "A Cultural Paradigm for the Second World". See also, for example, Stephen Slemon, "Unsettling the Empire"; Alan Lawson, "Postcolonial Theory and the 'Settler' Subject"; Penelope Ingram, "Can the Settler Speak?"; Penelope Ingram, "Racializing Babylon".

24. Daiva Stasiulis and Nira Yuval–Davis (eds), *Unsettling Settler Societies*, p. 1. On the contrary, some postcolonial scholars downplay the distance between colonial and settler colonial forms. Defining the notion

of "postcolonial literature", Bill Ashcroft, Gareth Griffiths and Helen Tiffin have noted that "the literatures of African countries, Australia, Bangladesh, Canada, Caribbean countries, India, Malaysia, Malta, New Zealand, Pakistan, Singapore, South Pacific Island countries, and Sri Lanka are all post-colonial literatures" and that the "literature or the USA should also be placed in this category. Perhaps because of its current position of power, and the neo-colonizing role it has played, its post-colonial nature has not been generally recognized. But its relationship with the metropolitan centre as it evolved over the last two centuries has been paradigmatic for Post-colonial literatures everywhere. What each of these literatures has in common beyond their special and distinctive regional characteristics is that they emerged in their present form out of the experience of colonization and asserted themselves by foregrounding the tension with the imperial power, and by emphasizing their differences from the assumptions of the imperial centre. It is this which makes them distinctively post-colonial". Bill Ashcroft, Gareth Griffiths, Helen Tiffin, *The Empire Writes Back*, p. 2.

25. Jürgen Osterhammel, *Colonialism*, p. 108. In *Colonialism and Neocolonialism* Jean Paul Sartre, for example, had formulated this notion when writing on the Algerian conflict: "in his rage, [the settler] sometimes dreams of genocide. But it is pure fantasy. He knows it, he is aware of his dependence". Jean Paul Sartre, *Colonialism and Neocolonialism*, p. 75.

26. Patrick Wolfe, *Settler Colonialism and the Transformation of Anthropology*, p. 163.

27. Anna Johnston and Alan Lawson, "Settler Colonies", p. 369.

28. See, for examples, A. R. Buck, John McLaren, and Nancy E. Wright (eds), *Land and Freedom*; P. G. McHugh, *Aboriginal Societies and the Common Law*; Peter Karsten, *Between Law and Custom*; John C. Weaver, *The Great Land Rush and the Making of the Modern World*; A. R. Buck, John McLaren, and Nancy E. Wright (eds), *Despotic Dominion*; Hamar Foster, Benjamin L. Berger, and A. R. Buck (eds), *The Grand Experiment*; Stuart Banner, *Possessing the Pacific* and *How the Indians Lost their Land*; and Lisa Ford, *Settler Sovereignty*. On the comparative environmental history of settler contexts see, for example, Thomas R. Dunlap, *Nature and the English Diaspora* and Tom Griffiths and Libby Robin (eds), *Ecology and Empire*.

29. See, for examples, Lynette Russell (ed.), *Colonial Frontiers*; Julie Evans, Patricia Grimshaw, David Philips, and Shurlee Swain, *Equal Subjects, Unequal Rights*; David Trigger and Gareth Griffiths (eds), *Disputed Territories*; Annie Coombes (ed.), *Rethinking Settler Colonialism*; Larissa Behrendt, Tracey Lindberg, Robert J. Miller, and Jacinta Ruru (eds), *Discovering Indigenous Lands*; and Penelope Edmonds, *Urbanizing Frontiers*.

30. Fifth Galway Conference on Colonialism: Settler Colonialism, National University of Ireland, Galway, June 2007, Conditions of Settler Colonialism Symposium, Chicago University, April 2008, and Alyosha Goldstein and Alex Lubin (eds), "Settler Colonialism". The *Journal of Colonialism and Colonial Studies* had published a special issue dedicated

to "White Settler Colonialisms and the Colonial Turn" in 2003. However, compared to the edited issue published by *South Atlantic Quarterly*,
this was a very different exercise. The 2003 collection is about ways
in which a gender aware analysis can help understanding transnational
settler colonialisms in the aftermath of the "colonial turn", the 2009 collection is about the ways in which a settler colonial paradigm *in its own
right* can help understanding transnational phenomena. See Fiona Paisley,
"Introduction".

31. See, for example, David Thelen, "The Nation and Beyond" and Ann
    Curthoys and Marilyn Lake (eds), *Connected Worlds*.
32. See, for example, Alan Lester, "Colonial Settlers and the Metropole".
33. Marilyn Lake, "White Man's Country", p. 352.
34. Marilyn Lake and Henry Reynolds, *Drawing the Global Colour Line*.
35. Caroline Elkins and Susan Pedersen, "Settler Colonialism", especially
    pp. 8–15.
36. Caroline Elkins and Susan Pedersen, "Settler Colonialism", pp. 6–7. A con-
    vincing call to look for settler colonialism in colonies rarely associated
    with settler colonial endeavours is also presented in Penny Edwards,
    "On Home Ground".
37. Robert J. C. Young, *The Idea of English Ethnicity*.
38. See James Belich, *Replenishing the Earth*, especially pp. 145–176.
39. For classical examples of this type of comparative constitutional history,
    see Alexander Brady, *Democracy in the Dominions*, and John Manning
    Ward, *Colonial self-Government*.
40. On the development of settler colonial nationalisms within the British
    Empire, see, for example, John Eddy and Deryck Schreuder (eds), *The Rise
    of Colonial Nationalism*.
41. On the comparative economics of the *"areas nuevas"*, see D. C. M. Platt
    and Guido di Tella (eds), *Argentina, Australia, and Canada*; J. W. McCarthy,
    "Australia as a Region of Recent Settlement in the Nineteenth Cen-
    tury"; Carl E. Solberg, *The Prairies and the Pampas*; Jeremy Adelman,
    Frontier Development. For a comparative analysis of class development and
    labour relations, see Gary Cross, "Labour in Settler State Democracies",
    and Bryan D. Palmer, "Nineteenth-Century Canada and Australia".
    An overview of the comparative historical geography of settler societies
    is presented in Graeme Wynn, "Settler Societies in Geographical Focus".
    On environmental history and settler colonialism, see Alfred W. Crosby,
    Ecological Imperialism, and Jared Diamond, *Guns, Germs, and Steel*.
42. On the reproductive regimes of settler colonialism, see Richard Phillips,
    "Settler Colonialism and the Nuclear Family"; on settler colonialism's
    "logic of elimination", see Patrick Wolfe, "Settler Colonialism and the
    Elimination of the Native".
43. For an example of settler colonialism's ongoing invisibility, see Peter Pels,
    "The Anthropology of Colonialism", pp. 172–174. This sophisticated arti-
    cle contains a section on settlers, but does not talk about them! One
    paragraph is dedicated to the *"marxisant"* historiography of the planta-
    tion economies, one to 1980s feminist contributions on the experience

of white women in colonial settings, one to the contradictions between settler demands for cheap labour and the "administrative interest in a colony's strategic stability" (and the opposition between the "ethnocidal policies of settler colonies" and the need for "salvage ethnography"), and one more on the need to further develop the study of colonial culture at large.

44. On the connection between settlement and ethnic cleansing (and its disavowal), see Grant Farred, "The Unsettler". Appreciating an unavoid-able link between the two, however, is certainly not new and was not lost, for example, on Francis Bacon: "I like a plantation in a pure soil; that is, where people are not displaced to the end to plant in others. For else it is rather an extirpation than a plantation". Quoted, for example, in Sarah Irving, "In a Pure Soil", p. 258.

45. On this point, see, for example, Amy Kaplan, "Left Alone With America", which outlines "the ways in which imperialism has been simultaneously *formative* and *disavowed* in the foundational discourse of American stud-ies" (p. 5, my emphasis). See also Lorenzo Veracini, *Israel and Settler Society*.

46. Giovanni Arrighi recently referred to Gareth Stedman Jones' contention that the United States did not initiate settler colonial traditions over-seas because *it was* a settler colonial order. "American historians who speak complacently of the absence of the settler-type colonialism char-acteristic of the European powers merely conceal the fact that the whole *internal* history of United States imperialism was one vast process of ter-ritorial seizure and occupation. The absence of territorialism 'abroad' was founded on an unprecedented territorialism 'at home'". Quoted in Giovanni Arrighi, "Hegemony Unravelling – II", p. 103, n. 40 (emphasis in original).

47. Ava Baron, "On Looking at Men", p. 150.

48. Ruth Frankenberg has similarly argued for sustained critical engagement with "whiteness". Failing to do so entails "a continued failure to displace the 'unmarked marker' status of whiteness, a continued inability to 'color' the seeming transparency of white positionings", she notes. To "leave whiteness unexamined is to perpetuate a kind of asymmetry that has marred even many critical analyses of racial formation and cultural prac-tice. Here the modes of alterity of everyone-but-the-white-people are subjected to ever more meticulous scrutiny, celebratory or not, while whiteness remains unexamined – unqualified, essential, homogeneous, seemingly self-fashioned, and apparently unmarked by history or prac-tice". There are risks, I argue, also in not focusing on settler colonialism as a specific formation. We should focus on "settlerness" in order to unsettle the "unmarked marker" status of being a settler in a settler society (and to produce a critique of the "seeming transparency" of settler positionings). Frankenberg calls for the " 'revealing' of the unnamed – the exposure of whiteness masquerading as universal". We should operate similarly with regards to settlers: settler colonialism is not normal or natural. It is made

so in a settler colonial context. Ruth Frankenberg, "Local Whitenesses, Localizing Whiteness", pp. 1, 3.

49. See Frederick E. Hoxie, "Retrieving the Red Continent".

50. For examples of transnational scholarship involving the history of the United States, see Max Savelle, *Empires to Nations*; Alan Taylor, *American Colonies*; Jorge Cañizares-Esguerra, *How to Write the History of the New World*; and Anthony DePalma, *Here*. For a history of the notion of "Atlantic history", including an appraisal of its links with post-Second World War transatlantic relations, see Bernard Bailyn, *Atlantic History*.

1 Population

1. On "protection" as a global colonial form, see, for example, Alan Lester and Fae Dussart, "Trajectories of Protection". Lester and Dussart trace the global trajectory of "protection" from the British Caribbean colony of Trinidad to the Cape and Australasian colonies. "Protection", however, was an ancient colonial form that the British had adopted from Spanish practice (Trinidad had been a Spanish colony).

2. For a survey of various technologies of indigenous governance and a sustained call for sharing administrative expertise between settler polities, see A. Grenfell Price, *White Settlers and Native Peoples*.

3. Indeed, the political traditions of settler colonialism routinely auto-define themselves by way of a series of successive negations: settler colonialism is not the "Old World", and not a "colonial" world; not what is displaced by the establishment of a colonial order (i.e., a "despotic" Asiatic tyranny), and not what is displaced by the establishment of a settler colonial order (i.e., an indigenous "republic"). Finally, settlers also define their endeavours in specific contradistinction against alternative settler orders. No wonder that stubborn recurring notions of inherent exceptionalism retain extraordinary strength in settler contexts! On exceptionalist intellectual traditions in two settler societies, see, for example, Gary Cross, "Comparative Exceptionalism".

4. Quoted in John Lynch, *The Spanish American Revolutions*, pp. 24–25.

5. A triangular interpretative framework reproduces sociologist David Pearson's rendition of community relations in "British" settler societies. Pearson suggests that "settler and post-settler society citizenship is best conceptualized and described by examining the linked processes of [. . .] the aboriginalization (of aboriginal minorities), the ethnification (of immigrant minorities) and the indigenization (of settler majorities)". David Pearson, "Theorizing Citizenship in British Settler Societies", p. 990. See also David Pearson, *The Politics of Ethnicity in Settler Societies*. Pearson's approach was recently criticised by Hawaiian scholar Candace Fujikane, who, on the contrary, noting that *all* non-natives partake of the advantages of a particular colonial regime, emphasised the indigenous/non-indigenous divide. See Candace Fujikane, "Introduction".

6. Jürgen Osterhammel, *Colonialism*, p. 108, and Partha Chatterjee, *The Nation and its Fragments*, pp. 10, 14. See also Bill Ashcroft, Gareth Griffith, and Helen Tiffin, "Binarism".

7. An emphasis on triangular relations as they pertain to the settler colonial situation also differs from Patrick Wolfe's reconstruction of the relationship between "settler" and "indigenous", where the desire to erase and/or assimilate indigenous peoples coexists with the symbolic necessity of an ongoing indigenous presence. In Wolfe's analysis, an indigenous counterpoint to settler identity sustains a binary logic contrasting "virtuous" settler and "dysfunctional" indigenous person. As it underpins settler identity, he argues, the indigenous antithesis inevitably remains a crucial part of settler discourse. See Patrick Wolfe, "Settler Colonialism and the Elimination of the Native", especially p. 389. Settler identity, however, is also recurrently sustained by other dialectical counterpoints besides an indigenous one: actual, *bona fide*, settler versus absentee speculator, "old hand" versus "new chum", "better" Britonism versus decadent, constraining "Old World" ways, "free" labour versus labour that is variously perceived as subject or unassimilable, honourable, virtuous, settler manhood versus settlers who have "gone native", and so on.

8. For a comprehensive critique of the Zionist rhetoric of a "return" to Palestine, see Shlomo Sand, *The Invention of the Jewish People*, especially pp. 129–189. For constructions of the settler occupation of Algeria as a "return", see Patricia Lorcin, "Rome and France in Africa". However, reference to settler "indigeneity" is a crucial feature of all settler colonial representational regimes, and settlers see themselves as returning as well as moving forward: returning to the land, returning to a social and gendered order that they deem appropriate, and moving forward to a locale that is interpreted as the pre-ordained home of the settler collective. Unlike other migrants, settlers "remove" to regain a status that they perceive, from where they are, as irretrievably disrupted.

9. For similar diagrams assisting "the discussion by graphically representing the progression of the idea", see, for example, Charles W. Mills, "Intersecting Contracts", pp. 170–174. For other examples, see Jack P. Greene, *Pursuits of Happiness*, pp. 167, 173, and Caroline Elkins and Susan Pedersen, "Settler Colonialism", p. 5.

10. See George Lakoff and Mark Johnson, *Metaphors We Live By*, especially pp. 14–22.

11. See Gershom Gorenberg, *The Accidental Empire*, p. 65.

12. Johannes Fabian, *Time and the Other*, p. 31.

13. As the exogenous Others category is defined primarily by its not belonging to the settler and indigenous collective, this category encompasses a number of remarkably different groups: enslaved peoples, other imported labour, and subaltern migrants on the one hand, and metropolitan colonisers on the other.

14. A similar point is also made in Anthony Moran, "As Australia Decolonizes", especially pp. 1028–1029.

15. See, for example, Michèle Dominy, "Hearing Grass, Thinking Grass"; Catherine Nash, "Setting Roots in Motion". Other constitutive ambivalences of the settler colonial condition include, for example, being at once European and non-European, deliberately establishing new lifestyles and ostensibly reproducing old ones, being colonised and colonising at the same time, and so on. In the same way, D. H. Lawrence had noted in 1924 the inherent and unresolved paradox of an American indigenising/Europeanising expectation to at once enjoy "civilised" order and "savage" freedom. Quoted in Philip J. Deloria, *Playing Indian*, p. 3.

16. On settler "indigenisation", see, for example, Terry Goldie, *Fear and Temptation*, p. 13, David Pearson, "Theorizing Citizenship in British Settler Societies", and Pal Ahluwalia, "When Does a Settler Become a Native?".

17. Or at least, "we successfully adapted to this land". On the long-lasting project of making of a "new man" in a new (Australian) climate, see, for example, Warwick Anderson, *The Cultivation of Whiteness*. On nationalising indigenisations, see Eric Kaufmann, "'Naturalizing the Nation'".

18. On the dialectical interplay between "experience and inheritance", and on a "self-conscious effort to anglicize colonial life through the deliberate imitation of metropolitan institutions, values, and culture", see Jack P. Greene, *Pursuits of Happiness*, pp. 174–176. Quotations at pp. 175, 176.

19. See, for example, Eliga H. Gould, "A Virtual Nation". For an insightful analysis of this unresolved contradiction in Turner's text, see Henry Nash Smith, *Virgin Land*, pp. 250–260.

20. Reflecting on the national and cultural patterns of the "collectivities" of the New World, Gérard Bouchard has emphasised the importance of "rupture" and "continuity" as possibilities *vis à vis* the European metropole. This tension, he argues, informs the development of the founding collectivities. Quite importantly, these possibilities do not mutually rule each other out. On the contrary, he remarks, they are "likely to mix and to accommodate a large range of intermediary positions and configurations". Gérard Bouchard, *The Making of the Nations and Cultures of the New World*, pp. 13–14. Yet again, the recognition that continuity and rupture routinely coexist could be pursued further. A bidimensional appraisal of this tension (see Figure 1.2) suggests that they actually are a function of each other.

21. See Partha Chatterjee, *The Nation and its Fragments*. On deferral as a crucial colonial strategy, see also Alice Conklin, *A Mission to Civilize*.

22. See Louis Hartz, "A Theory of the Development of the New Societies", and, for example, Cole Harris, "The Simplification of Europe Overseas".

23. On Jacques Deridda's notion of "democracy to come", see, for example, Paul Patton, "Derrida, Politics and Democracy to Come".

24. This need creates a circumstance where the settler self is never ultimately free from its indigenous and exogenous counterpoints. Making a similar point, Philip J. Deloria concludes that American identity construction was never able to "effectively" develop "a positive, stand-alone identity

that did not rely heavily on either a British or an Indian foil". See Philip J. Deloria, *Playing Indian*, p. 36.

25. Benedict Anderson, *The Spectre of Comparisons*.

26. John C. Weaver's description of Canada's frontier encapsulates this tension: "[u]ntroubled by numerous and well stocked advance parties of pastoralists occupying extensive territory, Canada uniquely could organize settlement by procedures on the prairies that accentuated order." John C. Weaver, *The Great Land Rush and the Making of the Modern World*, p. 61.

27. A. A. Phillips's 1950 insight regarding the "Australian cringe" is worth quoting: "in the back of the Australian mind, there sits a minatory Englishman. He is not even the most suitable type of Englishman – not the rare pukka sahib with his deep still pool of imaginativeness, and his fine urbanity; not the common man with his blending of solidity and tenderness: but that Public School Englishman with his detection of a bad smell permanently engraved on his features […]". On the "Australian Cringe", see A. A. Phillips, *On The Cultural Cringe*. Quotation at p. 8.

28. An argument highlighting the ongoing tension between Europeanising elites and "Americanising" popular classes in the cultural history of French Canada is presented in Gérard Bouchard, *The Making of the Nations and Cultures of the New World*, pp. 58–147.

29. It is significant that in Canadian traditions the "French" element occupies both borderlands. French peculiarity thus confirms negatively Anglo settler normativity. On this point, see, for example, John Ralston Saul, *Reflections of a Siamese Twin*, Toronto, Viking, 1997, pp. 145–153.

30. See Russel Ward, *The Australian Legend*, and Douglas Pike, "The Smallholders' Place in the Australian Tradition". On Gauchos, see Jeane Delaney, "Making Sense of Modernity". Delaney explores the anti-immigrant climate in turn of the century Argentina; a shift that continued with inverted value signs the previous symbolic order. The new Argentinean nationalists glorified the gaucho as the national prototype and denigrated immigrants as comprehensively as nineteenth century liberals had previously endorsed immigration and its purported progressive civilisational input, and castigated the native rural population. In the Argentinean case, "barbarism" and "civilisation" (and indigenisation and Europeanisation) interconstitute each other even if they are valued differently in different periods/milieus.

31. There can be, however, exceptions to this pattern. Rejecting the "upward" indigenising dynamic that is expected of exogenous Others, non-Zionist orthodox Jews, for example, have migrated to Israel but have resisted the prospect of transforming into Zionist "new men". They could thus be seen as occupying a permanently separated sector in the exogenous Others section of a settler colonial population system.

32. Henry Nash Smith, *Virgin Land*, pp. 51–58. Quotation at p. 58.

33. Deloria's classification of possible representations of Indians corroborates an approach premised on two critical axes. "Indians could, for

example, signify civilized colonial philosophe (interior/noble), fearsome colonial soldier (interior/savage), noble, natural man (exterior/noble), or barbarous savage (exterior/savage)", he concludes. Philip J. Deloria, *Playing Indian*, p. 203, n. 29. See also pp. 20–21, 174.

34. See John L. Comaroff, "Images of Empire", and David Lambert and Alan Lester, "Geographies of Colonial Philanthropy".

35. Two idiomatic expressions from Canada and Australia respectively confirm "the settler population is a container" metaphor. "Leakage" describes a malfunctioning population economy, where settler "content" is dispersed into the wider population economy; "breeding out", on the contrary, describes the proper functioning of a settler population economy, where unwanted material is efficiently cast outside of the settler body politic.

36. On the "Caucasian Aborigines", see Warwick Anderson, *The Cultivation of Whiteness*, 2006, pp. 6, 193–194, 200–202, 204, 206.

37. See, for example, James Belich, "Myth, Race and Identity in New Zealand", and Tony Ballantyne, *Orientalism and Race*, especially pp. 56–82.

38. On "probationary" whiteness, see Matthew Frye Jacobson, *Whiteness of a Different Color*. In this context, it is significant that Japanese businessmen dealing with Apartheid South Africa should be officially considered "honorary" whites. Their position would then symmetrically replicate the "honorary" settler status of indigenous Maori in Aotearoa/New Zealand. See James Bennett, "Maori as Honorary Members of the White Tribe".

39. On the "colonisation" of freed African Americans, see, for example, P. J. Staudenraus, *The African Colonization Movement*. As Marilyn Lake has perceptively noted, the Commonwealth of Australia was actually inaugurated in coordinated acts of racial expulsion (the Immigration Restriction Act, excluding "non-whites" through a dictation test, and the Pacific Islands Labourers Act, enforcing the deportation of Kanak workers from Queensland). See Marilyn Lake, "The White Man under Siege".

40. For a transnational study of exclusion in settler colonial polities, see Marilyn Lake and Henry Reynolds, *Drawing the Global Colour Line*. It is significant that anti-Chinese hysteria in the United States was a specifically Western – that is, relatively *more* settler colonial – political phenomenon. See, for example, Andrew Gyory, *Closing the Gate*.

41. That is why indigenous activism has consistently and strategically attempted to bypass settler external mediation. On a long indigenous tradition of external appeal, see, for example, Ravi de Costa, *A Higher Authority*.

42. See Donald Denoon, "The Isolation of Australian History".

43. See Ronald Robinson, "Non-European Foundations of European Imperialism".

44. On the ways in which Britons settling the Dominions negotiated their relationship with the Empire and with "home", see, for example, Stuart Ward, "Imperial Identities Abroad".

45. In "Terms of Assimilation", Priscilla Wald appraises comparatively the *Cherokee Nation v. Georgia* (1831) and the *Dred Scott* (1857) Supreme Court cases. In quite different ways, both decisions were "attempts to legislate the disappearance of the 'Indians' and the 'descendents of Africans', respectively, by judging them neither citizens nor alien and therefore not legally representable" (this double negation confirms that indigenous and exogenous Others could not be ascribed to the upper segment of the population economy *or* to its outside). "Debates surrounding the extension of federal law into unincorporated territories generate both cases", she noted. "*Cherokee Nation* concerns Georgia's right to violate federal treaties and extend its legislation into Cherokee territory contained within the state's borders but exempt from state law. *Dred Scott* considers the status of slaves taken to dwell for an extended period in free territory". Thus, the first one deals with the assertion of a sovereign settler claim against *both* federal interference and indigenous resilience (the 1827 *Constitution of the Cherokee Nation* had constituted a body politics endowed with a sovereign charge modelled on and opposed to the settlers' – the nationalist Cherokee were *imitating* not *assimilating* settler institutions), while the latter deals with the assertion of a sovereign settler claim against federal interference *and* exogenous insurgency (*Dred Scott* confirmed "state rather than the federal government jurisdiction over domestic institutions, including slavery"). Priscilla Wald, "Terms of Assimilation". Quotations at pp. 59, 60, 75; on imitation rather than assimilation, see p. 68.
46. Homi Bhabha, of course, convincingly argued that cultural hybridity undermines colonial authority as well. And yet, as maintained by Lauren Benton and John Muth, for example, hybridity reinforces colonial dualism. This ambivalence is rarely available in settler colonial settings, where the reproduction of hybrid forms is incompatible with the need to imagine the eventual disappearance of all indigenous and exogenous alterities. See Homi Bhabha, "Of Mimicry and Man", and Lauren Benton and John Muth, "On Cultural Hybridity".
47. María Josefina Saldaña-Portillo, " 'How many Mexicans [is] a horse worth?' ", p. 812. On the other hand, Richard Gott has recently called for framing Latin American experiences in the context of settler colonial studies. See Richard Gott, "Latin America as a White Settler Society".
48. On miscegenation in settler colonial settings, see Victoria Freeman, "Attitudes Toward 'Miscegenation' in Canada, the United States, New Zealand, and Australia". Freeman notes (p. 53) that miscegenation, as well as a subversion of empire, can also be "an instrument of empire", and refers to French officials in New France promoting intermarriage "as a means to create a new people ideally suited for the new colony", and to Jeffersonian fantasies of miscegenation. Being "an instrument of empire", however, does not necessarily mean being an instrument of *settler* empire. In the end, mercantile New France was not primarily interested in settlement, and Jeffersonian America was not particularly interested in miscegenation.

49. On hybridity in the French empire, see Emmanuelle Saada, *Les enfants de la colonie*. Saada argues that Algeria and New Caledonia – the settler colonies were exceptions in the context of the French colonial empire.

50. Another way of establishing this sovereign control, of course, is the criminalisation and nullification of censurable marriages spanning both sides of the settler–indigenous or settler–exogenous divide. See Nancy F. Cott, "Marriage and Women's Citizenship in the United States", especially p. 1441, n. 2.

51. A Californian farmer's 1913 letter to a local newspaper on the subject of Japanese immigration poignantly expresses the settler nightmare of losing control: "Near my home is an 80-acre tract of as fine land as there is in California. On that land lives a Japanese. With that Japanese lives a white woman. In that woman's arms is a baby. What is that baby? It isn't a Japanese. It isn't white. I'll tell you what that baby is. It is a germ of the mightiest problem ever faced in this State; a problem that will make the black problem of the South look white". Quoted in Marilyn Lake and Henry Reynolds, *Drawing the Global Colour Line*, p. 267. Note that here the problem is that what is being described *is* an appropriate settler colonial environment; all *seems* well: the land is productive, the size of the farm is suitable, and the familial relations are also acceptable. The anxiety emanates *precisely* from the fact that all is well *except* from one (reproductive) detail that undermines the whole settler colonial structure. In this case, black difference is more acceptable because it is seen as incapable of *infiltrating* and subverting the settler population economy from within (i.e., it is perceived as abject Otherness).

52. For comparative outlooks on the practice of stealing and institutionalising indigenous and mixed children in settler colonial settings, see Margaret D. Jacobs, *White Mother to a Dark Race*, and Katherine Ellinghaus, *Taking Assimilation to Heart*. On Métis, see, for example, Gerhard J. Ens, *Homeland to Hinterland*, and D. N. Sprague, *Canada and the Métis*. On Griquas, see Martin Legassick, "The Northern Frontier to c. 1840". The dispossession and dispersal of the Cherokee nation should also be mentioned in this context.

53. See Patrick Wolfe, "Land, Labor, and Difference".

54. See also Anthony W. Marx, *Making Race and Nation*, which compares the experience of miscegenation in South Africa, the United States, and Brazil. It is significant that issue of indigenous difference is entirely suppressed in this analysis of racial oppression.

55. On this issue, Australian federal member of parliament Charles Carty Salmon noted in the 1930s: "We have been accustomed to look upon the half-caste as being partly a European product, but a reference to the reports will show that it is with the Eastern aliens that the admixture is taking place. [...] The admixture of European with Aboriginal blood is bad enough, but the admixture of the blood of Chinese, Japanese, and Malays of low caste with the blood of the Aboriginal race is too awful to contemplate. If we are to have a piebald Australia, let it be by the admixture of European blood with the blood of another race, not

by the mixture of alien blood with the blood of the aboriginal race, which would be more degrading and lowering to our status as a nation". Quoted in Robert van Krieken, "Rethinking Cultural Genocide", p. 141.

56. See Jack D. Forbes, *Black Africans and Native Americans*. Forbes's project was based on a determination to recover a repressed history of Indian-Black exchange, including genetic exchange. This is, of course, a most loaded field of historical inquiry. On the "African Cherokees", see, for example, Celia E. Naylor, *African Cherokees in Indian Territory*; on black-red exchange, see James F. Brooks (ed.), *Confounding the Color Line*.

57. See Rogers M. Smith, "Beyond Tocqueville, Myrdal, and Hartz". Then again, Smith's proposition could be pursued further: in the context of a settler colonial population economy, inclusion and exclusion do not merely interact, combine inconsistently, and oppose each other; they actually work together, advocating alternative strategies regarding different constituencies but sharing the need to imagine different peoples transiting from one condition to another (and agreeing on the need to ultimately empty the indigenous and exogenous sections of the population economy).

58. Epitomising settler control over indigenous reproductive sovereignty (and settler control over the population economy), settlers of East Hampton, Long Island, forced local Montauketts Indians in 1719 to sign an agreement that excluded exogenous Indians from the local area and surrendered absolute control of their population economy to local settlers. Montauketts would not "take any strange Indians in[,] nor suffer any such to be Muntoket to use or improve any part of said land directly or indirectly by taking of a squaw or squaws, if such Indians not be proper Muntokit Indians they shall not be allowed to use or improve any part of said land, they shall not enter to dwell on said Meantokit directly nor indirectly". These Indians could reside but could only reproduce with settler-approved partners, and indigenous people that could be construed as exogenous could not enter the population economy. Quoted in Ben Kiernan, *Blood and Soil*, pp. 242–243. Israeli authorities legislating in 2003 that spouses of Israeli Arab citizens could not enter Israel proper were enforcing an equally sovereign control of the population economy. The *Citizenship and Entry into Israel Law* also excluded indigenous people that could be construed as exogenous.

59. James Belich, *Replenishing the Earth*.

60. See Nur Masalha, *Expulsion of the Palestinians* and Israel Shahak, "A History of the Concept of 'Transfer' in Zionism".

61. See John Mack Faragher, *A Great and Noble Scheme*. Faragher (p. 473) defines the transfer of the Acadians as "the first episode of state-sponsored ethnic cleansing in North American history". What he means is that this was the first episode of state-sponsored ethnic cleansing of *exogenous* peoples in North American history. See also Naomi E. S. Griffiths, *From Migrant to Acadian*.

62. Beside obvious conceptual linkages, it is the very technology acquired in enacting one transfer that can be redeployed. The Australian government, for example, introduced a number of legislative acts in 2001 and

2002 excising parts of Australia's sovereign territory from its migratory zone. While this amounted to a type of administrative transfer (see p. 44) that established an area that is "Australia" for some and "not Australia" for others, a similar capacity to institute borders selectively affecting specific constituencies was replicated with the enactment of the Northern Territory Intervention in 2007. The Labour government that succeeded the Howard conservative administration in 2007 abandoned a number of the policies of the previous executive, but, significantly, retained both the excision and the intervention.

63. Leading seventeenth-century New England settler Emanuel Downing, for example, recommending a war against the Narragansetts Indians, outlined a whole population economy of replacement: "If upon a Just warre the Lord should deliver them into our hands, wee might easily have men woemen and children enough to exchange for Moores, which wilbe more gaynefull pilladge for us then we conceive, for I doe not see how wee can thrive until wee get into a stock of slaves sufficient to doe all our business, for our children's children will hardly see this great Continent filled with people, soe that our servants will still desire freedome to plant for themselves, and not stay but for verie great wages. And I suppose you know verie well how wee shall mayneteyne 20 Moores cheaper than one Englishe servant". Quoted in Francis Jennings, *Conquest of America*, p. 275.

64. As noted by Robert Blecher, Israeli Palestinians have had to face a complex variety of transferist policies and have articulated a multitude of "transfers" in their lexicon: "sedentary" transfer (when borders instead of bodies are moved, and people are deprived of rights without being deported), "transfer of rights" (where rights are moved instead of bodies or borders), "voluntary" transfers (where it is the will to retain residency that is moved), and "cultural transfer" (where is cultural practices that get pushed beyond borders). In this sense, Blecher concludes, transfer does not refer to a "single event of cataclysm finality but rather a set of ongoing practices". See Robert Blecher, "Citizens without Sovereignty", especially p. 728.

65. In the context of a comparative outline of the settler colonial practice of stealing and institutionalising children, Margaret Jacobs detects a crucial and recurring shift in settler colonial practice: "another common feature of settler colonialism involves the appropriation of indigenous symbols as emblems of the new nation at precisely the moment when indigenous people are characterized as nearly extinct", she concludes. Margaret D. Jacobs, *White Mother to a Dark Race*, p. 7. There is no way of precisely pinpointing this shift; and yet, this remains a crucial divide. It distinguishes between a settler society that is engaged in a conflict against indigenous resistance on the one hand, and a settler society that is actively repressing indigenous residues on the other.

66. The links between settler colonial phenomena and genocide are by now an established feature of the literature on mass murder. See, for example, Michael Mann, *The Dark Side of Democracy*, especially pp. 70–110; Dirk

Moses (ed.), *Empire, Colony, Genocide*; and Ben Kiernan, *Blood and Soil*, especially pp. 165–392.
67. See, for examples, Theda Perdue and Michael Green, *The Cherokee Nation and the Trail of Tears*, and Ilan Pappe, *The Ethnic Cleansing of Palestine*.
68. On this issue, see, for example, Donald F. Fixico, *Termination and Relocation*.
69. On nomadism as "a theoretical removal of [indigenous] pastoralists from their land", see John K. Noyes, "Nomadic Fantasies".
70. Alexis de Tocqueville, *Writings on Empire and Slavery*, p. 172.
71. Charles Robert Ageron, *Modern Algeria*, p. 72. Ageron emphasises how the Kabyle myth was functional to a colonial strategy of divide and rule. However, the Kabyle "myth" should also be seen as part of a settler colonial strategy of *transfer* and rule. On the "Kabyle myth", see also Patricia Lorcin, *Imperial Identities*, and Paul A. Silverstein, "The Kabyle Myth".
72. Russell McGregor, *Imagined Destinies*, p. 156.
73. See Shlomo Sand, *The Invention of the Jewish People*, pp. 185–187.
74. See Philippa Mein Smith, "New Zealand Federation Commissioners in Australia".
75. For a comparative survey of assimilationist policies in settler colonial contexts, see Andrew Armitage, *Comparing the Policy of Aboriginal Assimilation*.
76. See John Chesterman and Brian Galligan, *Citizens without Rights*, p. 132.
77. On the relationship between assimilation and biological absorption, see Katherine Ellinghaus, "Biological Absorption and Genocide". In the case of biological absorption as transfer, it is not bodies that are thrown across a border, it is their genetic makeup that is progressively effaced.
78. Indigenous agency, on the other hand, can also reinforce or undermine difference. Anthropologist Gillian Cowlishaw's work on Australian small town ethnic relations identified an Aboriginal "oppositional culture": oppositional to what she defines as the "implacable cultural domination" and the "coercive value consensus" of small town whites. Accordingly, Cowlishaw shows Aboriginal resistance developing an "arena of dignity independent of the judgements of the wider society", a strategy that necessitates deliberate bouts of scandalising behaviour. On the other hand, this underscoring of a separating limit, as argued by Tim Rowse, does not preclude autonomous Aboriginal engagement with assimilation. See Gillian Cowlishaw, *Black, White or Brindle*, and Tim Rowse, "Aboriginal Respectability".
79. Failure to envisage assimilation as an option for indigenous transfer significantly weakens the settler position. Zionism as a settler project, for example, could not think of assimilating indigenous Palestinians and needed to focus on other transfers. More generally, deprived of one effective way of imagining an indigenousless future, settler projects that insist on ethnoracial definitions of settlerness need to resort to permanently segregative practices. As they contain rather than manage the

population economy, as they cease imagining a dynamic environment and dream of permanent separation, these strategies are likely to fail in the long term.

80. On "statistical extermination – the use of legal definitions of indigenous identity to reduce the numbers of indigenous people", see, for example, Katherine Ellinghaus, "Strategies of Elimination". Quotation at p. 205.

81. See, for example, J. Kehaulani Kauanui, *Hawaiian Blood*, which notes blood quantum classification's ongoing applicability, its inconsistency with inclusive Kanaka Maoli genealogical and kinship practices, and its role in limiting the number of Hawaiians who can claim land and sovereignty.

82. On the other hand, criticising a scholarship that links any production of statistical knowledge with indigenous subjugation, Tim Rowse has recently noted how indigenous militancy can appropriate statistical knowledge to further its agendas. See Tim Rowse, "Official Statistics and the Contemporary Politics of Indigeneity". In an essay entitled "The Limits of 'Elimination' in the Politics of Population", Tim Rowse and Len Smith point out that the Australian government did not apply a "logic of elimination" in its census policy between 1961 and 1971. On the contrary, they note, its census policy "effectively enlarged the 'Aboriginal population": indigenous lobbying, technical considerations, and "social scientists' and bureaucrats' demand for better knowledge of Indigenous Australians" converged in ensuring that this would happen (p. 90). And yet, one could argue that while *in this specific instance* the logic of statistical elimination and its associated transfers were not activated, other transfers were operating. Assimilation, for example, requires detailed information on its target population.

83. See Arjun Appadurai, "Numbers in the Colonial Imagination".

84. See Ward Churchill, *A Little Matter of Genocide*, especially pp. 131–137.

85. See Paula Gerber, "Making Indigenous Australians 'Disappear' ".

86. Jewel Topsfield, "The Unbearable Heaviness of Being No One".

87. Patrick Wolfe, *Settler Colonialism and the Transformation of Anthropology*, p. 204. For a critique of repressive authenticity, see also Scott Richard Lyons, *X-Marks*, which argues that indigenous people should be able to embrace "nontraditional" ways *and* remain free from the fear of being perceived (transferred) as inauthentic.

88. On Eyre, see, for example, Catherine Hall, "Imperial Man".

89. On the complex operation of the Federal Acknowledgment Process in the United States, a system that can effectively transfer entire communities away from indigenous status, see, for example, Mark Edwin Miller, *Forgotten Tribes*.

90. Wolfe's reconstruction of the invention, diffusion, and transformation of the "Dreaming complex" in Australia outlines one specific example of this transfer: it is the "dreaming complex" that allows indigenous people and settlers to inhabit different temporalities. See Patrick Wolfe, "On Being Woken Up". Similarly, Deloria concludes that by "the 1830s,

American imaginings of the Indian had coalesced on a common theme: the past". Philip J. Deloria, *Playing Indian*, p. 63.

91. "Tide of history" legal arguments can be found in the Australia of *Yorta Yorta* (2002) and in the United States, where in *City of Sherrill v. Oneida Indian Nation of New York* (2005), the Supreme Court concluded that two centuries of non-Indian occupation annulled any unresolved claims. On *Yorta Yorta*, see Bruce Buchan, "Withstanding the Tide of History". On *City of Sherrill v. Oneida Indian Nation of New York*, see Alyosha Goldstein, "Where the Nation Takes Place", especially p. 834. More generally, see P. G. McHugh, *Aboriginal Societies and the Common Law*, especially pp. 12–15.

92. On how a romantic vision of a "courageous yet fateful last stand" is used in settler colonial contexts to disallow indigenous grievances, see Elizabeth Furniss, "Challenging the Myth of Indigenous Peoples' 'Last Stand' in Canada and Australia".

93. In *First Nations? Second Thoughts*, Tom Flanagan argues that First Nations should merely be seen as first Migrants. Even if the French arrived earlier than the British, he notes, they are not accorded special rights.

94. See, for an example of this tendency, Francis Jennings, *The Founders of America*. The extended subtitle of Jennings's book refers to Indians "discovering" the land, "pioneering" in it, and creating "classical civilizations". See also, James Belich's parallel insistence on English and Maori historical development and corresponding ethnogeneses in the opening of *Making Peoples*, pp. 13–19. The establishment of ethnohistory as a disciplinary field was a crucial moment in the comprehensive demise of Eurocentric assumptions about "peoples without history". The possibility of narrative transfer, however, should not be ignored.

95. On the relationship between "indigenous" and "multicultural" in a settler colonial setting, see, for example, Ann Curthoys, "An Uneasy Conversation".

96. See Stephen Turner, " 'Inclusive Exclusion' ".

97. See P. G. McHugh, *Aboriginal Societies and the Common Law*, especially p. 51.

98. On reserves, see, for example, Cole Harris, *Making Native Space*. The institution of reserves may, however, involve a combination of different transfers (see transfers (B), (F), (S), and (Y)).

99. See Katherine Ellinghaus, "Strategies of Elimination".

100. See Philip J. Deloria, *Playing Indian*, p. 106. Defining the notion of "domestic dependent nations" (note: "domestic", as in the government of a household), Judge Marshall in *Cherokee Nation* had pointed out that Indian "relation to the United States resembles that of a ward to his guardian. They look to our government for protection; rely upon its kindness and its power, appeal to it for relief of their wants; and address the president as their great father". Quoted in Priscilla Wald, "Terms of Assimilation", p. 68.

101. See Jessica R. Cattelino, "The Double Bind of American Indian-Need-based Sovereignty".
102. Quoted in Alyosha Goldstein, "Where the Nation Takes Place", p. 850.
103. Illinois governor Jim Thompson, for example, justified in 1990 his decision not to close an open Indian burial mound in Dixon by claiming that he was as much an Indian as the Indian protesters were, and that he was entitled to decide whether to display Indian remains as much as really existing Indians were. See Andrea Smith, *Conquest*, p. 11, and Katherine Ellinghaus, "Biological Absorption and Genocide", p. 71.
104. On settler "cultural plagiarism", see Stephen Turner, "Cultural Plagiarism and the New Zealand Dream of Home".
105. See Geoffrey Blainey, "Land Rights for All".
106. Transfer by performance can apply to exogenous alterity as well. In "White Like Me", Eric Lott outlines the "historical fact of white men literally assuming a 'black' self", which "began and continues to occur when the lines of 'race' appear both intractable and obstructive, when there emerges a collective desire (conscious or not) to bridge a gulf that is, however, perceived to separate the races absolutely". "Blackface, then, reifies and at the same time trespasses on the boundaries of 'race'", he notes, concluding that "our typical focus on the way 'blackness' in the popular imagination has been produced out of white cultural expropriation and travesty misses how necessary this process is to the making of white American manhood". I would suggest, however, that as well as crucially underpinning white identity, as well as demonstrating "the necessary *centrality and suppression* of 'blackness' in the making of American whiteness", this process actually *transfers* black people away. Eric Lott, "White Like Me". Quotations at pp. 475, 476, 485.
107. Official (apartheid) celebrations in 1988 of the 500th anniversary of Portuguese explorers reaching the Cape included whites masquerading as blacks – whites in black masks. See Leslie Witz, "History Below the Water Line".
108. See, for example, C. Richard King, Charles Fruehling Springwood (eds), *Team Spirits*.
109. Philip J. Deloria, *Playing Indian* and Shari M. Huhndorf, *Going Native*. Deloria refers (p. 191) to the "self-defining pairing of American truth with American freedom" resting "on the ability to wield power against Indians – social military, economic, and political – while simultaneously drawing power from them"; Huhndorf locates "going native" at the end of the nineteenth century and interprets it as one response to industrialisation and to the accomplished conquest of Native America. I would suggest, however, that going native and indigenising performance are critical features of all settler colonial settings, and as such they should not be seen as restricted to a specific national tradition or to these two moments.
110. However, as Deloria demonstrates throughout his book, indigenous people can also autonomously take advantage of a settler need for Indian playing in order to further their own agendas.

111. "Going native", of course, can help thinking the transfer of exogenous Others as well. Huhndorf's unpacking of Forrest Carter's acclaimed "Indian" autobiography (*The Education of Little Tree*, which was in reality a forgery authored by former Ku Klux Klan leader Asa Carter) is a case in point. White supremacism and "going native" are not conflicting tendencies: an opposition against exogenous alterity is necessarily premised on a marked degree of settler indigenisation. See Shari M. Huhndorf, *Going Native*, pp. 129–161.
112. See Mark Williams, "The Finest Race of Savages the World has Seen".
113. Donald Denoon, "Remembering Australasia", p. 297, and Gérard Bouchard, *The Making of the Nations and Cultures of the New World*, p. 70.
114. Name confiscation operates also to confuse identities. Russian novelist Mikhail Lermontov's 1841 *Kavkazets* (Caucasians) reflected on the phenomenon of Russian army personnel "going native" and posing as indigenous Caucasians. They were collectively known as "Caucasians". If "real" Caucasians are Russian poseurs, there are no indigenous Caucasians left. See Robert Geraci, "Genocidal Impulses and Fantasies in Imperial Russia", especially, pp. 356–357.
115. See Charles W. Mills, *The Racial Contract* (where Mills argues that social contract and its political theories are actually underpinned by an original racial contract).
116. On attempts to exchange indigenous for exogenous Others, see Ruth Wallis and Ella Wilcox Sekatau, "The Right to a Name". Working with town records, these authors expose sustained attempts to redefine indigenous people: "town officials stopped identifying native people as 'Indian' in the written record and began designating them as 'Negro' or 'black', thus committing a form of documentary genocide against them", they conclude (p. 437). Similarly, Virginia also enacted legislation that allowed indigenous people to be defined as "colored". See Katherine Ellinghaus, "Biological Absorption and Genocide" (p. 70).
117. According to Australian Aboriginal scholar Aileen Moreton Robinson, despite a commitment to denounce racism and its legacies, even Critical Whiteness studies as a disciplinary field is actively implicated in the attempt to "write off" indigenous sovereignty. See Aileen Moreton Robinson, "Introduction".
118. Marcia Langton, Maureen Tehan, Lisa Palmer, and Kathryn Shain have noted the "fiercely regional and cultural specific nature of solutions to the issue of reconciliation of settler and Aboriginal sovereignty". A fiercely guarded specificity may result from the awareness that even the prospect of disappearing within the "global indigeneity" category can be construed as indigenous transfer. Marcia Langton, Maureen Tehan, Lisa Palmer, and Kathryn Shain, *Honour Among Nations?*, p. 12.
119. Quoted in Ben Kiernan, *Blood and Soil*, p. 234.
120. See Ruth Wallis and Ella Wilcox Sekatau, "The Right to a Name", p. 433. On the practice of deliberately writing indigenous people out of existence and expunging them from the historical record, see also Jean M. O'Brien, *Firsting and Lasting*.

121. See Alan Lester and Fae Dussart, "Trajectories of Protection". Asserting their control over the population economy, however, settler concerns eventually displaced humanitarian ones, and "protection" became a byword for segregation and institutionalisation (i.e., other types of transfer).
122. See Hadie Gooder and Jane M. Jacobs, "On The Border of the Unsayable".
123. Zygmunt Bauman, "Making and Unmaking of Strangers", pp. 1, 2.
124. Zygmunt Bauman, "Making and Unmaking of Strangers", p. 2. Making a similar point, Terry Goldie has suggested that settler colonialism can operate *both* via "penetration (the forcible imposition of the dominator and his discursive system within the dominated space) and appropriation (the consumption enforced by the dominator of what belongs to the dominated)". See Terry Goldie, *Fear and Temptation*, p. 15.
125. Zygmunt Bauman, "Making and Unmaking of Strangers", p. 12.
126. See Nicolás Wey Gómez, *The Tropics of Empire*, especially p. 289.
127. Patrick Wolfe, *Settler Colonialism and the Transformation of Anthropology*, p. 163.
128. See, for example, Ronald Niezen, *The Origins of Indigenism*, and Makere Stewart-Harawira, *The New Imperial Order*.

2 Sovereignty

1. On coming "to stay", see Patrick Wolfe, *Settler Colonialism and the Transformation of Anthropology*, p. 2. On colonial sojourners, see Alan L. Karras, *Sojourners in the Sun*. Karras emphasises the colonial sojourners' intention to return.
2. Quoted in Nancy F. Cott, "Marriage and Women's Citizenship in the United States", p. 1448 (my emphasis).
3. Of course, *animus manendi* is one necessary condition but not a sufficient one: a settler colonial setting is also characterised, as noted, by an intrinsic drive towards supersession. There are committed settlers in all colonial settings; however, as well as expressing a determination to stay, these people want colonialism to also stay.
4. See, for example, Lauren Benton, *A Search for Sovereignty*, which emphasises the remarkable complexity and contingency of shifting sovereign forms in colonial settings. Benton concludes by noting that the "strength and persistence of arrangements of layered and divided sovereignty made a difference in the structure of the global regime" (p. 280).
5. For a similar approach to the study of colonial sovereignty, see Achille Mebmbe, "Necropolitics". In the first footnote of his essay (p. 11, n.1), Mbembe states his intention to depart from "traditional accounts of sovereignty" and from a scholarship that exclusively locates sovereignty "within the boundaries of the nation-state, within institutions empowered by the state, or within supranational institutions and networks".
6. See Sandro Petrucci, *Re in Sardegna, a Pisa cittadini*.

7. See Charles Verlinden, "Antonio da Noli and the Colonization of the Cape Verde Islands", especially pp. 168–169.

8. See the classical David H. Makinson, *Barbados*, and George Medcalf, *Royal Government and Political Conflict in Jamaica*.

9. Quoted in Frederick Jackson Turner, "Western State Making in the Revolutionary Era, II", p. 253 (my emphasis). This extended essay published in two parts, unlike Turner's most famous "frontier" piece, which had insisted on the ways in which the frontier shaped American democracy, presented a much more exciting argument outlining how frontiersmen actually operated *in explicit defiance* of American institutions. (Turner's work is used here as a *documentary source* in the context of an analysis of settler dispositions rather than as an authority on historical processes. While Turner is often seen as the initiator of an interpretative tradition, his enunciation of an American "frontier" should be also seen as collecting and articulating a particular sensitivity: a *culmination* rather than a beginning. The "frontier" as he described it did not exist, decades of scholarly activity focusing on ethnicity, class, rural–urban splits, local specificities, and other themes now prove it. The power of the images he evoked, however, did.)

10. Quoted in Frederick Jackson Turner, "Western State Making in the Revolutionary Era, I", p. 82.

11. Thomas Hobbes, *Leviathan*, pp. 221–222.

12. Jack P. Greene reaches a similar conclusion: "In colonial English America, the earliest settlers did not so much bring authority with them across the ocean as a license to create their own authorities. Hence, authority in the colonies did not devolve from England but emerged on the spot from colonising enterprises. [...] They also established pockets of authority by constructing settler legalities to preside over [the land]. The English state's lack of resources, both technical and coercive, meant that these *settler republics* – a concept chosen with full comprehension of its radical implications for a reconception of colonial history – were neither closely nor consistently monitored by the parent country". Jack P. Greene, "By Their Laws Shall Ye Know Them", pp. 251–252.

13. For a sustained argument interpreting early nineteenth-century South African history as fundamentally shaped by imperial attempts to gain access to *all* colonial subjects (and by protracted settler resistance to this assertion of imperial control over the population economy), see Timothy Keegan, *Colonial South Africa and the Origins of the Racial Order*. A similar argument, emphasising a settler determination to exclusively control slaves in eighteenth-century North American colonies against the centralising drive of the British state is presented in Andy Doolen, *Fugitive Empire*.

14. Marc Ferro, *Colonization: A Global History*, pp. 211–213. On colonist independence, see pp. 211–238. However, the end of white Rhodesia is certainly not the end of "colonist independence". Current separatist ferments in Santa Cruz de la Sierra and other regions of Bolivia, where calls for autonomy are framed in an inherent capacity to detach local (settler)

territorialised institutions from indigenous centralising control, and the very denial of legitimacy that a consistent section of the settler movement in the occupied West Bank is expressing *vis à vis* the very institutions of the Israeli state could be mentioned in this context.

15. See Louis Hartz, "A Theory of the Development of the New Societies". Tocqueville's 1831 impression of Lower Canada also conveyed an appreciation of unchanging mores: "Everywhere we were received [...] like children of Old France, as they say here. To my mind the epithet is badly chosen. Old France is in Canada, the new is with us [...]." Quoted in D. Gerhard, "The Frontier in Comparative View", p. 211.

16. See Ed Wright, *Ghost Colonies*, pp. 131–144, 190–203.

17. Francis Jennings, *The Invasion of America*, p. 35.

18. Jonathan Bardon, *A History of Ulster*, p. 130.

19. See Tiziano Bonazzi, *Il sacro esperimento*.

20. See Alan G. Brunger, "The Geographical Context of Planned Group Settlement in Cape Colony".

21. On the Group Settlements scheme, see Alan G. Brunger and J. Selwood, "Settlement and Land Alienation in Western Australia". On settler colonialism in pre-state Israel, see, for example, Gershon Shafir, "Zionism and Colonialism".

22. L. D. Scisco, "The Plantation Type Colony", pp. 260–261; Carter Goodrich and Sol Davison, "The Wage-Earner in the Westward Movement, I"; and Carter Goodrich and Sol Davison, "The Wage-Earner in the Westward Movement, II".

23. See Caroline Elkins and Susan Pedersen (eds), *Settler Colonialism in the Twentieth Century*.

24. Scholars have focused, for example, on different models of settler colonial expansion. However, emphasising antithetical patterns can obscure the fact that settlers were recurrently able to enforce *their respective* visions, whatever they may be. A settler sovereign charge is confirmed, not denied, by an analysis that is attentive to the regional diversity of early America. See Jack P. Greene, *Pursuits of Happiness*.

25. For an analysis of the new "imperial" sovereign form emerging from processes of colonial settlement, see Michael Hardt and Antonio Negri, *Empire*, especially pp. 167–172.

26. This is indeed a constitutive element of settler colonial political traditions. As confirmed by Andrew Fitzmaurice's analysis of early modern English reflections on colonisation, for example, the promoters of colonial ventures in America were serious in their ambivalence about profit. See Andrew Fitzmaurice, *Humanism and America*.

27. See, for example, Donald Harman Akenson, *God's Peoples*, p. 92.

28. On settler capitalism, see Philip McMichael, *Settlers and the Agrarian Question*. In a similar vein, Donald Denoon noted that "there was undeniably something capitalist in the structure of these [settler] colonies." Elsewhere, he quoted Paul Baran's remark in *The Political Economy of Growth* that Western Europeans settled new lands with "capitalism in their bones", and that "from the outset capitalist in its structure, unencumbered by the fetters and barriers of feudalism, [a settler] society

could single-mindedly devote itself to the development of its productive resources." Donald Denoon, *Settler Capitalism*, p. 35; Donald Denoon,
"Understanding Settler Societies", p. 511. For more recent arguments
emphasising the capitalist-driven nature of settler colonial expansion, see
Cole Harris, "How Did Colonialism Dispossess?".

29. For a sustained argument regarding the need to focus on the localised
nature of settler jurisdiction, see Lisa Ford, *Settler Sovereignty*. See also
Deborah A. Rosen, *American Indians and State Law*.

30. See John Mack Faragher, "HBO's *Deadwood*".

31. Peter Lambley, *The Psychology of Apartheid*, p. 34.

32. Jacqueline Rose, *The Question of Zion*.

33. As quoted in Francis Jennings, *The Invasion of America*, p. 180 (my
emphasis).

34. On the covenantal politics of settler colonial formations, see Donald
Harman Akenson, *God's Peoples*.

35. Alexis de Tocqueville, *Democracy in America*.

36. Woody Holton, *Unruly Americans and the Origins of the Constitution*,
p. 234.

37. On settler self-constitutions, see, for example, Peter S. Onuf, "State Making in Revolutionary America". Indeed, settler communities in a variety
of frontiers would recurrently settle disputes internally and according
to self-constituted practices. As Robert Ellickson has demonstrated in
Order Without Law, settlers were literally carrying the law as baggage.
Besides its practical uses, including the possibility of operating without
external judicial intervention, this baggage underscores a self-constitutive
sovereign capacity. See Robert C. Ellickson, *Order Without Law*. See also
John Phillip Reid, *Law for the Elephant*.

38. Theodore Roosevelt, *The Winning of the West, Volume Three*, p. 97.
Roosevelt admired the settler colonial foundation of the United States
but would be instrumental in abandoning this tradition for an explicitly colonial prospect. This was, as some of his opponents were pointing
out, a critical realignment. See Paul A. Kramer, "Empires, Exceptions, and
Anglo-Saxons".

39. George Henry Alden, "The State of Franklin", p. 271.

40. See, for example, Samuel Cole Williams, *History of the Lost State of Franklin*.

41. Quoted in Benjamin F. Shearer (ed.), *The Uniting States*, p. 1134 (my
emphasis).

42. Quoted in Frederick Jackson Turner, "Western State Making in the
Revolutionary Era, I", p. 83.

43. Quoted in Frederick Jackson Turner, "Western State Making in the
Revolutionary Era, I", p. 85.

44. And yet an assertion of separate settler sovereignty is recurrently accompanied by the selective incorporation and enactment of the judicial
practices of the parent polity. Clearly, in the context of settler colonial
political traditions, the issue is not the *content* of the law but the *location*
from where it emanates. On this point, historian of settler sovereignty
Lisa Ford perceptively notices the crucial importance played by the
institutions of local government. Juries and common law culture, she

argues, gave settlers a monopoly over local jurisdictional practice. See Lisa Ford, *Settler Sovereignty*. It is no coincidence that one crucial grievance against Britain prior to the American War of Independence had been the suspension of trial by jury.

45. Quoted in W. A. De Klerk, *The Puritans in Africa*, p. 22 (my emphasis).
46. On declarations of independence and on the role played by settler independence in spreading the "contagion" of sovereignty, see David Armitage, *Declarations of Independence*, especially pp. 103–104.
47. Hamilton's preoccupied reaction to the Louisiana Purchase confirms that Jeffersonians and Federalists actually shared an understanding of a settler sovereign capacity (the extension of America's sphere would, in his opinion, remove subjects from the coercive reach of the state). See Joyce Appleby, "Commercial Farming and the 'Agrarian Myth' in the Early Republic", p. 848.
48. Quoted in Frederick Jackson Turner, "Western State Making in the Revolutionary Era, II", p. 253.
49. Belich has recently argued that the Northwestern Ordinance had a pan-Angloworld impact. He quotes a British official stating in 1796 that "Good policy [...] requires that we should leave as little for [Canadians] to gain from separation as possible." See James Belich, "The Rise of the Angloworld", p. 53. See also James Belich, *Replenishing the Earth*, p. 169.
50. On this point, see Alan Atkinson, *The Europeans in Australia: Volume One*, p. xii. It is significant that this should be the starting point for an outline of Australian history also interested in emphasising "independence from the beginning" (p. xiii).
51. See Edward Gibbon Wakefield, *The Collected Works of Edward Gibbon Wakefield*.
52. Peter S. Onuf, *The Origins of the Federal Republic*, p. 145.
53. On the relationship between the consolidation of modern notions of sovereignty and colonialism, see, for example, Lauren Benton, *Law and Colonial Cultures*, and Ken MacMillan, *Sovereignty and Possession in the English New World*.
54. Patricia Seed, *Ceremonies of Possession in Europe's Conquest of the New World*. "Englishmen held that they acquired rights to the New World by physical objects, Frenchmen by gestures, Spaniards by speech, Portuguese by numbers, Dutch by description", she concludes (p. 179).
55. Damen Ward, "Colonial Communication".
56. Patrick Griffin, *American Leviathan*, p. 242. *American Leviathan* emphasises the crucial role played by settler violence against Indians and resistance against authority. Settler self-sovereignty developed, the author argues, in protracted parallel struggles against speculators and against Indians (i.e., to use a terminology that Griffin does not use, against both indigenous and exogenous Others in a multiplicity of settler locales). Griffin shows how settlers were prepared to assert their independence on the frontier should the government cease to be "accountable" (i.e., should the government prove to be unable to defend the settlements against Indian insurgencies). Settlers would prefer to exercise their sovereignty *beside*

the government's, but would consider exercising it entirely *independent* of it should this articulation prove unfeasible. The American government that emerged from the revolutionary struggle opted to remain "account-able" and extended military protection. Rather than the Union extending its authority over the outlying settlements, it was thus a case of the Western settlements extending their influence over the Union. It was in this sense, Griffin concludes, that the new American state was "an act of co-creation".

57. Eric Foner, *The Story of American Freedom*, p. 50.
58. See Peter S. Onuf and Leonard J. Sadosky, *Jeffersonian America*, p. 156.
59. Israeli settlers in the West Bank who in the context of discussions about possible solutions to the conflict find the "commandment" to settle the land more important than the principle of Israeli national sovereignty and declare a theoretical commitment to remain in an independent future Palestinian state fit in with this approach.
60. See Abraham Matthews, *Crónica de la colonia galesa de la Patagonia*.
61. See John F. Williams, Daniela Kraus, and Harry Knowles, "Flights from Modernity".
62. Scott Atran describes Mandatary Palestine as a case of "surrogate coloniza-tion": "to have *another people* colonize the territory for the Empire's sake". See Scott Atran, "The Surrogate Colonization of Palestine". Quotation at p. 720.
63. Quoted in Peter S. Onuf and Leonard J. Sadosky, *Jeffersonian America*, p. 17.
64. By emphasising a long-lasting "recolonial" phase that had begun in the 1880s (meat and dairy shipments – the "protein bridge" – had cemented an ongoing connection, and emotional and financial ties had been a consequence), Belich upset traditional narratives identifying a pattern of steadily progressing settler and national independence. See James Belich, *Paradise Reforged*, especially p. 66. More recently, in *Replenishing the Earth*, Belich applied this intuition to the whole of the "Angloworld" – and indeed beyond, his analysis also touches on Argentina, Siberia, Manchuria, and other locales – suggesting that recolonisation is a phe-nomenon affecting all the settler neo-Europes. And yet, even if his narrative of early settler independence followed by re-integration is con-vincing, as "colonisation" implies the subordination of the colonised, "isopolity" better than "recolonisation" may encapsulate a system of relations where a single political community is imagined encompass-ing two separate sovereign entities that operate concomitantly and interconstitute each other.
65. James Belich, *Replenishing the Earth*, p. 209; on "Greater Britain", see pp. 456–478.
66. Marilyn Lake, "The Brightness of Eyes and Quiet Assurance Which Seem to Say American", p. 35.
67. Carl Berger, *The Sense of Power*.
68. "Thus, for example, with a view to the peculiar status of American Indians, who are inhabitants, but are not citizens, of the United States,

care would have to be taken that the enactment of common citizenship did not confer on Canadian Indians, who are British subjects, greater rights, when passing into the United States, than are possessed there by American Indians", he proposed. Later, Dicey also suggested that an isopolitical move could be used against the migration in the United States of undesirables, a reminder that settler colonial forms are equally exclusive of indigenous and exogenous Others. Albert Venn Dicey, "A Common Citizenship for the English Race", pp. 458–459, 463–464.

69. Quoted in Eliga H. Gould, "A Virtual Nation", p. 487, n. 50.
70. See, for example, Judith Brett, *Robert Menzies' Forgotten People*. Similarly, Australian historian W. K. Hancock had written in the 1930s about "independent Australian Britons". W. K. Hancock, *Australia*.
71. Quoted in Daniel Gorman, "Wider and Wider Still?", paragraph 42. On the stubbornly exclusionary practices of the settler colonising peripheries, see Robert A. Huttenback, *Racism and Empire*.
72. On settler transnational networks, see, for example, Alan Lester, "Colonial Settlers and the Metropole", and Alan Lester, "British Settler Discourse and the Circuits of Empire". On the settler "archive" of the European imagination, see Lorenzo Veracini, "Colonialism and Genocides".
73. Indeed, the settler project can be even conceived as an *antidote* against state activity. Settlement promoter and radical Israeli politician Yitzhak Tabenkin believed that settlement activity and settler self-organisation *in itself* was the ultimate goal of Zionism. In his vision, the state and the army were only instrumental to its defence. On Tabenkin's "anarchic" theory of settlement, see, for example, Gershom Gorenberg, *The Accidental Empire*, especially pp. 15–17.
74. Lauren Benton, *A Search for Sovereignty*, p. 288.
75. Lisa Ford, for example, perceptively identifies a crucial global passage in the doctrines of sovereignty in the Anglophone settler polities. It is in the decades 1820s–1840s, and in the United States, Canada, New Zealand, and Australia, and not elsewhere, that sovereignty and territorial jurisdiction become coliminal (and previous traditions of colonial legal pluralism are discontinued). See Lisa Ford, *Settler Sovereignty*.
76. Ken MacMillan, *Sovereignty and Possession in the English New World*.
77. Philip J. Stern, "A Politie of Civill & Military Power", p. 255, n. 9.
78. Philip J. Stern, "A Politie of Civill & Military Power", pp. 256, 257.
79. Quoted in Philip J. Stern, "A Politie of Civill & Military Power", p. 259.
80. This is another defining trait separating colonial and settler colonial forms: if the establishment of colonial relations is one way to build the state, if colonialism is an exercise in state making, in settler colonial traditions, it is establishing the state that facilitates settlement. When it comes to the state, colonialism and settler colonialism operate differently: the state is paramount in the former and is minimal in the latter. It is ironic that colonialism can end up with failed states while settler colonialism builds remarkably resilient ones.

81. Woody Holton, *Unruly Americans and the Origins of the Constitution*. Holton detects a clear bias favouring the Framers. In his attempt to recover the agency of Anti-Federalism, he argues that they were not just opposing the ratification of the proposed Constitution and that their political ideology was not merely a negative one. His analysis of the relative invisibility of Anti-Federalism, however, should be integrated with an understanding of a special settler sovereignty. Anti-Federalists did not need to positively articulate their positions; after all, in the context of a settler localised body politic, a settler self-constitution is *the* constitution. For what could be defined as a recent anti-Madisonian historiographical turn, see also Terry Bouton, *Taming Democracy*, and Michael A. McDonnell, *The Politics of War*.

82. See James Belich, *Replenishing the Earth*.

3 Consciousness

1. I have especially relied on J. Laplanche and J. B. Pontalis, *The Language of Psycho-Analysis*.
2. See Lorenzo Veracini, "Colonialism and Genocides".
3. Jacqueline Rose, *States of Fantasy*, p. 10. On the need to include fantasy, projection, idealisation, and other psychic components in the analysis of the dynamic process of identification, see also Stuart Hall, "Introduction: Who Needs Identity".
4. Jürgen Osterhammel, *Colonialism*, p. 108.
5. See, for example, Dominique O. Mannoni, *Prospero and Caliban*; Frantz Fanon, *The Wretched of the Earth*; Frantz Fanon, *Black Skin White Masks*; Albert Memmi, *The Colonizer and the Colonized*; Ashis Nandy, *The Intimate Enemy*; and Homi Bhabha, "Of Mimicry and Man". On the psychology of slavery as a specific formation in the context of colonial practices, see Orlando Patterson, *Slavery and Social Death*. On the relationship between history and psychoanalysis, see, for example, Joy Damousi and Robert Reynolds (eds), *History on the Couch*, and Rudolph Binion, *Past Impersonal*. For an attempt to consider the specific psychoanalytical dynamics associated with settler colonialism, see Chris Prentice, "Some Problems of Response to Empire in Settler Post-Colonial Societies".
6. Moving on is not that easy. Historian John Hirst's positive (and influential) rendition of convict society in Australia, for example, can be seen as replacing one defensive mechanism with another: finally disposing of repression relating to the "convict stain" with its idealisation. After all, idealisation is one crucial defensive mechanism. See John Hirst, *Convict Society and its Enemies*.
7. See, for example, Roland Boer, "Political Myth, or Foreign Policy and the Fantasy of Israel", pp. 77–95.
8. On the psychology of settler Australia, for example, see Bernard Smith's groundbreaking *The Spectre of Truganini*. For an argument regarding "white colonial paranoia in Australia", see Ghassan Hage, *Against Paranoid Nationalism*, especially pp. 48–49.

9. On founding violence and political orders, see, for example, Renè Girard, *Violence and the Sacred* (where "founding violence" is interpreted as a symbolic concept), and Jacques Derrida, "Force of Law" (where "originary violence" is seen as inherent in the foundation of states). Carl Schmitt had also written about it in *The Nomos of the Earth in the International Law of the Jus Publicum Europaeum*.

10. For an argument about disavowal as a collective strategy shaped by social concerns, see Eviatar Zerubavel, *The Elephant in the Room*.

11. William Gilpin's 1846 description of a settler "marching republic" encapsulates this capacity: "Surrounded by his *wife and children*, equipped with wagon, ox-team, and provisions, such as the chase does not furnish, accompanied by his rifle and slender outfit of worldly goods, did these hard men embark upon the unmeasured waste before them. Plunged into the immense plains which slope up to the Rocky Mountains, contending with great rivers, and surrounded by the uncertain dangers of an Indian foe, *a government and a discipline, at once republican and military*, was created for the common safety, and implicitly obeyed by this moving people". Quoted in Henry Nash Smith, *Virgin Land*, p. 38 (my emphasis).

12. On heterotopias, see Michael Foucault, "Des espaces autres".

13. On settler Shanghai, see Robert Bickers, "Shanghailanders". On the Kanak insurrection of 1878, see Bronwen Douglas, "Winning and Losing?".

14. Both quoted in John K. Noyes, "Nomadic Landscapes and the Colonial Frontier", p. 201.

15. See Ana María Alonso "The Politics of Space, Time and Substance".

16. Quoted in John C. Weaver, *The Great Land Rush and the Making of the Modern World*, p. 164, and Robert Blecher, "Citizens Without Sovereignty", p. 735.

17. Alexis de Tocqueville, *Democracy in America*.

18. Ayse Deniz Temiz, "Dialogues with *A Forgetful Nation*".

19. Quoted in Benjamin Arditi, *Politics on the Edges of Liberalism*, p. 3. On territorialisation and ego formation, see, for example, Klaus Theweleit, *Male Fantasies*, vol. 1, pp. 322–323 and Gilles Deleuze and Félix Guattari, *Anti-Oedipus*.

20. The reverse can also be true. At times the settler project is premised, or largely premised, on the appropriation of indigenous labour. In these cases, appropriating land is primarily aimed at ensuring appropriate conditions for labour recruitment. However, as this is also a necessary requirement for the survival of the settler project, as it is one condition for its realisation, even in these cases the settler colonial situation is ultimately if not immediately reliant on settler territorialisation.

21. Jonathan Bardon, *A History of Ulster*, p. 132.

22. Jonathan Bardon, *A History of Ulster*, p. 132.

23. Whether or not concerns about worst case scenarios are founded or a paranoid construction should be less important: as Lacan remarked, a jealous husband's pathological disposition towards his wife remains pathological independently of whether she actually sleeps with other men or not. See Slavoj Žižek, *Iraq: The Borrowed Kettle*, p. 51. For settler

paranoias regarding Australia (for many reasons an especially nervous settler locale), see David Walker, *Anxious Nation*; Jennifer Rutherford, *The Gauche Intruder*; and Anthony Burke, *In Fear of Security*. On Australian diplomat's Alan Renouf's insightful notion of Australia as "the frightened country", see Peter Hartcher, "Bipolar Nation". On the other hand, but underscoring a similar dynamic, while the 2007 Australian federal election has been called the "first climate change election in the world", an Australian settler consciousness and a related stubborn uneasiness about Australian landscapes contribute to making climate change anxieties especially significant.

24. US Supreme Court justice Joseph Story encapsulated the vanishing Indian ideology in 1828: "By a law of nature they seem destined to a slow, but sure extinction. Everywhere, at the approach of the white man, they fade away. We hear the rustling of their footsteps, like that of the withered leaves of autumn, and they are gone for ever. They pass mournfully by us, and they return no more". Quoted in Philip J. Deloria, *Playing Indian*, p. 64.

25. Quoted in Marilyn Lake, "The White Man under Siege", p. 57. In a similar fashion, and utilising metaphors available in their local surroundings, the San Francisco *Alta California* and the *Sacramento Union* proclaimed indigenous disappearance unavoidable: they would vanish "like a dissipating mist before the morning sun", and melt away "as the snows of the mountains in June". Both quoted, in Ben Kiernan, *Blood and Soil*, pp. 350, 353.

26. Ubiquitous references comparing Australia to a "gentleman's park", for example, are generally understood in the context of an incapacity/unwillingness to recognise Aboriginal land management. However, for people that had the enclosures and their consequences hardwired in their system of perception, marvelling at a "gentleman's park" should also be recognised as an allusion to emptiness.

27. See Charles Burdett, "Journeys to Italian East Africa".

28. Quoted in Gershom Gorenberg, *The Accidental Empire*, p. 2 (my emphasis).

29. Quoted in John C. Weaver, *The Great Land Rush and the Making of the Modern World*, pp. 163–164 (my emphasis).

30. See Jonathan Bardon, *A History of Ulster*, p. 118.

31. Karen Kupperman, *Settling with the Indians*, p. 1.

32. For an argument identifying surveying as a crucial moment in the constitution of settler colonial space, see Giselle Byrnes, *Boundary Markers*.

33. Thomas L. Mitchell, *Three Expeditions into the Interior of Eastern Australia*.

34. Thomas L. Mitchell, *Three Expeditions into the Interior of Eastern Australia* (my emphasis).

35. Patrick Wolfe has also noted that settler perception and a genuine encounter are ultimately incompatible: in a settler context, he noted, the "horizontal relationship" (the encounter) is replaced by "the vertical reality of incorporation". See Patrick Wolfe, "On Being Woken Up", especially p. 214.

36. It is significant that the original characterisation of "frontier", the US Census Bureau's (it was the 1890 census and the announcement that the frontier had been "closed" that prompted Frederick Jackson Turner's 1894 "The Significance of the Frontier in American History"), should be about individuals and their location in space – individuals detached from social relations, and space devoid of defining features: an area inhabited by less than one person per square mile (i.e., less than one *exogenous/European* person per square mile). The concept of "frontier" as a contact zone or as a transition zone represents a reaction to this approach and reintroduces multiple agencies and regional specificities into the analytical frame. Reality *is* messy, and the vision of an "empty" frontier is only the final result of a series of successive transfers rather than an original condition. However, in the context of an analysis of settler perception what should be emphasised is an inclination to *see* a circumstance where the only encounter is between man and land: a non-encounter.
37. See Richard White, *The Middle Ground*.
38. See, for example, but the list could be extended, Urs Bitterli, *Cultures in Conflict*; James Axtell, *Beyond 1492*; Antony Pagden, *European Encounters With the New World*; Stephen Greenblatt (ed.), *New World Encounters*; James Axtell, "Columbian Encounters"; Stuart B. Schwartz (ed.), *Implicit Understandings*; Martin Daunton and Rick Halpern (eds), *Empire and Others* (and especially the essay by Philip D. Morgan, "Encounters between British and 'Indigenous' Peoples, c. 1500–c. 1800", which outlines a classification of encounters); John Sutton Lutz (ed.), *Myth and Memory* and Inga Clendinnen, *Dancing with Strangers*.
39. Conversely, it is exactly a determination to focus completely on the colonisation of Mars and its social and biological consequences that encourages Kim Stanley Robinson to discard the possibility of any indigenous life in his acclaimed Mars trilogy. Settler colonialism truly happens in a void. The first and last sentence of *Red Mars*' first paragraph set a typically settler colonial scene ("Mars was empty before we came. [. . .] We are all the consciousness that Mars has ever had"), and a two-page introductory passage ends with a classic account of settler constitution of space: "And so we came here [Mars]. It had been a power; now it became a place". Kim Stanley Robinson, *Red Mars*, pp. 13, 14.
40. Ray Bradbury, *The Martian Chronicles*, p. 110.
41. Ray Bradbury, *The Martian Chronicles*, p. 164.
42. Ray Bradbury, *The Martian Chronicles*, p. 168.
43. Slavoj Žižek, *Violence*, p. 50.
44. Frantz Fanon, *The Wretched of the Earth*, p. 36.
45. Ayse Deniz Temiz, "Dialogues with *A Forgetful Nation*".
46. Francis Jennings, *The Invasion of America*, p. 30.
47. Quoted in Ghada Karmi, *Married to Another Man*.
48. In *Two Treatises of Government* (1690), John Locke theorised a state of nature where there would be no property. If that was the case, if America *was* the beginning of the world and indigenous people and

their association with the land could be transferred away, no indigenous dispossession was logically possible. See John Locke, *Two Treatises of Government*, sections 48, 49.

49. Quoted in Jonathan Bardon, *A History of Ulster*, p. 123.
50. Donald D. Pease has noted how post-1968 critiques emphasising indigenous removal, violence, theft, classism, racism, misogyny, and environmental degradation actually established an "alternative primal scene" (i.e., alternative to previous intellectual traditions premised on the comprehensive disavowal of indigenous peoples). See Donald E. Pease, "New Perspectives on US Culture and Imperialism", pp. 24–25.
51. In a paper entitled " 'Unlocking the Fountains of the Heart' " John O'Leary has uncovered a surprisingly sizeable transnational settler colonial tradition of ventriloquised indigenous "lament" focusing on the "crying indigenous mother" and the "abandoned indigenous orphan" tropes. In order to produce a "sympathy effect", as well as indigenous suffering and pathos, these texts emphasise foundational similarities between indigenous sufferers and their target audience and establish what O'Leary calls a "community of righteous emotion" (p. 58). This tradition of literary mourning is genuine, O'Leary argues, even if is patronising and assimilatory; and yet, as Patrick Brantliger has highlighted, a "proleptic" elegy often actually conceals a death wish. See Patrick Brantlinger, *Dark Vanishings*, pp. 3–4. See also Laura Mielke, *Moving Encounters*; Susan Scheckel, *The Insistence of the Indian*; Henry Reynolds, *This Whispering in Our Hearts*.
52. Quoted in Ben Kiernan, *Blood and Soil*, p. 246. Indeed, as Henry Reynolds has reconstructed for Tasmania in *Fate of a Free People*, indigenous removal is routinely construed as a benevolent alternative to extermination.
53. Quoted in Derek Gregory, *The Colonial Present*, p. 9.
54. For example, Joan Peters argued in *From Time Immemorial* that Palestine was virtually empty before the beginning of Zionist colonisation. Edward Said and Norman Finkelstein have comprehensively demolished Peters's argument. In this context, however, the fact that the settler colonial situation compels a gaze that empties the landscape of its indigenous inhabitants should also be emphasised. See Joan Peters, *From Time Immemorial*; Edward Said, "Conspiracy of Praise", pp. 23–32; Norman Finkelstein, *Beyond Chutzpah*.
55. Andrew Zimmerman, " 'What Do You Really Want in German East Africa, *Herr Professor*'?", p. 420.
56. Inga Clendinnen, "The History Question", p. 3.
57. See Lorenzo Veracini, "Historylessness", pp. 271–285.
58. See Eviatar Zerubavel, *Time Maps*, pp. 91–93, 106. See also Jay Gonen, *A Psychohistory of Zionism*.
59. Jay Gitlin, "On Boundaries of Empire", p. 80.
60. Paul Carter, *The Road to Botany Bay*, p. 349.
61. Louis Hartz, "A Theory of the Development of the New Societies", p. 19.

62. According to Freud's *The Interpretation of Dreams* (1900), secondary revision occurs when the problematic or incoherent elements of a dream are reorganised into a plausible and logical narrative. While secondary revision is essential in the elaboration of "manifest" dreams, it is significant that the construction of settler national historical narratives is often premised on the notion of a "Manifest" Destiny.
63. See Anna Haebich, "The Battlefields of Aboriginal History", p. 2.
64. Raymond Evans, "Plenty Shoot 'Em", p. 167; Douglas Pike, *Australia*; and Russel Ward, *The Australian Legend*.
65. See, for example, Deborah Posel and Graeme Simpson (eds), *Commissioning the Past*. On the specific difficulties associated with deploying a reconciliation model in a settler colonial context, see, for example, Damien Short, "Reconciliation and the Problem of Internal Colonialism".
66. See, for example, Keith Windschuttle, *The Fabrication of Australian History, Vol. 1*, and Michael Connor, *The Invention of Terra Nullius*. In a sense, however, Windschuttle is right: if a settler society is characterised by a narcissistic rendition of its history, openly addressing a violent past is unbefitting of a settler society. On Australia's "history wars", see, for example, Robert Manne (ed.), *Whitewash* and Stuart Macintyre and Anna Clark, *The History Wars*.
67. Hadie Gooder and Jane M. Jacobs, " 'On The Border Of The Unsayable' ". On the politics of official regret for past injustice, see, for example, Roy Brooks (ed.), *When Sorry Isn't Enough*.
68. Debates surrounding legislative activity in France regarding the officially sanctioned memory of colonial pasts epitomise a split consciousness. The Taubira Law explicitly recognised slavery and the slave trade as "crimes against humanity" and instituted an official annual commemoration dedicated to this awareness. In 2005, however, another legislative act demanded that teachers and textbooks "acknowledge and recognise in particular the positive role of the French presence abroad, especially in North Africa". The official memory of colonialism is indeed easier to manage (and condemn) than the official memory of settler colonialism. On these debates, see, for example, Pascal Blanchard, Nicolas Bancel, and Sandrine Lemaire (eds), *La fracture coloniale*.
69. The soul, "when perfect and fully winged [...] soars upward, and orders the whole world; whereas the imperfect soul, losing her wings and drooping in her flight *at last settles on the solid ground – there, finding a home*, she receives an earthly frame which appears to be self-moved, but is really moved by her power". And yet, even if Harold North Flower's English translation uses "settles", "colonise" would probably be more appropriate. Plato, *Phaedrus*, p. 473 (my emphasis). On this point, see also Nicolás Wey Gómez, *The Tropics of Empire*, p. 92.
70. Quoted in Ben Kiernan, *Blood and Soil*, p. 219.
71. See A. Dirk Moses, "Genocide and Settler Society in Australian History".
72. Albert Memmi, *The Colonizer and the Colonized*, pp. 96–97.
73. Grant Farred, "The Unsettler".

4 Narrative

1. See Lorenzo Veracini, "Settler Colonialism and Decolonisation".
2. For an argument emphasising an unbroken continuity between "colonising" and "postcolonising" Australia, see Aileen Moreton Robinson, "I Still Call Australia Home".
3. Anna Johnston and Alan Lawson, "Settler Colonies", p. 369.
4. See, for example, David Carr, *Time, Narrative, and History*, especially pp. 4–5, and Nira Yuval-Davis, "Theorizing Identity".
5. Anthony D. Smith, *The Ethnic Origins of Nations*, p. 15.
6. For an argument regarding the importance of an awareness of the existence and operation of narrative forms, see, for example, William F. Lewis, "Telling America's Story".
7. On colonial narratives, see, for example, Azzedine Haddour, *Colonial Myths*. On captivity narratives and colonialism, see Linda Colley, *Captives*; Pauline T. Strong, *Captive Selves, Captivating Others*.
8. Mary Beard, "*Homer's The Iliad and The Odyssey: A Biography*, by Alberto Manguel". She then adds: "There is at first sight something faintly depressing about the idea that, almost 3000 years on, we are still enthralled – or, to put it more brutally, enslaved – to the works that first launched our literary tradition. And the notion that we are still busy reinventing Homer, from James Joyce to the Coen Brothers (in *O Brother, Where Art Thou?*), is almost shaming".
9. Emma Christopher, Cassandra Pybus and Marcus Rediker, "Introduction", pp. 1–2. On the middle passage, see also Herbert S. Klein, *The Middle Passage*.
10. Emma Christopher, Cassandra Pybus and Marcus Rediker, "Introduction", p. 17, n. 10, p. 2.
11. Quoted in Nigel Penn, "The Voyage Out", p. 87.
12. Quoted in Sacvan Bercovitch, *The Puritan Origin of the American Self*, p. 162. Henry David Thoueau also wrote in strikingly similar terms.
13. Richard Waswo's *The Founding Legend of Western Civilization* provides a compelling argument in this direction. John Docker has also noted that the *Aeneid* (like Exodus, see below), encompassing a succession of displacement, wandering, and conquest, is built upon an inherently settler colonial narrative structure. See John Docker, *The Origins of Violence*, especially pp. 113–144.
14. This point is made in Ben Kiernan, *Blood and Soil*, p. 234. Earlier (especially pp. 169–212), Kiernan had explored the ways in which a specific reading of Virgil's opus underpinned the formulation of English plans for the settler colonisation of Ireland during the second half of the sixteenth century.
15. A reference to *animus revertendi* and the possibility of colonialism is presented in Jennifer S. H. Brown, *Strangers in Blood*, p. xi. Brown notes that the fur traders' intention to return to their homelands in the more settled parts of Canada produced a non-colonial environment (see also p. 22). However, one could argue, on the contrary, that it is not the intention to

return that precludes a colonial predicament; it is the lack of an intention to stay that rules out a settler colonial one.

16. Benedict Anderson, *Imagined Communities*, pp. 55–56.
17. See, for example, see Steven Greenblatt, *Marvelous Possessions*; Mary Louise Pratt, *Imperial Eyes*; Nicholas Thomas, *Colonialism's Culture*.
18. Rebecca L. Stein has recently suggested that hiking could be theorised as a specifically settler form of travel, a movement that traverses the settler "home" without ever leaving it. See Rebecca L. Stein, "Travelling Zion".
19. See Donald Harman Akenson, *God's Peoples*.
20. Deborah Bird Rose, *Reports from a Wild Country*, pp. 56–57, 60–62.
21. Quoted in Sacvan Bercovitch, *The Puritan Origin of the American Self*, p. 148.
22. John Mack Faragher, "Americans, Mexicans, Métis", pp. 94–95. On the opposition between "declension" and "developmental" models of English colonisation in America, see Jack P. Greene, *Pursuits of Happiness*, especially pp. 55–98, 81–100.
23. See Catriona Elder, "Colonialism and Reenactment Television".
24. On the continuities between writing about the American West and imagining the American future, see Carl Abbott, *Frontiers Past and Future*.
25. Patricia Nelson Limerick, *Legacy of Conquest*, p. 19.
26. See Lorenzo Veracini, "Interacting Imaginaries in Israel and the United States".
27. On this point see, for example, Michael Walzer, *Exodus and Revolution*; Conor Cruise O'Brien, *God Land*; Jonathan Boyarin, "Reading Exodus into History"; Michael Prior, *The Bible and Colonialism*. For a convincing response to Walzer's argument, see Edward W. Said, "Michael Walzer's *Exodus and Revolution*".
28. See Christopher Churchill, "Camus and the Theatre of Terror".
29. Albert Camus, *The First Man*, p. 232.
30. Albert Camus, *The First Man*, p. 152. See also Robert Aldrich, *Greater France*, pp. 141–142.
31. On *The First Man* being at once an anti-colonial and a settler colonial text, see Gabriel Piterberg, "The Literature of Settler Societies".
32. Albert Camus, *The First Man*, pp. 140–141.
33. Carole Pateman, "The Settler Contract", pp. 55, 73. On the difficulties inherent in settler postcolonialities, see also P. H. Russell, *Recognizing Aboriginal Title*; Janna Thompson, *Taking Responsibility for the Past*. On the need to decolonise sovereignty and the international law that underpins it, see Antony Anghie, *Imperialism, Sovereignty, and the Making of International Law*. And yet, significantly, this denunciation of the colonial origins of sovereignty ultimately does not distinguish between colonial and settler colonial sovereign forms. Indigenous sovereignties are thus left out of a critique of a system of imperial sovereignties that is seen as enduring (Anghie refers [p. 8] to "the traditions of Critical Race Theory, Feminism, Lat-Crit theory and Third World Approaches to International law" but, not to indigenous peoples).

34. An example of this invisibility is provided by Dietmar Rothermund's *Routledge Companion to Decolonisation*. South Africa is beyond the *Companion's* brief because "it attained its independence before the period of post-war decolonization" (p. 177). While this characterisation of decolonisation allows a comprehensive disavowal of black and other South Africans' struggles against colonialism *and* settler colonialism, it also strategically blocks out the need to think about the decolonisation of settler colonial forms. Martin Shipway's *Decolonization and Its Impact* similarly neglects the decolonisation of settler colonialism, but of course, the list could be easily extended.
35. See, for example, Wm. Roger Louis, "Suez and Decolonization: Scrambling out of Africa and Asia".
36. Ann Curthoys's intuition that Australia, for example, is colonial and postcolonial at once, and colonising and decolonising at the same time, emphasises the inherent ambiguity of postcolonial passages in settler contexts. See Ann Curthoys, "An Uneasy Conversation".
37. A classic example of this type of disavowal is represented by Engels's position on decolonisation. Replying to an enquiry from Kautsky in 1982, Engels wrote: "In my opinion, the colonies proper, that is, the countries occupied by a European population – Canada, the Cape, Australia – will all become independent; on the other hand, the countries inhabited by a native population, which are simply subjugated – India, Algeria, the Dutch, Portuguese and Spanish possessions – must be taken over for the time being by the proletariat and led as rapidly as possible to independence". For Engels, a structural difference between colonial and settler colonial forms results in different avenues to independence. And yet, no decolonisation for the indigenous peoples of the "colonies proper" is envisaged. Quoted in Shlomo Avineri (ed.), *Karl Marx on Colonialism and Modernization*, p. 473.
38. Frantz Fanon, *The Wretched of the Earth*, p. 35.
39. See Eviatar Zerubavel, *Time Maps*, p. 30.
40. Augie Fleras, Jean Leonard Elliott, *The 'Nations Within'*.
41. See, for example, Paul Havemann (ed.), *Indigenous Peoples' Rights in Australia, Canada and New Zealand*; Duncan Ivison, Paul Patton, Will Sanders (eds), *Political Theory and the Rights of Indigenous Peoples*; Maureen Tehan, Lisa Palmer, Marcia Langton, Odette Mazel (eds), *Settling with Indigenous People*.
42. Alan Lawson, "Postcolonial Theory and the 'Settler' Subject".
43. Iris Marion Young, "Hybrid Democracy".
44. On the unsuitability of Third World decolonisations as models for the liberation of indigenous peoples, see Ward Churchill, "Self-Determination and the Fourth World".
45. Deborah Bird Rose, "Land Rights and Deep Colonising". Similarly, even if in another context, reflecting on the concept of "Renaissance", Joan Kelly has concluded that "events that further the historical development of men, liberating them form, natural, social, or ideological constraints, have quite different, even opposite, effects upon women". Joan Kelly,

Women, History and Theory, pp. xii–xiii. A parallel conclusion can be drawn as regards the settler colonial situation: settler independence, depriving indigenous peoples of the possibility of metropolitan interposition between them and the settlers, creates a situation in which there is no possible decolonisation for indigenous peoples.

46. See James Tully, "The Struggles of Indigenous Peoples for and of Freedom".
47. For a recent critique of attempts to project "sovereignty" onto indigenous forms of governance in the context of the "politics of recognition" in settler societies, see Paul Muldoon, "The Sovereign Exceptions".
48. Mahmood Mamdani, "When Does a Settler Become a Native?", p. 7.
49. Mahmood Mamdani, "When Does a Settler Become a Native?", p. 7.
50. See, for examples, Henry Reynolds, *The Law of the Land*, and Alan Ward, *An Unsettled History*.
51. For an example of this interpretative pattern, see A. D. Smith, "State-Making and Nation-Building". Smith distinguishes (p. 241) between different patterns of nation-formation: the Western, the immigrant (but he means the settler colonial), "where small part-*ethnie* are beneficiaries of a state of their own, with or without a struggle, and they then seek to absorb and assimilate waves of new immigrants from different cultures into what becomes increasingly a territorial nation and a political community, as in America, Argentina, Australia", the ethnic, and the colonial.
52. See Lorenzo Veracini, *Negotiating a Bicultural Past*. An outline of changing historical narratives in the context of Treaty practice in New Zealand is presented, for example, in Michael Belgrave, *Historical Frictions*.
53. W. H. Oliver, "The Future behind Us". On juridical history see Andrew Sharp, "Recent Juridical and Constitutional Histories of Maori", pp. 31–32, and, more generally, Ann Curthoys, Ann Genovese, and Alexander Reilly, *Rights and Redemption*.
54. Bain Attwood, *"The Law of the Land* or the Law of the Land?", p. 1.
55. Nigel Penn, "The Northern Cape Frontier Zone in South African Frontier Historiography", p. 39.
56. This is a vast scholarly field. See, among others, Karen Kupperman, *Settling with the Indians*; Richard White, *The Middle Ground*; Edward Countryman, "Indians, the Colonial Order, and the Social Significance of the American Revolution"; Colin G. Calloway, *New Worlds for All*; Colin G. Calloway, *The American Revolution in Indian Country*; Lucy Eldersveld Murphy, *A Gathering of Rivers*; Patricia Nelson Limerick, *Something in the Soil*; Daniel K. Richter, *Facing East from Indian Country*; Susan Sleeper-Smith, *Indian Women and French Men*; Jane T. Merritt, *At the Crossroads*; Alan Taylor, *The Divided Ground*. In *The Bowl with One Spoon*, for example, Tony Hall espoused the "treaty traditions" and "multicultural conservatism" emerging from the strategic alliance between European monarchs and indigenous nations. "Old World" indigenous and European Covenant Chain diplomatic traditions were not entirely displaced or discontinued by the emerging "New World" United States, certainly not in Canada,

and, Hall argues, should be restored. For this line of historical inquiry, see also Francis Jennings, *Empire of Fortune*.

57. See, for example, Paul Muldoon, "Reconciliation and Political Legitimacy".
58. Todd Shepard, *The Invention of Decolonization*, pp. 2, 4, 7.
59. Kevin Bruyneel, *The Third Space of Sovereignty*, pp. 128, 124. See also Thomas Biolsi, "Imagined Geographies".
60. Vine Deloria quoted in Kevin Bruyneel, *The Third Space of Sovereignty*, p. 152.
61. It should be emphasised that a crucial narrative gap characterises locales beyond the contemporary settler colonial world. As Mahmood Mamdani has repeatedly argued, a settler-indigenous dichotomy fundamentally shapes most colonial and postcolonial contexts as well. While he has consistently emphasised the need to overcome the colonially determined distinction between "natives" and "settlers" (the latter are defined by Mamdani as those who do not have a tribal homeland or those who have a tribal homeland elsewhere), his critique has focused on the postcolonial nationalist elites's incapacity to move away from it. See, for example, Mahmood Mamdani, "Beyond Settler and Native as Political Identities".
62. This text was crucially framed in the comparative context of settler societies. In a crucial passage the apology was justified by mentioning "settler societies elsewhere". See Kevin Rudd, "Apology to Australia's Indigenous Peoples".
63. Frantz Fanon, *The Wretched of the Earth*, p. 40.
64. Carole Pateman, "The Settler Contract". On indigenous sovereignties, see, for example (this is, however, a rapidly growing literature), Taiaiake Alfred, *Peace, Power, Righteousness*; Paul Keal, *European Conquest and the Rights of Indigenous Peoples*; Steven Curry, *Indigenous Sovereignty and the Democratic Project*; Joanne Barker (ed.), *Sovereignty Matters*.
65. Quoted in Mark McKenna, "A History for our Time?", p. 5.

Bibliography

Carl Abbott, *Frontiers Past and Future: Science Fiction and the American West*, Lawrence, KA, University Press of Kansas, 2006.

Jeremy Adelman, *Frontier Development: Land, Labour and Capital on the Wheatlands of Argentina and Canada, 1890–1914*, New York, Oxford University Press, 1994.

Charles Robert Ageron, *Modern Algeria: A History from 1830 to the Present*, London, C. Hurst & Co. Publishers, 1991.

Pal Ahluwalia, "When Does a Settler Become a Native? Citizenship and Identity in a Settler Society", *Pretexts: Literary and Cultural Studies*, 10(1), 2001, pp. 63–73.

Donald Harman Akenson, *God's Peoples: Covenant and Land in South Africa, Israel and Ulster*, Ithaca, NY, Cornell University Press, 1992.

George Henry Alden, "The State of Franklin", *American Historical Review*, 8(2), 1903, pp. 271–289.

Robert Aldrich, *Greater France: A History of French Overseas Expansion*, Basingstoke, Palgrave Macmillan, 1996.

Taiaiake Alfred, *Peace, Power, Righteousness: An Indigenous Manifesto*, New York, Oxford University Press, 2009.

Ana María Alonso, "The Politics of Space, Time and Substance: State Formation, Nationalism and Ethnicity", *Annual Review of Anthropology*, 23, 1994, pp. 379–405.

Benedict Anderson, *Imagined Communities: Reflections on the Origins and Spread of Nationalism*, London, Verso, 1991.

———, *The Spectre of Comparisons: Nationalism, Southeast Asia, and the World*, London, Verso, 1998.

Warwick Anderson, *The Cultivation of Whiteness: Science, Health, and Racial Destiny in Australia*, Durham, NC, Duke University Press, 2006.

Antony Anghie, *Imperialism, Sovereignty, and the Making of International Law*, Cambridge, Cambridge University Press, 2005.

Arjun Appadurai, "Numbers in the Colonial Imagination", in C. A. Breckenridge, P. van der Veer (eds), *Orientalism and the Postcolonial Predicament*, Philadelphia, University of Pennsylvania Press, 1993, pp. 314–339.

Joyce Appleby, "Commercial Farming and the 'Agrarian Myth' in the Early Republic", *The Journal of American History*, 68(4), 1982, pp. 833–849.

Benjamin Arditi, *Politics on the Edges of Liberalism: Difference, Populism, Revolution, Agitation*, Edinburgh, Edinburgh University Press, 2007.

Andrew Armitage, *Comparing the Policy of Aboriginal Assimilation: Australia, Canada, and New Zealand*, Vancouver, UBC Press, 1995.

David Armitage, *Declarations of Independence: A Global History*, Cambridge, MA, Harvard University Press, 2008.

Giovanni Arrighi, "Hegemony Unravelling – II", *New Left Review*, 33, 2005, pp. 83–116.

Bill Ashcroft, Gareth Griffiths, Helen Tiffin, *The Empire Writes Back: Theory and Practice in post-Colonial Literatures*, London, Routledge, 1989.

———, "Binarism", in Bill Ashcroft, Gareth Griffith, Helen Tiffin (eds), *Key Concepts in Post-Colonial Studies*, London, Routledge, 1998, pp. 23–27.

Alan Atkinson, *The Europeans in Australia, Volume One: The Beginning*, Melbourne, Oxford University Press, 1997.

Scott Atran, "The Surrogate Colonization of Palestine, 1917–1939", *American Ethnologist*, 16(4), 1989, pp. 719–744.

Bain Attwood, *"The Law of the Land* or the Law of the Land? History, Law and Narrative in a Settler Society", *History Compass*, 2, 2004, pp. 1–30.

Shlomo Avineri (ed.), *Karl Marx on Colonialism and Modernization*, Garden City, NY, Doubleday, 1969.

James Axtell, *Beyond 1492: Encounters in Colonial North America*, New York, Oxford University Press, 1992.

———, "Columbian Encounters: 1992–1995", *The William and Mary Quarterly*, 52(4), 1995, pp. 649–696.

Bernard Bailyn, *Atlantic History: Concept and Contours*, Cambridge, MA, Harvard University Press, 2005.

Georges Balandier, "The Colonial Situation: A Theoretical Approach", in Immanuel Wallerstein (ed.), *Social Change: The Colonial Situation*, New York, John Wiley & Sons, 1966, pp. 34–61.

Tony Ballantyne, *Orientalism and Race: Aryanism in the British Empire*, Basingstoke, Palgrave Macmillan, 2002.

Stuart Banner, *Possessing the Pacific: Land, Settlers, and Indigenous People from Australia to Alaska*, Cambridge, MA, Harvard University Press, 2007.

———, *How the Indians Lost their Land: Law and Power of the Frontier*, Cambridge, MA, Harvard University Press, 2007.

Jonathan Bardon, *A History of Ulster*, Belfast, Blackstaff Press, 1992.

Joanne Barker (ed.), *Sovereignty Matters: Locations of Contestation and Possibility in Indigenous Struggles for Self-Determination*, Lincoln, NE, University of Nebraska Press, 2005.

Ava Baron, "On Looking at Men: Masculinity and the Making of a Gendered Working Class History", in Ann-Louise Shapiro (ed.), *Feminists Revision History*, New Brunswick, NJ, Rutgers University Press, 1994, pp. 146–171.

Zygmunt Bauman, "Making and Unmaking of Strangers", *Thesis Eleven*, 43, 1995, pp. 1–16.

Mary Beard, *"Homer's The Iliad and The Odyssey: A Biography*, by Alberto Manguel", *The Sunday Times*, 4 November 2007.

Larissa Behrendt, Tracey Lindberg, Robert J. Miller, Jacinta Ruru (eds), *Discovering Indigenous Lands: The Doctrine of Discovery in the English Colonies*, Oxford, Oxford University Press, 2010.

Michael Belgrave, *Historical Frictions: Maori Claims and Reinvented Histories*, Auckland, Auckland University Press, 2005.

James Belich, *Making Peoples: A History of the New Zealanders from Polynesian Settlement to the End of the Nineteenth Century*, Auckland, Allen Lane/Penguin Press, 1996.

———, "Myth, Race and Identity in New Zealand", *New Zealand Journal of History*, 31(1), 1997, pp. 6–22.

———, *Paradise Reforged: A History of the New Zealanders from the 1880s to the Year 2000*, Auckland, Allen Lane, 2001.

———, "The Rise of the Angloworld: Settlement in North America and Australasia, 1784–1918", in Phillip Buckner, R. Douglas Francis (eds), *Rediscovering the British World*, Calgary, University of Calgary Press, 2005, pp. 39–57.

———, *Replenishing the Earth: The Settler Revolution and the Rise of the Angloworld*, Oxford, Oxford University Press, 2009.

James Bennett, "Maori as Honorary Members of the White Tribe", *Journal of Imperial and Commonwealth History*, 29(3), 2001, pp. 33–53.

Lauren Benton, *Law and Colonial Cultures: Legal Regimes in World History, 1400–1900*, Cambridge, Cambridge University Press, 2002.

———, *A Search for Sovereignty: Law and Geography in European Empires, 1400–1900*, Cambridge, Cambridge University Press, 2010.

Lauren Benton, John Muth, "On Cultural Hybridity: Interpreting Colonial Authority and Performance", *Journal of Colonialism and Colonial History*, 1(1), 2000.

Sacvan Bercovitch, *The Puritan Origin of the American Self*, New Haven, CT, Yale University Press, 1975.

Carl Berger, *The Sense of Power: Studies in the Ideas of Canadian Imperialism, 1867–1914*, Toronto, Toronto University Press, 1970.

Homi Bhabha, "Of Mimicry and Man: The Ambivalence of Colonial Discourse", *October*, 28, 1984, pp. 125–133.

Robert Bickers, "Shanghailanders: The Formation and Identity of the British Settler Community in Shanghai, 1843–1937", *Past and Present*, 159, 1998, pp. 161–211.

Rudolph Binion, *Past Impersonal: Group Process in Human History*, DeKalb, IL, Northern Illinois University Press, 2005.

Thomas Biolsi, "Imagined Geographies: Sovereignty, Indigenous Space, and American Indian Struggle", *American Ethnologist*, 32(2), 2005, pp. 239–259.

Urs Bitterli, *Cultures in Conflict: Encounters between European and Non-European Cultures, 1492–1800*, Stanford, CA, Stanford University Press, 1989.

Geoffrey Blainey, "Land Rights for All", *The Age*, 10 November 1993.

Pascal Blanchard, Nicolas Bancel, Sandrine Lemaire (eds), *La fracture coloniale. La société française au prisme de l'héritage colonial*, Paris, La Découverte, 2005.

Robert Blecher, "Citizens Without Sovereignty: Transfer and Ethnic Cleansing in Israel", *Comparative Studies in Society and History*, 47(4), 2005, pp. 725–754.

Roland Boer, "Political Myth, or Foreign Policy and the Fantasy of Israel", *Arena Journal*, 23, 2005, pp. 77–95.

Tiziano Bonazzi, *Il sacro esperimento. Teologia e politica nell'America puritana*, Bologna, Il Mulino, 1970.

Gérard Bouchard, *The Making of the Nations and Cultures of the New World: An Essay in Comparative History*, Montreal, McGill-Queen's University Press, 2008.

Terry Bouton, *Taming Democracy: "The People", The Founders, and the Troubled Ending of the American Revolution*, Oxford, Oxford University Press, 2007.

Jonathan Boyarin, "Reading Exodus into History", *New Literary History*, 23(3), 1992, pp. 523–554.

Ray Bradbury, *The Martian Chronicles*, London, Harper Collins, 2001.

Alexander Brady, *Democracy in the Dominions: A Comparative Study in Institutions*, Toronto, University of Toronto Press, 1958.

Patrick Brantlinger, *Dark Vanishings: Discourses on the Extinction of Primitive Races, 1800–1930*, Ithaca, NY, Cornell University Press, 2003.

Judith Brett, *Robert Menzies' Forgotten People*, Sydney, Sun Australia, 1993.

James F. Brooks (ed.), *Confounding the Color Line: The Indian-Black Experience in North America*, Lincoln, NE, University of Nebraska Press, 2002.

Roy Brooks (ed.), *When Sorry Isn't Enough: The Controversy over Apologies and Reparations for Human Injustice*, New York, New York University Press, 1999.

Jennifer S. H. Brown, *Strangers in Blood: Fur Trade Company Families in Indian Country*, Norman, OK, University of Oklahoma Press, 1996.

Alan G. Brunger, "The Geographical Context of Planned Group Settlement in Cape Colony: The 1820s British Emigrants", *Journal of Historical Geography*, 29(1), 2003, pp. 51–72.

Alan G. Brunger, J. Selwood, "Settlement and Land Alienation in Western Australia: The Shire of Denmark", *Journal of Historical Geography*, 23, 1997, pp. 478–495.

Kevin Bruyneel, *The Third Space of Sovereignty: The Postcolonial Politics of U.S.–Indigenous Relations*, Minneapolis, University of Minnesota Press, 2007.

Bruce Buchan, "Withstanding The Tide of History: The *Yorta Yorta* Case and Indigenous Sovereignty", *borderlands e-journal*, 1(2), 2002.

A. R. Buck, John McLaren, Nancy E. Wright (eds), *Land and Freedom: Law, Property Rights and the British Diaspora*, Aldershot, Ashgate, 2001.

―――― (eds), *Despotic Dominion: Property Rights in British Settler Societies*, Vancouver, UBC Press, 2005.

Charles Burdett, "Journeys to Italian East Africa, 1936–1941", *Journal of Modern Italian Studies*, 5(2), 2000, pp. 207–226.

Anthony Burke, *In Fear of Security: Australia's Invasion Anxiety*, Sydney, Pluto Press, 2001.

Edmund Burke, *The Writings and Speeches of Edmund Burke*, Oxford, Clarendon Press, 1991.

Giselle Byrnes, *Boundary Markers: Land Surveying and the Colonisation of New Zealand*, Wellington, Bridget Williams Books, 2001.

Colin G. Calloway, *The American Revolution in Indian Country: Crisis and Diversity in Native American Communities*, Cambridge, Cambridge University Press, 1995.

———, *New Worlds for All: Indians, Europeans, and the Remaking of Early America*, Baltimore, Johns Hopkins University Press, 1997.

Albert Camus, *The First Man*, London, Penguin, 1996.

Jorge Cañizares-Esguerra, *How to Write the History of the New World: Histories, Epistemologies, and Identities in the Eighteenth-Century Atlantic World*, Stanford, CA, Stanford University Press, 2001.

David Carr, *Time, Narrative, and History*, Bloomington, Indiana University Press, 1986.

Paul Carter, *The Road to Botany Bay: An Exploration of Landscape and History*, Chicago, University of Chicago Press, 1987.

Jessica R. Cattelino, "The Double Bind of American Indian-Need-based Sovereignty", *Cultural Anthropology*, 25, 2010, pp. 235–262.

Paulomi Chakraborty, "Framing 'Always Indigenize' beyond the Settler-Colony: 'Indigenising' in India", *ESC*, 30(3), 2004, pp. 17–28.

Partha Chatterjee, *The Nation and its Fragments: Colonial and Postcolonial Histories*, Princeton, NJ, Princeton University Press, 1993.

John Chesterman, Brian Galligan, *Citizens without Rights: Aborigines and Australian Citizenship*, Cambridge, Cambridge University Press, 1997.

Emma Christopher, Cassandra Pybus, Marcus Rediker, "Introduction", in Emma Christopher, Cassandra Pybus, Marcus Rediker (eds), *Many Middle Passages: Forced Migration and the Making of the Modern World*, Berkeley, CA, University of California Press, 2007, pp. 1–19.

Christopher Churchill, "Camus and the Theatre of Terror: Artaudian Dramaturgy and Settler Society in the Works of Albert Camus", *Modern Intellectual History*, 7(1), 2010, pp. 93–121.

Ward Churchill, *A Little Matter of Genocide: Holocaust and Denial in the Americas 1492 to the Present*, San Francisco, City Lights, 1997.

———, "Self-Determination and the Fourth World: An Introductory Survey", in Arlo Kempf (ed.), *Breaching the Colonial Contract: Anti-colonialism in the US and Canada*, Dordrecht, Springer, 2009, pp. 35–52.

Inga Clendinnen, *Dancing with Strangers*, Melbourne, Text Pub., 2003.

———, "The History Question: Who Owns the Past", *Quarterly Essay*, 23, 2006.

Linda Colley, *Captives*, New York, Pantheon Books, 2002.

Frederick Cooper, "Decolonizing Situations: The Rise, Fall, and Rise of Colonial Studies", *French Politics, Culture & Society*, 20(2), 2002, pp. 47–76.

John L. Comaroff, "Images of Empire: Models of Colonial Domination in South Africa", in Frederick Cooper, Ann Laura Stoler (eds), *Tensions of Empire: Colonial Cultures in a Bourgeois World*, Berkeley, CA, University of California Press, 1997, pp. 163–197.

Alice Conklin, *A Mission to Civilize: The Republican Idea of Empire in France and West Africa, 1895–1930*, Stanford, CA, Stanford University Press, 1997.

Michael Connor, *The Invention of Terra Nullius: Historical and Legal Fictions on the Foundation of Australia*, Sydney, Macleay Press, 2005.

Annie Coombes (ed.), *Rethinking Settler Colonialism: History and Memory in Australia, Canada, New Zealand and South Africa*, Manchester, Manchester University Press, 2006.

Nancy F. Cott, "Marriage and Women's Citizenship in the United States, 1830–1934", *The American Historical Review*, 103(5), 1998, pp. 1440–1474.

Edward Countryman, "Indians, the Colonial Order, and the Social Significance of the American Revolution", *William and Mary Quarterly*, LIII(2), 1996, pp. 342–362.

Gillian Cowlishaw, *Black, White or Brindle: Race in Rural Australia*, Cambridge, Cambridge University Press, 1988.

Alfred W. Crosby, *Ecological Imperialism: The Biological Expansion of Europe, 900–1900*, Cambridge, Cambridge University Press, 1986.

Gary Cross, "Comparative Exceptionalism: Rethinking the Hartz Thesis in the Settler Societies of Nineteenth Century United States and Australia", *Australasian Journal of American Studies*, 14, 1995, pp. 15–43.

———, "Labour in Settler State Democracies: Comparative Perspectives on Australia and the US, 1860–1920", *Labour History*, 70, 1996, pp. 1–24.

Steven Curry, *Indigenous Sovereignty and the Democratic Project*, Aldershot, Ashgate, 2004.

Ann Curthoys, "An Uneasy Conversation: The Multicultural and the Indigenous", in John Docker, Gerhard Fischer (eds), *Race, Colour and Identity in Australia and New Zealand*, Sydney, UNSW Press, 2000, pp. 21–36.

Ann Curthoys, Ann Genovese, Alexander Reilly, *Rights and Redemption: History, Law, and Indigenous Peoples*, Sydney, UNSW Press, 2008.

Ann Curthoys, Marilyn Lake (eds), *Connected Worlds: History in Transnational Perspective*, Canberra, ANU E-Press, 2005.

Joy Damousi, Robert Reynolds (eds), *History on the Couch: Essays in History and Psychoanalysis*, Melbourne, Melbourne University Press, 2003.

Charles Darwin, *Voyage of the Beagle*, London, Penguin Classics, 1989.

Martin Daunton, Rick Halpern (eds), *Empire and Others: British Encounters with Indigenous Peoples, 1600–1850*, London, UCL Press, 1999.

Ravi de Costa, *A Higher Authority: Indigenous Transnationalism and Australia*, Sydney, UNSW Press, 2006.

W. A. De Klerk, *The Puritans in Africa: A Story of Afrikanerdom*, Rex Collings, London, 1975.

Gilles Deleuze, Félix Guattari, *Anti-Oedipus: Capitalism and Schizophrenia*, New York, Viking, 1977.

Jeane Delaney, "Making Sense of Modernity: Changing Attitudes toward the Immigrant and the Gaucho in Turn-Of-The-Century Argentina", *Comparative Studies in Society and History*, 38(3), 1996, pp. 434–459.

Philip J. Deloria, *Playing Indian*, New Haven, CT, Yale University Press, 1998.

Donald Denoon, "Understanding Settler Societies", *Historical Studies*, 18(73), 1979, pp. 511–527.

———, *Settler Capitalism: The Dynamics of Dependent Development in the Southern Hemisphere*, Oxford, Oxford University Press, 1983.

———, "The Isolation of Australian History", *Historical Studies*, 87, 1986, pp. 252–260.

———, "Remembering Australasia: A Repressed Memory," *Australian Historical Studies*, 122, 2003, pp. 290–304.

Anthony DePalma, *Here: A Biography of the New American Continent*, New York, Public Affairs, 2001.

Jacques Derrida, "Force of Law: The Mystical Foundation of Authority", *Cardoza Law Review*, 11, 1989, pp. 919–1045.

Jared Diamond, *Guns, Germs, and Steel: The Fates of Human Societies*, New York, W. W. Norton, 1997.

Albert Venn Dicey, "A Common Citizenship for the English Race", *Contemporary Review*, LXXI, April 1897, pp. 457–476.

Michèle Dominy, "Hearing Grass, Thinking Grass: Postcolonialism and Ecology in Aotearoa New Zealand", in David Trigger, Gareth Griffiths (eds), *Disputed Territories: Land Culture and Identity in Settler Societies*, Hong Kong, Hong Kong University Press, 2003, pp. 53–80.

Andy Doolen, *Fugitive Empire: Locating Early American Imperialism*, Minneapolis, University of Minnesota Press, 2005.

Bronwen Douglas, "Winning and Losing? Reflections on the War of 1878–79 in New Caledonia", *Journal of Pacific History*, 26, 1991, pp. 213–233.

John Eddy, Deryck Schreuder (eds), *The Rise of Colonial Nationalism: Australia, New Zealand, Canada and South Africa First Assert their Nationalities, 1880–1914*, Sydney, Allen & Unwin, 1988.

John Docker, *The Origins of Violence: Religion, History and Genocide*, Sydney, University of New South Wales Press, 2008.

Thomas R. Dunlap, *Nature and the English Diaspora: Environment and History in the United States, Canada, Australia, and New Zealand*, Cambridge, Cambridge University Press, 1999.

Penelope Edmonds, *Urbanizing Frontiers: Indigenous Peoples and Settlers in 19th-Century Pacific Rim Cities*, Vancouver, University of British Columbia Press, 2010.

Penny Edwards, "On Home Ground: Settling Land and Domesticating Difference in the 'Non-Settler' Colonies of Burma and Cambodia", *Journal of Colonialism and Colonial History*, 4(3), 2003.

Catriona Elder, "Colonialism and Reenactment Television: Imagining Belonging in *Outback House*", in Vanessa Agnew, Jonathan Lamb (eds), *Settler and Creole Re-Enactment*, Basingstoke, Palgrave Macmillan, 2009, pp. 193–207.

Caroline Elkins, Susan Pedersen, "Settler Colonialism: A Concept and its Uses", in Caroline Elkins, Susan Pedersen (eds), *Settler Colonialism in the Twentieth Century: Projects, Practices, Legacies*, New York, Routledge, 2005, pp. 1–20.

——— (eds), *Settler Colonialism in the Twentieth Century: Projects, Practices, Legacies*, New York, Routledge, 2005.

Lucy Eldersveld Murphy, *A Gathering of Rivers: Indians, Métis, and Mining in the Western Great Lakes, 1737–1832*, Lincoln, NE, University of Nebraska Press, 2000.

Robert C. Ellickson, *Order Without Law: How Neighbors Settle Disputes*, Cambridge, MA, Harvard University Press, 1991.

Katherine Ellinghaus, *Taking Assimilation to Heart: Marriages of Whiten Women and Indigenous Men in the United States and Australia, 1887–1937*, Lincoln, NE, University of Nebraska Press, 2006.

——, "Strategies of Elimination: 'Exempted' Aborigines, 'Competent' Indians, and Twentieth-Century Assimilation Policies in Australia and the United States", *Online Journal of the CHA*, 18(2), 2007, pp. 202–225.

——, "Biological Absorption and Genocide: A Comparison of Indigenous Assimilation Policies in the United States and Australia", *Genocide Studies and Prevention*, 4(1), 2009, pp. 59–79.

Arghiri Emmanuel, "White–Settler Colonialism and the Myth of Investment Imperialism", *New Left Review*, 73(1), 1972, pp. 35–57.

Stanley L. Engerman, Jacob Metzer (eds), *Land Rights, Ethno-Nationality and Sovereignty in History*, London, Routledge, 2004.

Gerhard J. Ens, *Homeland to Hinterland: The Changing Worlds of the Red River Métis*, Toronto, University of Toronto Press, 1996.

Julie Evans, Patricia Grimshaw, David Philips, Shurlee Swain, *Equal Subjects, Unequal Rights: Indigenous Peoples in British Settler Colonies, 1830–1910*, Manchester, Manchester University Press, 2003.

Raymond Evans, "Plenty Shoot 'Em: The Destruction of Aboriginal Societies along the Queensland Frontier", in A. Dirk Moses (ed.), *Genocide and Settler Society: Frontier Violence and Stolen Indigenous Children in Australian History*, New York, Berghahn Books, 2004, pp. 150–173.

Johannes Fabian, *Time and the Other: How Anthropology Makes its Object*, New York, Columbia University Press, 1983.

Frantz Fanon, *The Wretched of the Earth*, Harmondsworth, Penguin Books, 1967.

——, *Black Skin, White Masks*, St. Albans, Paladin, 1970.

John Mack Faragher, "Americans, Mexicans, Métis: A Community Approach to the Comparative Study of North American Frontiers", in William Cronon, George Miles, Jay Gitlin (eds), *Under an Open Sky: Rethinking America's Past*, New York, Norton & Company, 1992, pp. 90–109.

——, *A Great and Noble Scheme: The Tragic Story of the Expulsion of the French Acadians from their American Homeland*, New York, W. W. Norton & Co., 2005.

——, "HBO's *Deadwood*: Not Your Typical Western", *Montana: The Magazine of Western History*, 57(3), 2007, pp. 60–65.

Grant Farred, "The Unsettler", *South Atlantic Quarterly*, 107(4), 2008, pp. 791–808.

Marc Ferro, *Colonization: A Global History*, London, Routledge, 1997.

D. K. Fieldhouse, *The Colonial Empires: A Comparative Survey from the Eighteenth Century*, London, Weidenfeld & Nicolson, 1966.

Norman Finkelstein, *Beyond Chutzpah: On the Misuse of Anti-Semitism and the Abuse of History*, Berkeley, CA, University of California Press, 2005.

M. I. Finley, "Colonies – An attempt at a Typology", *Transactions of the Royal Historical Society*, 26, 1976, pp. 167–188.

Andrew Fitzmaurice, *Humanism and America: An Intellectual History of English Colonization, 1500–1625*, Cambridge, Cambridge University Press, 2003.

Donald F. Fixico, *Termination and Relocation: Federal Indian Policy, 1945–1960*, Albuquerque, NM, University of New Mexico Press, 1986.

Tom Flanagan, *First Nations? Second Thoughts*, Montreal, McGill-Queen's University Press, 2008.

Angie Fleras, Joan Leonard Elliott, *The "Nations Within": Aboriginal-State Relations in Canada, the United States, and New Zealand*, Toronto, Oxford University Press, 1992.

Eric Foner, *The Story of American Freedom*, New York, W. W. Norton & Company, 1998.

Jack D. Forbes, *Black Africans and Native Americans: Color, Race, and Caste in the Evolution of Red-Black Peoples*, New York, Basil Blackwell, 1988.

Lisa Ford, *Settler Sovereignty: Jurisdiction and Indigenous People in America and Australia, 1788–1836*, Cambridge, MA, Harvard University Press, 2010.

Hamar Foster, Benjamin L. Berger, A. R. Buck (eds), *The Grand Experiment: Law and Legal Culture in British Settler Societies*, Vancouver, UBC Press, 2008.

Michael Foucault, "Des espaces autres", *Architecture, Mouvement, Continuité*, 5, 1984, pp. 46–49.

Ruth Frankenberg, "Local Whitenesses, Localizing Whiteness", in Ruth Frankenberg (ed.), *Displacing Whiteness: Essays in Social and Cultural Criticism*, Durham, NC, Duke University Press, 1997, pp. 1–34.

George M. Fredrickson, "Colonialism and Racism," in *The Arrogance of Race: Historical Perspectives on Slavery, Racism, and Social Inequality*, Middletown, CT, Wesleyan University Press, 1988, pp. 216–235.

Victoria Freeman, "Attitudes Toward 'Miscegenation' in Canada, the United States, New Zealand, and Australia, 1860–1914", *Native Studies Review*, 16(1), 2005, pp. 41–69.

Candace Fujikane, "Introduction: Asian Settler Colonialism in the U.S, Colony of Hawai'i", in Candace Fujikane, Jonathan Y. Okamura (eds), *Asian Settler Colonialism: From Local Governance to the Habits of Everyday Life in Hawaii*, Honolulu, University of Hawai'i Press, 2008, pp. 1–42.

Elizabeth Furniss, "Challenging the Myth of Indigenous Peoples' 'Last Stand' in Canada and Australia: Public Discourse and the Conditions of Silence", in Annie Coombes (ed.), *Rethinking Settler Colonialism: History and Memory in Australia, Canada, New Zealand and South Africa*, Manchester, Manchester University Press, 2006, pp. 172–192.

Daniel Gaido, "Settler Colonialism and the Bourgeois Revolutions", in Daniel Gaido, *The Formative Period of American Capitalism: A Materialist Interpretation*, New York, Routledge, 2006, pp. 3–28.

Robert Geraci, "Genocidal Impulses and Fantasies in Imperial Russia", in A. Dirk Moses (ed.), *Empire, Colony, Genocide: Conquest, Occupation, and Subaltern Resistance in World History*, New York, Berghahn, pp. 343–371.

Paula Gerber, "Making Indigenous Australians 'Disappear': Problems arising from our Birth Registration Systems", *Alternative Law Journal*, 34(3), 2009, pp. 15–162, 167.

D. Gerhard, "The Frontier in Comparative View", *Comparative Studies in Society and History*, 1, 1959, pp. 205–229.

Renè Girard, *Violence and the Sacred*, Baltimore, Johns Hopkins University Press, 1977.

Jay Gitlin, "On Boundaries of Empire: Connecting the West to its Imperial Past", in William Cronon, George Miles, Jay Gitlin (eds), *Under an Open Sky: Rethinking America's Past*, New York, Norton & Company, 1992, pp. 71–89.

Terry Goldie, *Fear and Temptation: The Image of the Indigene in Canadian, Australian and New Zealand Literatures*, Montreal, McGill-Queens University Press, 1989.

Alyosha Goldstein, "Where the Nation Takes Place: Proprietary Regimes, Antistatism, and U.S. Settler Colonialism", *South Atlantic Quarterly*, 107(4), 2008, pp. 833–861.

Alyosha Goldstein, Alex Lubin (eds), "Settler Colonialism", special issue of *South Atlantic Quarterly*, 107(4), 2008.

Jay Gonen, *A Psychohistory of Zionism*, New York, New American Library, 1976.

Hadie Gooder, Jane M. Jacobs, " 'On The Border Of The Unsayable': The Apology in Postcolonizing Australia", *Interventions*, 2(2), 2000, pp. 229–247.

Carter Goodrich, Sol Davison, "The Wage-Earner in the Westward Movement, I", *Political Science Quarterly*, 1935, pp. 161–185.

———, "The Wage-Earner in the Westward Movement, II", *Political Science Quarterly*, 1936, pp. 61–116.

Gershom Gorenberg, *The Accidental Empire: Israel and the Birth of the Settlements, 1967–1977*, New York, Henry Holt and Company, 2006.

Daniel Gorman, "Wider and Wider Still? Racial Politics, Intra-Imperial Immigration and the Absence of an Imperial Citizenship in the British Empire", *Journal of Colonialism and Colonial History*, 3(3), 2002.

Richard Gott, "Latin America as a White Settler Society", *Bulletin of Latin American Research*, 26(2), 2007, pp. 269–289.

Eliga H. Gould, "A Virtual Nation: Greater Britain and the Imperial Legacy of the American Revolution", *American Historical Review*, 104(2), 1999, pp. 476–489.

Stephen Greenblatt, *Marvelous Possessions: The Wonder of the New World*, Chicago, University of Chicago Press, 1991.

——— (ed.), *New World Encounters*, Berkeley, CA, University of California Press, 1993.

Jack P. Greene, " 'By Their Laws Shall Ye Know Them': Law and Identity in Colonial British America", *Journal of Interdisciplinary History*, 33, 2, 2002, pp. 247–260.

——— *Pursuits of Happiness: The Social Development of Early Modern British Colonies and the Formation of American Culture*, Chapel Hill, NC, University of North Carolina Press, 1988.

Derek Gregory, *The Colonial Present: Afghanistan, Palestine, Iraq*, Malden, MA, Blackwell Publishers, 2004.

Patrick Griffin, *American Leviathan: Empire, Nation, and Revolutionary Frontier*, New York, Hill and Wang, 2007.

Naomi E. S. Griffiths, *From Migrant to Acadian: A North American Border People, 1604–1755*, Montreal, McGill-Queen's University Press, 2005.

Tom Griffiths, Libby Robin (eds), *Ecology and Empire: Environmental History of Settler Societies*, Melbourne, Melbourne University Press, 1997.

Andrew Gyory, *Closing the Gate: Race, Politics, and the Chinese Exclusion Act*, Chapel Hill, NC, University of North Carolina Press, 1998.

Azzedine Haddour, *Colonial Myths: History and Narrative*, Manchester, Manchester University Press, 2000.

Anna Haebich, "The Battlefields of Aboriginal History", in Martyn Lyons, Penny Russell (eds), *Australia's History: Themes and Debates*, Sydney, UNSW Press, 2005, pp. 1–21.

Ghassan Hage, *Against Paranoid Nationalism: Searching for Hope in a Shrinking Society*, Sydney, Pluto Press, 2003.

Catherine Hall, "Imperial Man: Edward Eyre in Australia and the West Indies, 1833–66", in Bill Schwarz (ed.), *The Expansion of England: Race, Ethnicity and Cultural History*, London, Routledge, 1996, pp. 142–148.

——, *Civilising Subjects: Metropole and Colony in the English Imagination, 1830–1867*, Cambridge, Polity, 2002.

Stuart Hall, "Introduction: Who Needs Identity", in Stuart Hall, Paul de Gay (eds), *Questions of Cultural Identity*, London, Sage, 1996, pp. 1–17.

Tony Hall, *The Bowl with One Spoon*, Montreal, McGill-Queen's University Press, 2003.

W. K. Hancock, *Australia*, New York, Charles Scribner's Sons, 1930.

Michael Hardt, Antonio Negri, *Empire*, Cambridge, MA, Harvard University Press, 2000.

Cole Harris, "The Simplification of Europe Overseas", *Annals of the Association of American Geographers*, 67(4), 1977, pp. 469–483.

——, *Making Native Space: Colonialism, Resistance, and Reserves in British Columbia*, Vancouver, University of British Columbia Press, 2002.

——, "How Did Colonialism Dispossess? Comments from an Edge of Empire", *Annals of the Association of American Geographers*, 94(1), 2004, pp. 165–182.

Peter Hartcher, "Bipolar Nation: How to Win the 2007 Election", *Quarterly Essay*, 25, 2007.

Louis Hartz, "A Theory of the Development of the New Societies", in Louis Hartz (ed.), *The Founding of New Societies: Studies in the History of the United States, Latin America, South Africa, Canada, and Australia*, San Diego, Harvest/HBJ, 1964, pp. 3–23.

Paul Havemann (ed.), *Indigenous Peoples' Rights in Australia, Canada and New Zealand*, Auckland, Oxford University Press, 1999.

Adam J. Hirsch, "The Collision of Military Cultures in Seventeenth-Century New England", *The Journal of American History*, 74(4), 1988, pp. 1187–1212.

John Hirst, *Convict Society and its Enemies: A History of Early New South Wales*, Sydney, George Allen & Unwin, 1983.

Thomas Hobbes, *Leviathan*, Cambridge, Cambridge University Press, 1996.

Woody Holton, *Unruly Americans and the Origins of the Constitution*, New York, Hill and Wang, 2007.

A. G. Hopkins, "Back to the Future: From National History to Imperial History", *Past and Present*, 164, 1999, pp. 198–243.

Ronald J. Horvath, "A Definition of Colonialism", *Current Anthropology*, 13(1), 1972, pp. 45–57.

Frederick E. Hoxie, "Retrieving the Red Continent: Settler Colonialism and the History of American Indians in the US", *Ethnic and Racial Studies*, 31(6), 2008, pp. 1153–1167.

Shari M. Huhndorf, *Going Native: Indians in the American Cultural Imagination*, Ithaca, NY, Cornell University Press, 2001.

Robert A. Huttenback, *Racism and Empire: White Settlers and Colored Immigrants in the British Self-Governing Colonies, 1830–1910*, Ithaca, NY, Cornell University Press, 1976.

Penelope Ingram, "Can the Settler Speak? Appropriating Subaltern Silence in Janet Frame's 'The Carpathians' ", *Cultural Critique*, 41, 1999, pp. 79–107.

———, "Racializing Babylon: Settler Whiteness and the 'New Racism' ", *New Literary History*, 32(1), 2001, pp. 157–176.

Sarah Irving, " 'In a Pure Soil': Colonial Anxieties in the Work of Francis Bacon", *History of European Ideas*, 32, 2006, pp. 249–262.

Duncan Ivison, Paul Patton, Will Sanders (eds), *Political Theory and the Rights of Indigenous Peoples*, Cambridge, Cambridge University Press, 2000.

Margaret D. Jacobs, *White Mother to a Dark Race: Settler Colonialism, Maternalism, and the Removal of Indigenous Children in the American West and Australia, 1880–1940*, Lincoln, NE, University of Nebraska Press, 2009.

Matthew Frye Jacobson, *Whiteness of a Different Color: European Immigrants and the Alchemy of Race*, Cambridge, MA, Harvard University Press, 1998.

Francis Jennings, *The Invasion of America: Indians, Colonialism, and the Cant of Conquest*, New York, Norton, 1976.

———, *Empire of Fortune: Crowns, Colonies, and Tribes in the Seven Years War in America*, New York, Norton, 1988.

———, *The Founders of America: How Indians Discovered the Land, Pioneered in it, and Created Great Classical Civilizations, How they were Plunged into a Dark Age by Invasion and Conquest, and How they are Reviving*, New York, Norton, 1993.

Anna Johnston, Alan Lawson, "Settler Colonies", in Henry Schwarz, Sangeeta Ray (eds), *A Companion to Postcolonial Studies*, Malden, MA, Blackwell, 2000, pp. 360–376.

Amy Kaplan, " 'Left Alone With America': The Absence of Empire in the Study of American Culture", in Amy Kaplan, Donald E. Pease (eds), *Cultures of United States Imperialism*, Durham, NC, Duke University Press, 1993, pp. 3–21.

Amy Kaplan, Donald E. Pease (eds), *Cultures of United States Imperialism*, Durham, NC, Duke University Press, 1993.

Ghada Karmi, *Married to Another Man: Israel's Dilemma in Palestine*, London, Pluto Press, 2007.

Alan L. Karras, *Sojourners in the Sun: Scottish Migrants in Jamaica and the Chesapeake, 1740–1800*, Ithaca, NY, Cornell University Press, 1992.

Peter Karsten, *Between Law and Custom: High and Low Legal Cultures in the Lands of the British Diaspora – The United States, Canada, Australia, and New Zealand, 1600–1900*, Cambridge, Cambridge University Press, 2002.

J. Kehaulani Kauanui, *Hawaiian Blood: Colonialism and the Politics of Sovereignty and Indigeneity*, Durham, NC, Duke University Press, 2008.

Eric Kaufmann, "'Naturalizing the Nation' The Rise of Naturalistic Nationalism in the United States and Canada", *Comparative Studies in Society and History*, 40(4), 1998, pp. 666–695.

Paul Keal, *European Conquest and the Rights of Indigenous Peoples: The Moral Backwardness of International Society*, Cambridge, Cambridge University Press, 2003.

Timothy Keegan, *Colonial South Africa and the Origins of the Racial Order*, Charlottesville, VA, University Press of Virginia, 1996.

Joan Kelly, *Women, History and Theory: The Essays of Joan Kelly*, Chicago, University of Chicago Press, 1984.

Ben Kiernan, *Blood and Soil: A World History of Genocide and Extermination from Sparta to Darfur*, New Haven, CT, Yale University Press, 2007.

C. Richard King, Charles Fruehling Springwood (eds.), *Team Spirits: The Native American Mascots Controversy*, Lincoln, NE, University of Nebraska Press, 2001.

Herbert S. Klein, *The Middle Passage: Comparative Studies in the Atlantic Slave Trade*, Princeton, NJ, Princeton University Press, 1978.

Paul A. Kramer, "Empires, Exceptions, and Anglo-Saxons: Race and Rule between the British and United States Empires, 1880–1910", *The Journal of American History*, 88(4), 2002, pp. 1315–1353.

Udo Krautwurst, "What is Settler Colonialism? An Anthropological Meditation of Frantz Fanon's 'Concerning Violence'", *History and Anthropology*, 14(1), 2003, pp. 55–72.

Karen Kupperman, *Settling with the Indians: The Meeting of English and Indian Cultures in America, 1580–1640*, Totowa, NJ, Littlefield, 1980.

Marilyn Lake, "White Man's Country: The Trans-National History of a National Project", *Australian Historical Studies*, 122, 2003, pp. 346–363.

———, "The White Man under Siege: New Histories of Race in the Nineteenth Century and the Advent of White Australia", *History Workshop Journal*, 58, 2004, pp. 41–62.

———, "'The Brightness of Eyes and Quiet Assurance Which Seem to Say American': Alfred Deakin's Identification with Republican Manhood", *Australia Historical Studies*, 129, 2007, pp. 32–51.

Marilyn Lake, Henry Reynolds, *Drawing the Global Colour Line: White Men's Countries and the Question of Racial Equality*, Melbourne, Melbourne University Press, 2008.

George Lakoff, Mark Johnson, *Metaphors We Live By*, Chicago, University of Chicago Press, 2003.

David Lambert, Alan Lester, "Geographies of Colonial Philanthropy", *Progress in Human Geography*, 28(3), 2004, pp. 320–341.

Peter Lambley, *The Psychology of Apartheid*, Athens, GA, University of Georgia Press, 1980.

Marcia Langton, Maureen Tehan, Lisa Palmer, Odette Mazel (eds), *Settling with Indigenous People: Modern Treaty and Agreement-Making*, Sydney, Federation Press, 2007.

Marcia Langton, Maureen Tehan, Lisa Palmer, *Honour Among Nations? Treaties and Agreements with Indigenous People*, Melbourne, Melbourne University Press, 2004.

J. Laplanche, J. B. Pontalis, *The Language of Psycho-analysis*, New York, W. W. Norton & Company, 1973.

Alan Lawson, "A Cultural Paradigm for the Second World", *Australian-Canadian Studies*, 9(1–2), 1991, pp. 67–78.

———, "Postcolonial Theory and the 'Settler' Subject", *Essays on Canadian Writing*, 56, 1995, pp. 20–36.

Martin Legassick, "The Northern Frontier to c. 1840: The Rise and Decline of the Griqua People", in Richard Elphick, Hermann Giliomee (eds), *The Shaping of South African Society, 1652–1840*, Middletown, CT, Wesleyan University Press, 1988, pp. 358–420.

Alan Lester, "British Settler Discourse and the Circuits of Empire", *History Workshop Journal*, 54, 2002, pp. 25–48.

———, "Colonial Settlers and the Metropole: Racial Discourse in the Early 19th-Century Cape Colony, Australia and New Zealand", *Landscape Research*, 27(1), 2002, pp. 39–49.

Alan Lester, Fae Dussart, "Trajectories of Protection: Protectorates of Aborigines in Early 19th Century Australia and Aotearoa New Zealand", *The New Zealand Geographer*, 64(3), 2008, pp. 205–220.

William F. Lewis, "Telling America's Story: Narrative Form and the Reagan Presidency", *Quarterly Journal of Speech*, 73, 1987, pp. 280–302.

John Locke, *Two Treatises of Government: A Critical Edition with an Introduction and Apparatus*, New York, Cambridge University Press, 1965.

Patricia Lorcin, *Imperial Identities: Stereotyping, Prejudice and Race in Colonial Algeria*, London, I. B. Tauris, 1995.

———, "Rome and France in Africa: Recovering Colonial Algeria's Latin Past", *French Historical Studies*, 25(2), 2002, pp. 295–329.

Wm. Roger Louis, "Suez and Decolonization: Scrambling out of Africa and Asia", in Wm. Roger Louis, *Ends of British Imperialism: The Scramble for Empire, Suez and Decolonization*, London, I. B. Tauris, 2006, pp. 1–31.

John Sutton Lutz (ed.), *Myth and Memory: Stories of Indigenous-European Contact*, Vancouver, UBC Press, 2007.

John Lynch, *The Spanish American Revolutions, 1808–1826*, New York, Norton, 1973.

Scott Richard Lyons, *X-Marks: Native Signatures of Assent*, Minneapolis, University of Minnesota Press, 2010.

Stuart Macintyre, Anna Clark, *The History Wars*, Melbourne, Melbourne University Press, 2003.

Ken MacMillan, *Sovereignty and Possession in the English New World: The Legal Foundations of Empire, 1576–1640*, Cambridge, Cambridge University Press, 2006.

David H. Makinson, *Barbados: A Study of North-American-West-Indian Relations, 1739–1789*, London, Mouton, 1964.

Mahmood Mamdani, "When Does a Settler Become a Native? Reflections of the Colonial Roots of Citizenship in Equatorial and South Africa", inaugural lecture as A C Jordan Professor of African Studies, University of Cape Town, 13 May 1998. The URL for this lecture is: http://hrp.bard.edu/resource_pdfs/mamdani.settler.pdf.

———, "Beyond Settler and Native as Political Identities: Overcoming the Political Legacy of Colonialism", *Comparative Studies in Society and History*, 43, 4, 2001, pp. 651–664.

Michael Mann, *The Dark Side of Democracy: Explaining Ethnic Cleansing*, New York, Cambridge University Press, 2004.

Robert Manne (ed.), *Whitewash: On Keith Windschuttle's Fabrication of Aboriginal History*, Melbourne, Black Inc, 2003.

Dominique O. Mannoni, *Prospero and Caliban: The Psychology of Colonisation*, London, Methuen, 1956.

Anthony W. Marx, *Making Race and Nation: A Comparison of South Africa, the United States, and Brazil*, Cambridge, Cambridge University Press, 1998.

Karl Marx, Friederich Engels, *The Communist Manifesto*, London, Verso, 1998.

Nur Masalha, *Expulsion of the Palestinians: The Concept of 'Transfer' in Zionist Political Thought, 1882–1984*, Washington, DC, Institute of Palestine Studies, 1991.

Abraham Matthews, *Crónica de la colonia galesa de la Patagonia*, Buenos Aires, Ed. Alfonsina, 1995.

Achille Mebmbe, "Necropolitics", *Public Culture*, 15(1), 2003, pp. 11–40.

J. W. McCarthy, "Australia as a Region of Recent Settlement in the Nineteenth Century", *Australian Economic History Review*, 13, 1973, pp. 148–167.

Michael A. McDonnell, *The Politics of War: Race, Class, and Conflict in Revolutionary Virginia*, Chapel Hill, NC, University of North Carolina Press, 2007.

P. G. McHugh, *Aboriginal Societies and the Common Law: A History of Sovereignty, Status, and Self-Determination*, Oxford, Oxford University Press, 2004.

Mark McKenna, "A History for our Time? The Idea of the People in Australian Democracy", *History Compass*, 1, 2003, pp. 1–15.

Philip McMichael, *Settlers and the Agrarian Question: Foundations of Capitalism in Colonial Australia*, Cambridge, Cambridge University Press, 1984.

George Medcalf, *Royal Government and Political Conflict in Jamaica, 1729–1783*, London, Longmans, 1965.

Philippa Mein Smith, "New Zealand Federation Commissioners in Australia: One Past, Two Historiographies", *Australian Historical Studies*, 122, 2003, pp. 305–325.

Albert Memmi, *The Colonizer and the Colonized*, London, Earthscan, 2003.

Jane T. Merritt, *At the Crossroads: Indians and Empires on a Mid-Atlantic Frontier, 1700–1763*, Chapel Hill, NC, University of North Carolina Press, 2003.

Laura Mielke, *Moving Encounters: Sympathy and the Indian Question in Antebellum Literature*, Amherst, MA, University of Massachusetts Press, 2008.

Mark Edwin Miller, *Forgotten Tribes: Unrecognized Indians and the Federal Acknowledgment Process*, Lincoln, NE, University of Nebraska Press, 2004.

Charles W. Mills, *The Racial Contract*, Ithaca, NY, Cornell University Press, 1997.

———, "Intersecting Contracts", in Carole Pateman, Charles W. Mills (eds), *Contract and Domination*, Cambridge, Polity, 2007, pp. 165–199.

Thomas L. Mitchell, *Three Expeditions into the Interior of Eastern Australia: With Descriptions of the Recently Explored Region of Australia Felix, and of the Present Colony of New South Wales*, Adelaide, Libraries Board of South Australia, 1965.

Anthony Moran, "As Australia Decolonizes: Indigenizing Settler Nationalism and the Challenges of Settler/Indigenous Relations", *Ethnic and Racial Studies*, 25(6), 2002, pp. 1013–1042.

Aileen Moreton Robinson, "I Still Call Australia Home: Indigenous Belonging and Place in a White Postcolonizing Society", in Sara Ahmed (ed.), *Uprootings/Regroundings: Questions of Home and Migration*, New York, Berg Publishers, 2003, pp. 23–40.

———, "Introduction", in Aileen Moreton Robinson (ed.), *Sovereign Subjects: Indigenous Sovereignty Matters*, Sydney, Allen & Unwin, 2007, pp. 1–14.

Philip D. Morgan, "Encounters between British and 'Indigenous' Peoples, c. 1500–c. 1800", in Martin Daunton, Rick Halpern (eds), *Empire and Others: British Encounters with Indigenous Peoples, 1600–1850*, London, UCL Press, 1999, pp. 42–78.

A. Dirk Moses, "Genocide and Settler Society in Australian History", in A. Dirk Moses (ed.), *Genocide and Settler Society: Frontier Violence and Stolen Indigenous Children in Australian History*, New York, Berghahn, 2004, pp. 3–48.

——— (ed.), *Empire, Colony, Genocide: Conquest, Occupation, and Subaltern Resistance in World History*, New York, Berghahn, 2008.

Paul Muldoon, "Reconciliation and Political Legitimacy: The Old Australia and the New South Africa", *Australian Journal of Politics and History*, 49(2), 2003, pp. 182–196.

———, "The Sovereign Exceptions: Colonization and the Foundation of Society", *Social & Legal Studies*, 17(1), 2008, pp. 59–74.

Ashis Nandy, *The Intimate Enemy: Loss and Recovery of Self under Colonialism*, Delhi, Oxford University Press, 1983.

Catherine Nash, "Setting Roots in Motion: Genealogy, Geography and Identity", in David Trigger, Gareth Griffiths (eds), *Disputed Territories: Land Culture and Identity in Settler Societies*, Hong Kong, Hong Kong University Press, 2003, pp. 29–52.

Celia E. Naylor, *African Cherokees in Indian Territory: From Chattel to Citizens*, Chapel Hill, NC, University of North Carolina Press, 2008.

Patricia Nelson Limerick, *Legacy of Conquest*, New York, Norton, 1987, p. 19.

———, *Something in the Soil: Legacies and Reckonings in the New West*, New York, Norton, 2000.

Ronald Niezen, *The Origins of Indigenism*, Berkeley, CA, University of California Press, 2003.

John K. Noyes, "Nomadic Fantasies: Producing Landscapes of Mobility in German Southwest Africa", *Ecumene*, 7, 2000, pp. 47–66.

———, "Nomadic Landscapes and the Colonial Frontier: The Problem of Nomadism in German South Africa", in Lynette Russell (ed.), *Colonial Frontiers: Indigenous-European Encounters in Settler Societies*, Manchester, Manchester University Press, 2001, pp. 198–215.

Conor Cruise O'Brien, *God Land: Reflections on Religion and Nationalism*, Cambridge, MA, Harvard University Press, 1988.

Jean M. O'Brien, *Firsting and Lasting: Writing Indians out of Existence in New England*, Minneapolis, University of Minnesota Press, 2010.

W. H. Oliver, "The Future Behind Us: The Waitangi Tribunal's Retrospective Utopia", in Andrew Sharp, Paul McHugh (eds), *Histories, Power and Loss: Uses of the Past – A New Zealand Commentary*, Wellington, Bridget Williams Books, 2001, pp. 9–29.

Peter S. Onuf, "State Making in Revolutionary America: Independent Vermont as a Case Study", *The Journal of American History*, 67(4), 1981, pp. 797–815.

———, *The Origins of the Federal Republic: Jurisdictional Controversies in the United States, 1775–1787*, Philadelphia, University of Pennsylvania Press, 1983.

Peter S. Onuf, Leonard J. Sadosky, *Jeffersonian America*, Malden, MA, Blackwell Publishers, 2002.

Jürgen Osterhammel, *Colonialism: A Theoretical Overview*, Princeton, NJ, Markus Wiener Publishers, 1997.

Antony Pagden, *European Encounters With the New World: From Renaissance to Romanticism*, New Haven, CT, Yale University Press, 1993.

Thomas Paine, *Common Sense*, London, Penguin Classics, 1986.

Fiona Paisley, "Introduction: White Settler Colonialisms and the Colonial Turn: An Australian Perspective", *Journal of Colonialism and Colonial History*, 4, 3, 2003.

Bryan D. Palmer, "Nineteenth-Century Canada and Australia: The Paradoxes of Class Formation", *Labour/Le Travail*, 38, 1996, pp. 16–36.

Ilan Pappe, *The Ethnic Cleansing of Palestine*, Oxford, Oneworld, 2006.

Carole Pateman, "The Settler Contract", in Carole Pateman, Charles W. Mills, *Contract and Domination*, Cambridge, Polity, 2007, pp. 35–78.

Orlando Patterson, *Slavery and Social Death: A Comparative Study*, Cambridge, MA, Harvard, University Press, 1982.

Paul Patton, "Derrida, Politics and Democracy to Come", *Philosophy Compass*, 2(6), 2007, pp. 766–780.

David Pearson, *The Politics of Ethnicity in Settler Societies: States of Unease*, Houndmills, Palgrave, 2001.

———, "Theorizing Citizenship in British Settler Societies", *Ethnic and Racial Studies*, 25(6), 2002, pp. 989–1012.

Donald E. Pease, "New Perspectives on US Culture and Imperialism", in Amy Kaplan, Donald E. Pease, (eds), *Cultures of United States Imperialism*, Durham, NC, Duke University Press, 1993, pp. 22–38.

See Peter Pels, "The Anthropology of Colonialism: Culture, History, and the Emergence of Western Governmentality", *Annual Review of Anthropology*, 26, 1997, pp. 163–183.

Nigel Penn, "The Voyage Out: Peter Kolb and VOC Voyages to the Cape", in Emma Christopher, Cassandra Pybus, Marcus Rediker (eds), *Many Middle Passages: Forced Migration and the Making of the Modern World*, Berkeley, CA, University of California Press, 2007, pp. 72–91.

———, "The Northern Cape Frontier Zone in South African Frontier Historiography", in Lynette Russell (ed.), *Colonial Frontiers: Indigenous–European Encounters in Settler Societies*, Manchester, Manchester University Press, 2001, pp. 19–46.

Theda Perdue, Michael Green, *The Cherokee Nation and the Trail of Tears*, New York, Viking, 2007.

Joan Peters, *From Time Immemorial: The Origins of the Arab-Jewish Conflict over Palestine*, New York, Harper and Row, 1984.

Sandro Petrucci, *Re in Sardegna, a Pisa cittadini. Ricerche sui "domini Sardinae" pisani*, Bologna, Cappelli, 1988.

A. A. Phillips, *On The Cultural Cringe*, Melbourne, Melbourne University Press, 2006.

Richard Phillips, "Settler Colonialism and the Nuclear Family", *The Canadian Geographer*, 53(2), 2009, pp. 239–253.

Douglas Pike, *Australia: The Quiet Continent*, Cambridge, Cambridge University Press, 1962.

———, "The Smallholders' Place in the Australian Tradition", *Tasmanian Historical Research Association*, 10(2), 1962, pp. 28–33.

Plato, *Phaedrus*, Cambridge, MA, Harvard University Press, 1914.

Gabriel Piterberg, "The Literature of Settler Societies: Camus, S. Yizhar and Amos Oz", paper delivered at the Invasion is a Structure not an Event: Settler Colonialism Past and Present Conference, Center for Near Eastern Studies, UCLA, 30 November 2009.

D. C. M. Platt, Guido di Tella (eds), *Argentina, Australia, and Canada: Studies in Comparative Development, 1870–1965*, New York, St. Martin's Press, 1985.

Deborah Posel, Graeme Simpson (eds), *Commissioning the Past: Understanding South Africa's Truth and Reconciliation Commission*, Johannesburg, Witwatersrand University Press, 2002.

Mary Louise Pratt, *Imperial Eyes: Travel Writing and Transculturation*, London, Routledge, 1992.

Chris Prentice, "Some Problems of Response to Empire in Settler Post-Colonial Societies", in Chris Tiffin, Alan Lawson (eds), *De-Scribing Empire: Post-Colonialism and Textuality*, London, Routledge, 1994, pp. 45–59.

A. Grenfell Price, *White Settlers and Native Peoples; An Historical Study of Racial Contacts between English-speaking Whites and Aboriginal Peoples in the United States, Canada, Australia, and New Zealand*, Westport, CT, Greenwood Press, 1972.

Micheal Prior, *The Bible and Colonialism: A Moral Critique*, Sheffield, Sheffield Academic Press, 1997.

David Prochaska, *Making Algeria French: Colonialism in Bône, 1870–1920*, Cambridge, Cambridge University Press, 1990.

John Phillip Reid, *Law for the Elephant. Property and Social Behavior on the Overland Trail*, San Marino, CA, Huntington Library, 1997.

Henry Reynolds, *The Law of the Land*, Melbourne, Penguin, 1987.

——, *Fate of a Free People*, Melbourne, Penguin, 1995.

——, *This Whispering in Our Hearts*, Sydney, Allen & Unwin, 1998.

Daniel K. Richter, *Facing East from Indian Country: A Native History of Early America*, Cambridge, MA, Harvard University Press, 2001.

Kim Stanley Robinson, *Red Mars*, New York, Bantam Books, 1993.

Ronald Robinson, "Non-European Foundations of European Imperialism: Sketch for a Theory of Collaboration", in R. Owen, B. Sutcliffe (eds), *Studies in the Theory of Imperialism*, London, Longmans, 1972, pp. 117–140.

Theodore Roosevelt, *The Winning of the West, Volume Three: The Founding of the Trans-Alleghany Commonwealths, 1784–1790*, New York, G. P. Putnam's Sons, 1894.

Deborah Bird Rose, "Land Rights and Deep Colonising: The Erasure of Women", *Aboriginal Law Bulletin*, 3(85), 1996, pp. 6–13.

——, *Reports From a Wild Country: Ethics for Decolonisation*, Sydney, UNSW Press, 2004.

Jacqueline Rose, *States of Fantasy*, Oxford, Clarendon Press, 1996.

——, *The Question of Zion*, Princeton, NJ, Princeton University Press, 2005.

Deborah A. Rosen, *American Indians and State Law: Sovereignty, Race, and Citizenship, 1790–1880*, Lincoln, NE, University of Nebraska Press, 2007.

Dietmar Rothermund, *The Routledge Companion to Decolonization*, London, Routledge, 2006.

Tim Rowse, "Aboriginal Respectability", in Tim Rowse (ed.), *Contesting Assimilation*, Perth, API Network, 2005, pp. 49–67.

——, "Official Statistics and the Contemporary Politics of Indigeneity", *Australian Journal of Political Science*, 44(2), 2009, pp. 193–211.

Tim Rowse, Len Smith, "The Limits of 'Elimination' in the Politics of Population", *Australian Historical Studies*, 41(1), 2010, pp. 90–106.

Kevin Rudd, "Apology to Australia's Indigenous Peoples", House of Representatives, Parliament House, Canberra, 13 February 2008. The URL for this text is: http://www.pm.gov.au/media/Speech/2008/speech_0073.cfm.

Lynette Russell (ed.), *Colonial Frontiers: Indigenous-European Encounters in Settler Societies*, Manchester, Manchester University Press, 2001.

P. H. Russell, *Recognizing Aboriginal Title: The Mabo Case and Indigenous Resistance to English Settler Colonialism*, Toronto, Toronto University Press, 2005.

Jennifer Rutherford, *The Gauche Intruder: Freud, Lacan and the White Australian Fantasy*, Melbourne, Melbourne University Press, 2000.

Emmanuelle Saada, *Les enfants de la colonie. Les métis de l'Empire français entre sujétion et citoyenneté*, Paris, Découverte, 2007.

Edward Said, "Conspiracy of Praise", in Edward Said, Christopher Hitchens (eds), *Blaming the Victims: Spurious Scholarship and the Palestine Question*, London, Verso, 1988, pp. 23–32.

———, "Michael Walzer's *Exodus and Revolution*: A Canaanite Reading", in Edward W. Said, Christopher Hitchens (eds), *Blaming the Victims: Spurious Scholarship and the Palestinian Question*, London, Verso, 1988, pp. 161–178.

María Josefina Saldaña-Portillo, "How many Mexicans [is] a horse worth?" The League of United Latin American Citizens, Desegregation Cases, and Chicano Historiography", *South Atlantic Quarterly*, 107(4), 2008, pp. 809–831.

Shlomo Sand, *The Invention of the Jewish People*, London, Verso, 2009.

Jean Paul Sartre, *Colonialism and Neocolonialism*, London, Routledge, 2001.

Max Savelle, *Empires to Nations: Expansion in America, 1713–1824*, Minneapolis, University of Minnesota Press, 1974.

Carl Schmitt, *The Nomos of the Earth in the International Law of the Jus Publicum Europaeum*, New York, Telos Press, 2003.

Stuart B. Schwartz (ed.), *Implicit Understandings: Observing, Reporting, and Reflecting on the Encounters between Europeans and Other Peoples in the Early Modern Era*, Cambridge, Cambridge University Press, 1994.

L. D. Scisco, "The Plantation Type Colony", *American Historical Review*, 8(2), 1903, pp. 260–270.

Patricia Seed, *Ceremonies of Possession in Europe's Conquest of the New World, 1492–1640*, Cambridge, Cambridge University Press, 1995.

Gershon Shafir, "Zionism and Colonialism: A Comparative Approach", in Ilan Pappe (ed.), *The Israel/Palestine Question*, London, Routledge, 1999, pp. 81–96.

Israel Shahak, "A History of the Concept of 'Transfer' in Zionism", *Journal of Palestine Studies*, 18(3), 1989, pp. 22–37.

Andrew Sharp, "Recent Juridical and Constitutional Histories of Maori", in Andrew Sharp, Paul McHugh (eds), *Histories, Power and Loss: Uses of the Past – A New Zealand Commentary*, Wellington, Bridget Williams Books, 2001, pp. 31–60.

Benjamin F. Shearer (ed.), *The Uniting States: The Story of Statehood for the Fifty United States*, Westport, CT, Greenwood Press, 2004.

Susan Scheckel, *The Insistence of the Indian: Race and Nationalism in Nineteenth-Century American Culture*, Princeton, NJ, Princeton University Press, 1998.

Todd Shepard, *The Invention of Decolonization: The Algerian War and the Remaking of France*, Ithaca, NY, Cornell University Press, 2006.

Martin Shipway, *Decolonization and Its Impact: A Comparative Approach to the End of the Colonial Empires*, Malden, MA, Blackwell Publishing, 2008.

Damien Short, "Reconciliation and the Problem of Internal Colonialism", *Journal of Intercultural Studies*, 26(3), 2005, pp. 267–282.

Paul A. Silverstein, "The Kabyle Myth: Colonization and the Production of Ethnicity", in Brian Keith Axel (ed.), *From the Margins: Historical Atnrhopology and Its Futures*, Durham, NC, Duke University Press, 2002, pp. 122–155.

Susan Sleeper-Smith, *Indian Women and French Men: Rethinking Cultural Encounter in the Western Great Lakes*, Amherst, MA, University of Massachusetts Press, 2001.

Stephen Slemon, "Unsettling the Empire: Resistence Theory for the Second World", *Journal of Postcolonial Writing*, 30, 2, 1990, pp. 30–41.

Andrea Smith, *Conquest: Sexual Violence and American Indian Genocide*, Cambridge, MA, South End Press, 2005.

Anthony D. Smith, "State Making and Nation-Building", in J. Hall, *States in History*, Oxford, Blackwell, 1986, pp. 228–263.

——, *The Ethnic Origins of Nations*, Oxford, Blackwell, 1986.

Bernard Smith, *The Spectre of Truganini*, Sydney, The Australian Broadcasting Commission, 1980.

Henry Nash Smith, *Virgin Land: The American West as Symbol and Myth*, Cambridge, MA, Harvard University Press, 1950.

Rogers M. Smith, "Beyond Tocqueville, Myrdal, and Hartz: The Multiple Traditions in America", *The American Political Science Review*, 87(3), 1993, pp. 549–566.

Carl E. Solberg, *The Prairies ad the Pampas: Agrarian Policy in Canada and Argentina, 1880–1939*, Stanford, CA, Stanford University Press, 1987.

D. N. Sprague, *Canada and the Métis, 1869–1885*, Waterloo, Ont., Wilfrid Laurier University Press, 1988.

Daiva Stasiulis, Nira Yuval–Davis (eds), *Unsettling Settler Societies: Articulations of Gender, Race, Ethnicity and Class*, London, Sage, 1995.

P. J. Staudenraus, *The African Colonization Movement, 1816–1865*, New York, Octagon Books, 1980.

Rebecca L. Stein, "Travelling Zion: Hiking and Settler-Nationalism in pre-1948 Palestine", *Interventions*, 11(3), 2009, pp. 334–351.

Philip J. Stern, " 'A Politie of Civill & Military Power': Political Thought and the Late Seventeenth-Century Foundations of the East India Company-State", *Journal of British Studies*, 47, 2008, pp. 253–283.

Makere Stewart-Harawira, *The New Imperial Order: Indigenous Responses to Globalization*, London, Zed Books, 2005.

Ann Laura Stoler, Frederick Cooper, "Between Metropole and Colony: Rethinking a Research Agenda," in Ann Laura Stoler, Frederick Cooper (eds), *Tensions of Empire*, Berkeley, CA, University of California Press, 1997, pp. 1–56.

Pauline T. Strong, *Captive Selves, Captivating Others: The Politics and Poetics of Colonial American Captivity Narratives*, Boulder, CO, Westview Press, 2000.

Alan Taylor, *American Colonies: The Settling of North America*, New York, Viking, 2001.

——, *The Divided Ground: Indians, Settlers and the Northern Borderland of the American Revolution*, New York, Alfred A. Knopf, 2006.

Ayse Deniz Temiz, "Dialogues with *A Forgetful Nation*: Genealogy of Immigration Discourses in the US", *Borderlands e-journal*, 5(3), 2006.

David Thelen, "The Nation and Beyond: Transnational Perspective on United States History", *Journal of American History*, 86(3), 1999, pp. 965–975.

Klaus Theweleit, *Male Fantasies*, Minneapolis, University of Minnesota Press, 1987.

Nicholas Thomas, *Colonialism's Culture: Anthropology, Travel and Government*, Princeton, NJ, Princeton University Press, 1994.

Janna Thompson, *Taking Responsibility for the Past: Reparation and Historical Injustice*, Cambridge, Polity Press, 2002.

Alexis de Tocqueville, *Democracy in America*, Chicago, University of Chicago Press, 2000.

——, *Writings on Empire and Slavery*, Baltimore, Johns Hopkins University Press, 2001.

Jewel Topsfield, "The Unbearable Heaviness of Being No One", *The Age*, 23 January 2009.

James Tully, "The Struggles of Indigenous Peoples for and of Freedom", in Duncan Ivison, Paul Patton, Will Sanders (eds), *Political Theory and the Rights of Indigenous Peoples*, Cambridge, Cambridge University Press, 2000, pp. 36–59, 260–264.

Frederick Jackson Turner, "Western State Making in the Revolutionary Era, I", *American Historical Review*, I, 1895, pp. 70–87.

——, "Western State Making in the Revolutionary Era, II", *American Historical Review*, II, 1896, pp. 251–269.

Stephen Turner, "Cultural Plagiarism and the New Zealand Dream of Home", *Landfall*, 214, 2007, pp. 85–90.

——, " 'Inclusive Exclusion': Managing Identity for the Nation's Sake in Aotearoa/New Zealand", *Arena Journal*, 28, 2007, pp. 87–106.

Robert van Krieken, "Rethinking Cultural Genocide: Aboriginal Child Removal and Settler-Colonial State Formation", *Oceania*, 75, 2004, pp. 125–151.

Lorenzo Veracini, *Negotiating a Bicultural Past: An Historiographical Revolution 1980s Aotearoa/New Zealand*, Wellington, Treaty of Waitangi Research Unit, 2001.

——, *Israel and Settler Society*, London, Pluto Press, 2006.

——, "Historylessness: Australia as a Settler Colonial Collective", *Postcolonial Studies*, 10(3), 2007, pp. 271–285.

——, "Interacting Imaginaries in Israel and the United States", in Ned Curthoys, Debjani Ganguly (eds), *Edward Said: Debating the Legacy of a Public Intellectual*, Melbourne, Melbourne University Press, 2007, pp. 293–312.

——, "Settler Colonialism and Decolonisation", *borderlands e-journal*, 6(2), 2007.

——, "Colonialism and Genocides: Towards an Analysis of the Settler Archive of the European Imagination", in A. Dirk Moses (ed.), *Empire, Colony, Genocide: Conquest, Occupation, and Subaltern Resistance in World History*, New York, Berghahn, 2008, pp. 148–161.

Charles Verlinden, "Antonio da Noli and the Colonization of the Cape Verde Islands", in Charles Verlinden, *The Beginnings of Modern Colonization: Eleven Essays with an Introduction*, Ithaca, NY, Cornell University Press, 1970, pp. 161–180.

Edward Gibbon Wakefield, *The Collected Works of Edward Gibbon Wakefield*, Glasgow, Collins, 1968.

Priscilla Wald, "Terms of Assimilation: Legislating Subjectivity in the Emerging Nation", in Amy Kaplan, Donald E. Pease, (eds), *Cultures of United States Imperialism*, Durham, NC, Duke University Press, 1993, pp. 59–84.

Ruth Wallis, Ella Wilcox Sekatau, "The Right to a Name: The Narragansett People and Rhode Island Officials in the Revolutionary Era", *Ethnohistory*, 44(3) 1997, pp. 433–462.

David Walker, *Anxious Nation: Australia and the Rise of Asia 1850–1939*, Brisbane, University of Queensland Press, 1999.

Michael Walzer, *Exodus and Revolution*, New York, Basic Books, 1985.

Alan Ward, *An Unsettled History: Treaty Claims in New Zealand Today*, Wellington, Bridget William Books, 1999.

Damen Ward, "Colonial Communication: Creating Settler Public Opinion in Crown Colony South Australia and New Zealand", in Simon J. Potter (ed.), *Imperial Communication: Australia, Britain and the British Empire, c. 1830–1850*, London, Menzies Centre for Australian Studies, 2005, pp. 7–46.

John Manning Ward, *Colonial self-Government: The British Experience, 1759–1856*, Toronto, University of Toronto Press, 1976.

Russel Ward, *The Australian Legend*, Melbourne, Oxford University Press, 1958.

Stuart Ward, "Imperial Identities Abroad", in Sarah Stockwell (ed.), *The British Empire: Themes and Perspectives*, Malden, MA, Blackwell, 2008, pp. 219–243.

Richard Waswo, *The Founding Legend of Western Civilization: From Virgil to Vietnam*, Hanover, NH, Wesleyan University Press/University Press of New England, 1997.

John C. Weaver, *The Great Land Rush and the Making of the Modern World, 1650–1900*, Montreal, McGill-Queen's University Press, 2003.

Nicolás Wey Gómez, *The Tropics of Empire: Why Columbus Sailed South to the Indies*, Cambridge, MA, MIT Press, 2008.

Richard White, *The Middle Ground: Indians, Empires, and Republics in the Great Lakes Region, 1650–1815*, New York, Cambridge University Press, 1991.

John F. Williams, Daniela Kraus, Harry Knowles, "Flights from Modernity: German and Australian Utopian Colonies in Paraguay, 1886–1896", *Journal of Australian Studies*, 69(20), 2001, pp. 49–62, 189–191.

Mark Williams, " 'The Finest Race of Savages the World has Seen': How Empire Turned Out Differently in Australia and New Zealand", in Vanessa Agnew, Jonathan Lamb (eds), *Settler and Creole Re-Enactment*, Houndmills, Palgrave Macmillan, 2009, pp. 223–244.

Samuel Cole Williams, *History of the Lost State of Franklin*, Philadelphia, Porcupine Press, 1974.

Keith Windschuttle, *The Fabrication of Australian History, Vol. 1: Van Dieman's Land, 1803–1847*, Sydney, Macleay Press, 2002.

Leslie Witz, "History Below the Water Line: The Making of Apartheid's Last Festival", in Vanessa Agnew, Jonathan Lamb (eds), *Settler and Creole Re-Enactment*, Houndmills, Palgrave Macmillan, 2009, pp. 138–155.

Patrick Wolfe, "On Being Woken Up: The Dreamtime in Anthropology and in Australian Settler Culture", *Comparative Studies in Society and History*, 33(2), 1991, pp. 197–224.

———, *Settler Colonialism and the Transformation of Anthropology: The Politics and Poetics of an Ethnographic Event*, London, Cassell, 1999.

———, "Land, Labor, and Difference: Elementary Structures of Race", *American Historical Review*, 106, 2001, pp. 866–905.

———, "Settler Colonialism and the Elimination of the Native", *Journal of Genocide Research*, 8(4), 2006, pp. 387–409.

Ed Wright, *Ghost Colonies*, Sydney, Murdoch Books, 2009.

Graeme Wynn, "Settler Societies in Geographical Focus", *Australian Historical Studies*, 20, 1983, pp. 353–366.

Iris Marion Young, "Hybrid Democracy: Iroquois Federalism and the Postcolonial Project", in Duncan Ivison, Paul Patton, Will Sanders (eds), *Political Theory and the Rights of Indigenous Peoples*, Cambridge, Cambridge University Press, 2000, pp. 237–258, 280–281.

Robert J. C. Young, *The Idea of English Ethnicity*, Malden, MA, Blackwell Publishing, 2008.

Nira Yuval-Davis, "Theorizing Identity: Beyond the 'Us' and 'Them' Dichotomy", *Patterns of Prejudice*, 44, 3, 2010, pp. 261–280.

Eviatar Zerubavel, *Time Maps: Collective Memory and the Social Shape of the Past*, Chicago, University of Chicago Press, 2003.

———, *The Elephant in the Room: Silence and Denial in Everyday Life*, New York, Oxford University Press, 2006.

Andrew Zimmerman, " 'What Do You Really Want in German East Africa, *Herr Professor*'? Counterinsurgency and the Science Effect in Colonial Tanzania", *Comparative Studies in Society and History*, 48(2), 2006, pp. 419–461.

Slavoj Žižek, *Iraq: The Borrowed Kettle*, London, Verso, 2003.

———, *Violence*, London, Profile Books, 2008.

Index

Lightning Source UK Ltd.
Milton Keynes UK
UKHW021118050921
389957UK00005B/399